User Story Mapping

Jeff Patton

Beijing · Cambr   Tokyo   **O'REILLY®**

User Story Mapping

by Jeff Patton

Printed in the United States of America.

Published by O'Reilly Media, Inc., 1005 Gravenstein Highway North, Sebastopol, CA 95472.

O'Reilly books may be purchased for educational, business, or sales promotional use. Online editions are also available for most titles (*http://safaribooksonline.com*). For more information, contact our corporate/institutional sales department: 800-998-9938 or *corporate@oreilly.com*.

Editors: Mary Treseler and Amy Jollymore   **Indexer:** Ellen Troutman
Production Editor: Kara Ebrahim   **Cover Designer:** Ellie Volckhausen
Copyeditor: Rachel Monaghan   **Interior Designer:** David Futato
Proofreader: Elise Morrison   **Illustrator:** Rebecca Demarest

September 2014:   First Edition

Revision History for the First Edition:

2014-09-05:   First release

See *http://oreilly.com/catalog/errata.csp?isbn=9781491904909* for release details.

ISBN: 978-1-491-90490-9

[LSI]

For Stacy, Grace, and Zoe who are my biggest supporters and make all my effort worthwhile.

And in memory of Luke Barrett, a dear colleague and mentor of mine. Luke made a difference in my life as he did countless others.

Table of Contents

Foreword by Martin Fowler. xi

Foreword by Alan Cooper. xiii

Foreword by Marty Cagan. xvii

Preface. xxi

Read This First. xxix

1. The Big Picture. 1
    The "A" Word   1
    Telling Stories, Not Writing Stories   3
    Telling the Whole Story   3
    Gary and the Tragedy of the Flat Backlog   5
    Talk and Doc   6
    Frame Your Idea   8
    Describe Your Customers and Users   9
    Tell Your Users' Stories   10
    Explore Details and Options   14

2. Plan to Build Less. 21
    Mapping Helps Big Groups Build Shared Understanding   22
    Mapping Helps You Spot Holes in Your Story   25
    There's Always Too Much   26
    Slice Out a Minimum Viable Product Release   27
    Slice Out a Release Roadmap   28
    Don't Prioritize Features—Prioritize Outcomes   29
    This Is Magic—Really, It Is   30
    Why We Argue So Much About MVP   32
    The New MVP Isn't a Product at All!   34

3. Plan to Learn Faster. **37**

Start by Discussing Your Opportunity   38
Validate the Problem   39
Prototype to Learn   40
Watch Out for What People Say They Want   41
Build to Learn   41
Iterate Until Viable   44
How to Do It the Wrong Way   44
Validated Learning   46
Really Minimize Your Experiments   48
Let's Recap   48

4. Plan to Finish on Time. **51**

Tell It to the Team   52
The Secret to Good Estimation   53
Plan to Build Piece by Piece   54
Don't Release Each Slice   56
The Other Secret to Good Estimation   56
Manage Your Budget   57
    What Would da Vinci Do?   59
Iterative AND Incremental   62
Opening-, Mid-, and Endgame Strategy   63
Slice Out Your Development Strategy in a Map   64
It's All About Risk   64
Now What?   65

5. You Already Know How. **67**

1. Write Out Your Story a Step at a Time   67
    Tasks Are What We Do   68
    My Tasks Are Different Than Yours   69
    I'm Just More Detail-Oriented   70
2. Organize Your Story   71
    Fill in Missing Details   72
3. Explore Alternative Stories   72
    Keep the Flow   74
4. Distill Your Map to Make a Backbone   75
5. Slice Out Tasks That Help You Reach a Specific Outcome   76
That's It! You've Learned All the Important Concepts   77
Do Try This at Home, or at Work   78
It's a Now Map, Not a Later Map   79
Try This for Real   81

With Software It's Harder   82
The Map Is Just the Beginning   84

6. **The Real Story About Stories**. 89
Kent's Disruptively Simple Idea   89
Simple Isn't Easy   91
Ron Jeffries and the 3 Cs   92
    1. Card   93
    2. Conversation   93
    3. Confirmation   94
Words and Pictures   95
That's It   96

7. **Telling Better Stories**. 97
Connextra's Cool Template   97
Template Zombies and the Snowplow   102
A Checklist of What to Really Talk About   104
Create Vacation Photos   107
It's a Lot to Worry About   108

8. **It's Not All on the Card**. 109
Different People, Different Conversations   109
We're Gonna Need a Bigger Card   110
Radiators and Ice Boxes   113
That's Not What That Tool Is For   116
    Building Shared Understanding   116
    Remembering   118
    Tracking   119

9. **The Card Is Just the Beginning**. 121
Construct with a Clear Picture in Your Head   122
Build an Oral Tradition of Storytelling   123
Inspect the Results of Your Work   124
It's Not for You   126
Build to Learn   127
It's Not Always Software   128
Plan to Learn, and Learn to Plan   129

10. **Bake Stories Like Cake**. 131
Create a Recipe   132
Breaking Down a Big Cake   133

11. Rock Breaking.. **137**
Size Always Matters   137
Stories Are Like Rocks   139
Epics Are Big Rocks Sometimes Used to Hit People   140
Themes Organize Groups of Stories   142
Forget Those Terms and Focus on Storytelling   142
Start with Opportunities   143
Discover a Minimum Viable Solution   144
Dive into the Details of Each Story During Delivery   146
Keep Talking as You Build   148
Evaluate Each Piece   149
Evaluate with Users and Customers   150
Evaluate with Business Stakeholders   152
Release and Keep Evaluating   153

12. Rock Breakers.. **155**
Valuable-Usable-Feasible   156
A Discovery Team Needs Lots of Others to Succeed   158
The Three Amigos   159
Product Owner as Producer   163
This Is Complicated   164

13. Start with Opportunities... **167**
Have Conversations About Opportunities   167
Dig Deeper, Trash It, or Think About It   168
Opportunity Shouldn't Be a Euphemism   173
Story Mapping and Opportunities   173
Be Picky   179

14. Using Discovery to Build Shared Understanding.............. **181**
Discovery Isn't About Building Software   181
Four Essential Steps to Discovery   182
  1. Frame the Idea   183
  2. Understand Customers and Users   183
  3. Envision Your Solution   186
  4. Minimize and Plan   196
Discovery Activities, Discussions, and Artifacts   199
Discovery Is for Building Shared Understanding   200

15. Using Discovery for Validated Learning....................... **201**
We're Wrong Most of the Time   201

The Bad Old Days   203
Empathize, Focus, Ideate, Prototype, Test   204
How to Mess Up a Good Thing   208
Short Validated Learning Loops   209
How Lean Startup Thinking Changes Product Design   210
   Start by Guessing   211
   Name Your Risky Assumptions   212
   Design and Build a Small Test   212
   Measure by Running Your Test with Customers and Users   214
   Rethink Your Solution and Your Assumptions   215
Stories and Story Maps?   215

16. Refine, Define, and Build. **217**
Cards, Conversation, More Cards, More Conversations…   217
Cutting and Polishing   218
Workshopping Stories   218
Sprint or Iteration Planning?   222
Crowds Don't Collaborate   225
Split and Thin   227
Use Your Story Map During Delivery   232
Use a Map to Visualize Progress   233
Use Simple Maps During Story Workshops   234

17. Stories Are Actually Like Asteroids. **239**
Reassembling Broken Rocks   241
Don't Overdo the Mapping   243
Don't Sweat the Small Stuff   244

18. Learn from Everything You Build. **247**
Review as a Team   247
Review with Others in Your Organization   251
Enough   253
Learn from Users   254
Learn from Release to Users   255
Outcomes on a Schedule   255
Use a Map to Evaluate Release Readiness   256

The End, or Is It? **259**

Acknowledgments. **261**

References. 265

Index. 267

Foreword by Martin Fowler

One of the beneficial consequences of the rise of Agile software development is the notion of splitting up large sets of requirements into smaller chunks. These chunks—stories—enable much more visibility into the progress of a development project. When a product is built story-by-story, with each story's implementation fully integrated into the software product, everyone can see the product grow. By using stories that make sense to users, developers can steer the project by determining which stories to build next. This greater visibility helps encourage greater participation from users—no longer do they have to wait a year or more to see what the development team's been up to.

But this chunking has some negative consequences. One of these is that it's easy to lose the big picture of what a software system should do. You can end up with a jumble of pieces that don't fit into a coherent whole. Or you can end up building a system that isn't really helpful to the users, because you've missed the essence of what's needed by getting lost in the details.

Story mapping is a technique that provides the big picture that a pile of stories so often misses.

That's it, really—the description of this book in a single sentence. And that sentence carries with it the promise of a lot of value. A big picture helps communicate effectively with users, it helps everyone involved avoid building unnecessary features, and it provides an orientation for a coherent user experience. When I talk to my colleagues at Thought-Works about what they do to develop their stories, story mapping regularly comes up as a core technique. Often they've learned that technique from workshops run by Jeff, because he's the one who developed the technique and can best communicate it. This book allows more people to understand this technique directly from its source.

But this isn't just a book for people who have something like "business analyst" on their business card or online profile. Perhaps the biggest disappointment for me in the decade of the adoption of Agile methods is the way that many programmers see stories as a one-way communication from analysts to them. Right from the beginning, stories were supposed to spark *conversations*. If you really want to come up with effective software to support an activity, then you need to look to those who build software as a vital source of ideas for its capabilities, because it's programmers who know best what software can do. Programmers need to understand what their users are trying to achieve and should collaborate in building the stories that capture those users' needs. A programmer who understands story mapping can better see the broader user context and can participate in framing the software—leading to a better job.

When Kent Beck (who originated the notion of a "story") developed his ideas on software development, he called out communication as a key value of effective teams. Stories are the building blocks of communication between developers and those who use their work. Story maps organize and structure these building blocks, and thus enhance this communication process—which is the most critical part of software development itself.

—Martin Fowler
June 18, 2014

Foreword by Alan Cooper

In Mary Shelley's famous science-fiction novel, *Frankenstein*, the mad Doctor Frankenstein builds a creature from disparate pieces of dead humans and brings the creature to life with the then-new technology of electricity. Of course, we know that this is not actually possible. You cannot create life by sewing together random body parts.

Yet this is what software developers attempt to do all the time. They add good features to software, one at a time, and then wonder why few users love their product. The heart of the conundrum is that developers are using their construction method as a design tool, but the two are not interchangeable.

It's entirely reasonable that programmers *build* software one feature at a time. That's a perfectly good strategy, proven over the years. What has also been proven over the years is that, when used as a method for designing the behavior and scope of a digital product, one-feature-at-a-time yields a Frankenstein monster of a program.

While they are intimately related, the practice of designing software behavior and the practice of building that software are distinctly different, and are typically performed by different people with different skill sets. The many hours that interaction designers spend observing users and mapping behavior patterns would drive most programmers batty. Conversely, the hours of sweating over algorithms are too solitary for most designers.

But when the two strains of practice—design and development—collaborate, the work becomes electric and has the potential to create a living, breathing product. Teamwork breathes life into the monster and makes people love it.

While the idea of collaboration is neither new nor particularly insightful, it is actually very difficult to do effectively. The way that developers work—their pace, language, and rhythm—is quite different from that of interaction designers.

Practitioners in each of the two fields are strong, capable, and internally well disciplined, yet they share a single, common weakness. It is really hard to express a design problem in programming terms, and it is equally hard to express a development problem in design terms. The two sister disciplines lack a common tongue. And that junction between the two disciplines is precisely where Jeff Patton lives.

Jeff's method of story mapping makes sense to developers, and it makes equal sense to designers. Story mapping is the Rosetta Stone for our digital age.

Despite protestations to the contrary, Agile development is not a very useful design tool. It is a way of thinking about development that is design-friendly, which is a very good thing, but by itself it won't get you to a product that users love. On the other hand, so many times we have seen good designs, well documented, given to developers—Agile or not—who manage to kill the essence of the design in the process of implementation.

Patton's story mapping approach is the bridge over this chasm. Interaction design is all about finding the user's truth and telling it as a narrative. Software development is all about breaking those narratives into tiny, functional chunks and implementing and integrating them. It's so ridiculously easy for the essence of the narrative to slip away during this complex process. Yes, the functions are implemented, but the patient dies on the operating room table.

By mapping out the user's stories, the design retains its narrative structure yet can still be deconstructed for effective implementation. The designer's story, which is a formalized version of the user's story, remains intact throughout the development.

The conventional corporate world has proven that it is nearly impossible for a team of two or three hundred people to build a product that people love. Meanwhile the startup community has proven that a team of four or five people *can* build small products that people love, but even these little products eventually grow big and lose their spark. The challenge we face is creating big software that people love. Big software serves large audiences doing complex, commercially viable jobs. It's ridiculously hard to make such software fun to use and easy to learn.

The only way we are going to build big software that is not a Frankenstein monster is by learning how to integrate the disciplines of software design and development. Nobody knows how to do that better than Jeff Patton.

—Alan Cooper

June 17, 2014

Foreword by Marty Cagan

I've had the extremely good fortune to be able to work with many of the very best technology product teams in the world. People creating the products you use and love every day. Teams that are literally changing the world.

I've also been brought in to try to help companies that are not doing so well. Startups racing to get some traction before the money runs out. Larger companies struggling to replicate their early innovation. Teams failing to continuously add value to their business. Leaders frustrated with how long it takes to go from idea to reality. Engineers exasperated with their product owners.

What I've learned is that there is a profound difference between how the very best product companies create technology products, and the rest. And I don't mean minor differences. I mean everything from how leaders behave to the level of empowerment of teams; to the way teams work together; to how the organization thinks about funding, staffing, and producing products; to the culture; to how product, design, and engineering collaborate to discover effective solutions for their customers.

This book is titled *User Story Mapping*, but you'll soon see it is about much more than this powerful yet simple technique. This book gets to the heart about how teams collaborate, communicate, and ultimately come up with good stuff to build.

Many of you have never had a chance to see up close how a strong product team operates. All you may know is what you've seen at your company or where you've worked before. So what I'd like to do here is to try to give you a flavor of just how different the best teams are from the rest.

With a grateful nod to Ben Horowitz's *Good Product Manager, Bad Product Manager*, here's a glimpse into some of the important differences between strong product teams and weak teams:

Good teams have a compelling product vision that they pursue with a missionary-like passion. Bad teams are mercenaries.

Good teams get their inspiration and product ideas from their scorecard KPIs, from observing customers struggle, from analyzing the data customers generate from using their product, and from constantly seeking to apply new technology to solve real problems. Bad teams gather requirements from sales and customers.

Good teams understand who their key stakeholders are, they understand the constraints that these stakeholders operate in, and they are committed to inventing solutions that not only work for users and customers, but also work within the constraints of the business. Bad teams gather requirements from stakeholders.

Good teams are skilled in the many techniques to rapidly try out product ideas to determine which ones are truly worth building. Bad teams hold meetings to generate prioritized roadmaps.

Good teams love to have brainstorming discussions with smart thought leaders from across the company. Bad teams get offended when someone outside their team dares to suggest they do something.

Good teams have product, design, and engineering sit side-by-side, and embrace the give and take between the functionality, the user experience, and the enabling technology. Bad teams sit in their respective functional areas, and ask that others make requests for their services in the form of documents and scheduling meetings.

Good teams are constantly trying out new ideas in order to innovate, but doing so in ways that protect the revenue and the brand. Bad teams are still waiting for permission to run a test.

Good teams insist they have the skill sets necessary to create winning products, such as strong interaction design. Bad teams don't even know what interaction designers are.

Good teams ensure that their engineers have time to try out the discovery prototypes every day so that they can contribute their thoughts on how to make the product better. Bad teams show the prototypes to the engineers during sprint planning so they can estimate.

Good teams engage directly with end users and customers every week to better understand their customers, and to see the customer's response to their latest ideas. Bad teams think they are the customer.

Good teams know that many of their favorite ideas won't end up working for customers, and even the ones that could will need several iterations to get to the point where they provide the desired outcome. Bad teams just build what's on the roadmap and are satisfied with meeting dates and ensuring quality.

Good teams understand the need for speed and how rapid iteration is the key to innovation, and they understand this speed comes from the right techniques and not forced labor. Bad teams complain they are slow because their colleagues are not working hard enough.

Good teams make high-integrity commitments after they've evaluated the request and ensured they have a viable solution that will actually work for the customer and the business. Bad teams complain about being a sales-driven company.

Good teams instrument their work so that they can immediately understand how their product is being used and make adjustments based on the data. Bad teams consider analytics and reporting a "nice to have."

Good teams integrate and release continuously, knowing that a constant stream of smaller releases provides a much more stable solution for their customers. Bad teams test manually at the end of a painful integration phase and then release everything at once.

Good teams obsess over their reference customers. Bad teams obsess over competitors.

Good teams celebrate when they achieve a significant impact to the business KPIs. Bad teams celebrate when they finally release something.

I realize you might be wondering what all this has to do with story maps. I think you'll be surprised. And that's precisely why I am a fan of story maps.

I have met only a few Agile experts whom I consider qualified to actually help a serious product team raise its game to the level its company needs and deserves. Jeff Patton is one of them. I have observed him working hands on in the trenches with teams in the midst of product discovery. I introduce him into companies because he is effective. Teams love him because he is knowledgeable yet humble.

The days of product managers gathering up and documenting requirements, designers scrambling just to put some lipstick on the product, and engineers sheltered in the basement, coding, are long gone for the best teams. And it's time they are gone for your team, too.

—Marty Cagan
June 18, 2014

Preface

Live in it, swim in it, laugh in it, love in it / Removes embarrassing
stains from contour sheets, that's right / And it entertains visiting
relatives, it turns a sandwich into a banquet.

— Tom Waits, "Step Right Up"

This book was supposed to be a small thing...a pamphlet, really.

I set out to write about a simple practice I called *story mapping*. I, and
lots of other folks, build simple maps to help us work together with
others and to imagine the experience of using a product.

*Story mapping keeps us focused on users and
their experience, and the result is a better
conversation, and ultimately a better
product.*

Building a map is dead simple. Working together with others, I'll tell
the story of a product, writing each big step the users take in the story
on sticky notes in a left-to-right flow. Then, we'll go back and talk

about the details of each step, and write those details down on sticky notes and place them vertically under each step. The result is a simple grid-like structure that tells a story from left to right, and breaks it into details from top to bottom. It's fun and fast. And those details make a better backlog of stories for our Agile development projects.

How complicated could writing a book about this be?

But it turns out that even the simple things can be pretty sophisticated. And writing about why you would want to build a story map, what's going on when you build one, and all the different ways you can use one took me a lot of pages. There was more to this simple practice than I thought.

If you're using an Agile development process, you're likely filling backlogs with user stories. I'd assumed that since stories were such a common practice, it'd be a waste of time for me to write about them in this book. But I was wrong. In the decade and a half since stories were first described by Kent Beck, they're more popular—and more misunderstood and misused—than ever before. That makes me sad. And, what's more, it kills all the benefit we get from story mapping.

So, in this book, I would like to correct as many big misconceptions as I can about stories and the way they're used in Agile and Lean software development. That's why, in the words of Tom Waits, I've turned this "sandwich into a banquet."

Why Me?

I like making things. What motivates me is the joy I get from creating a piece of software and seeing people use it and benefit from it. I'm a reluctant methodologist. I found I needed to learn how process and practice work to get better at them. I'm only now learning after 20-plus years in software development how to teach what I've learned. And I know that what I teach is a moving target. What I understand changes every week. How best to explain it changes almost as fast. All that's kept me from writing a book for years.

But it's time.

Stories and story maps are such a good idea. They've benefited so many people. They've made their lives better, and the products they build better. But while some people's lives are getting better, there are more people struggling with stories than ever before. I want to help stop that.

This book is something I can make to help. And, if it improves the work lives of even a few, I'll celebrate.

This Book Is for You If You're Struggling with Stories

Because so many organizations have adopted Agile and Lean processes, and stories along with them, you may fall into one or more of the traps caused by misconceptions about stories. Traps like these:

- Because stories let you focus on building small things, it's easy to *lose sight of the big picture*. The result is often a "Franken-product" where it's clear to everyone using the product that it's assembled from mismatched parts.

- When you're building a product of any significant size, building one small thing after another leaves people *wondering when you'll ever be done, or what exactly you'll deliver*. If you're the builder, you wonder, too.

- Because stories are about conversations, *people use that idea to avoid writing anything down*. Then they forget what they talked about and agreed to in the conversations.

- Because good stories are supposed to have acceptance criteria, we focus on getting acceptance criteria written, but there's still not a common understanding of what needs to be built. As a consequence, *teams don't finish the work they plan on in the timeframe they planned to*.

- Because good stories are supposed to be written from a user's perspective, and there are lots of parts that users never see, team members argue that "*our product doesn't have users, so user stories won't work here.*"

If you've fallen into any of those traps, then I'll try to wipe away the misconceptions that lead to those traps in the first place. You'll learn how to think of the big picture, how to plan and estimate in the large (and in the small), and how to have productive conversations about what users are trying to accomplish, as well as what a good piece of software needs to do to help them.

Who Should Read This Book?

You should, of course. Especially if you bought it. I, for one, think you've made a wise investment. If you're just borrowing it, you should order your own now, and return the one you've borrowed when the new one arrives at your door.

However, reading this book offers specific reasons and benefits for practitioners in specific roles:

- *Product managers and user experience (UX) practitioners in commercial product companies* should read this book to help them bridge the gap between thinking about whole products and user experience and thinking about tactical plans and backlog items. If you've been struggling to get from the vision you're imagining to the details your teams can build, story maps will help. If you've been struggling to help others imagine the experience of—and empathize with—the users of your product, story mapping will help. If you've been struggling to figure out how to incorporate good UX and product design practice, this book will help. If you've been working to incorporate Lean Startup–style experimentation in the way you work, this book will help.

- *Product owners, business analysts, and project managers in information technology (IT) organizations* should read this book to help them bridge the gap between their internal users, stakeholders, and developers. If you've been struggling to convince lots of stakeholders in your company to get on the same page, then story maps will help. If you've been struggling to help developers see the big picture, story maps will help.

- *Agile and Lean process coaches* with the goal of helping individuals and teams improve should read this book. And, as you do, think about the misconceptions people in your organization have about stories. Use the stories, simple exercises, and practices described in this book to help your teams improve.

- *Everyone else.* When using Agile processes, we often look to roles like product owners or business analysts to steer a lot of the work with stories, but effective use of stories requires that *everyone* get the basics. When people don't understand the basics, you hear complaints that "stories aren't well written" or that they're "too big," or that they "don't have enough detail." This book will help, but not in the way you think. You and everyone else will learn that stories aren't a way to write better requirements, but a way to organize and have better conversations. This book will help you understand what kinds of conversations you should be having to help you get the information you need when you need it.

I'm hoping you identify with one or more of the groups I just described. If you don't, give this book to someone who does.

If you do, let's get started.

A Few Conventions Used in This Book

I suspect this isn't the only book on software development you've ever read, so nothing should surprise you.

The Headings Inside Each Chapter Guide You Through the Subject

Use them to find your way or skip over stuff you're not interested in right now.

Key points look like this. Imagine me saying these a bit louder than all the other text.

If you're skimming, read the key points. If you like them, or they're not dead obvious, read the text before and after them. That should make them clear.

Sidebars are used to describe:

- *Interesting but not critical concepts*. These should be fun distractions. At least I hope they are.
- *Recipes for specific practices*. You should be able to use these recipes to help you get started with a specific practice.
- *Stories and examples contributed by others*. You should get some good ideas from these that you could try in your organization.

The book is organized into specific sections. You could read it a section at a time, or use the sections to help you find ideas for a specific challenge you have right now.

How This Book Is Organized

I bought a cool new color laser printer a while back. I opened the box, and sitting on top of the printer was a pamphlet with "Read This First" in big red letters on it. I wondered, "Should I *really* read this first?" because I usually don't do as I'm told. But I'm glad I did, because there were lots of plastic guards in various places inside the printer to keep it safe during shipping, and if I'd plugged it in before removing them, I might have damaged the printer.

This story might sound like a tangent, but it's not.

This book contains a "Read This First" chapter because there are two critical concepts and associated vocabulary that I'll use throughout the rest of the book. I'd like you to have those concepts in your head before you get started. If you start to story map before you understand them, I can't guarantee your safety.

Story Mapping from 10,000 Feet

Chapters 1–4 will give you a high-level view of story mapping. If you've been using stories for a while and played with a story map before, this section should give you enough to get going right away.

Chapter 5 gives you a nifty exercise to help you learn the key concepts used to create a great story map. Try it out with a group in your office, and everyone who participates will get it. And I promise you the maps they create for your products will come out better afterward.

Grokking User Stories

Chapters 6–12 tell the story behind stories, how they really work, and how to make good use of them in Agile and Lean projects. Inside story maps are lots of little stories you can use to drive day-to-day development. Even if you're an Agile veteran, I promise you'll learn something about stories you didn't already know. And, if you're new to stories, you'll learn enough to surprise the Agile know-it-alls at your office.

Better Backlogs

Chapters 13–15 dive deep into the lifecycle of a story. I'll discuss specific practices that help you use stories and story maps, starting with big opportunities and moving through the discovery work to identify a backlog full of stories that describe a viable product. You'll learn how story maps and lots of other practices can help you every step of the way.

Better Building

Chapters 16–18 dive deeper into using stories tactically, iteration-by-iteration or sprint-by-sprint. You'll learn how to get stories ready, to pay attention while they're built, to really get them done, and to really learn from each story you convert to working software.

I find that the last few chapters of many software development books are the extra junk. I can usually ignore them. Unfortunately, I didn't write any of those chapters. You'll need to read the whole book. My only consolation to you is that you'll get some useful nuggets out of every chapter that you can put to work right away.

Let's get to it.

Safari® Books Online

 *Safari Books Online* is an on-demand digital library that delivers expert content in both book and video form from the world's leading authors in technology and business.

Technology professionals, software developers, web designers, and business and creative professionals use Safari Books Online as their primary resource for research, problem solving, learning, and certification training.

Safari Books Online offers a range of plans and pricing for enterprise, government, education, and individuals.

Members have access to thousands of books, training videos, and pre-publication manuscripts in one fully searchable database from publishers like O'Reilly Media, Prentice Hall Professional, Addison-Wesley Professional, Microsoft Press, Sams, Que, Peachpit Press, Focal Press, Cisco Press, John Wiley & Sons, Syngress, Morgan Kaufmann, IBM Redbooks, Packt, Adobe Press, FT Press, Apress, Manning, New Riders, McGraw-Hill, Jones & Bartlett, Course Technology, and hundreds more. For more information about Safari Books Online, please visit us online.

How to Contact Us

Please address comments and questions concerning this book to the publisher:

O'Reilly Media, Inc.
1005 Gravenstein Highway North
Sebastopol, CA 95472
800-998-9938 (in the United States or Canada)
707-829-0515 (international or local)
707-829-0104 (fax)

We have a web page for this book, where we list errata, examples, and any additional information. You can access this page at *http://bit.ly/user-story-mapping*.

To comment or ask technical questions about this book, send email to *bookquestions@oreilly.com*.

For more information about our books, courses, conferences, and news, see our website at *http://www.oreilly.com*.

Find us on Facebook: *http://facebook.com/oreilly*

Follow us on Twitter: *http://twitter.com/oreillymedia*

Watch us on YouTube: *http://www.youtube.com/oreillymedia*

Read This First

This book has no introduction.

Yes, you read that right. Now, you might immediately ask yourself, "Why doesn't Jeff's book have an introduction? Did he forget to write it? Is he beginning to slip after all these years?! Did the dog eat it?"

No, I didn't forget to write an introduction to this book. And, no, I'm not beginning to slip. At least I don't think I am. And my dog didn't eat it (although my daughter's guinea pig looks suspicious). It's just that I've long believed that authors spend too much time convincing me I should read their book, and a great deal of that convincing lives in the introduction. The meat of most books usually doesn't start until Chapter 3. And I'm sure it's not only me who does this, but I usually skip the introduction.

This book actually starts here.

And you're not allowed to skip this because it really *is* the most important part. In fact, if you only get two points from this book, I'll be happy. And those two points are right here in this chapter:

- The goal of using stories isn't to write better stories.
- The goal of product development isn't to make products.

Let me explain.

The Telephone Game

I'm sure you remember when you were a kid and you played this weird "telephone game" where you whispered something to somebody, who whispered it to someone else, and so on around the group, until the last person reveals the totally garbled message and everyone laughs. Today, my family still plays this game at home with my kids around the dinner table. Note to parents: this is a good activity to occupy kids bored with adult dinner conversation.

In the grown-up world, we've continued this game—only we don't whisper to each other. We write lengthy documents and create official-looking presentations that we hand off to someone, who proceeds to get something completely different out of it than we intended. And that person uses that document to create more documents to give to different people. However, unlike that game we played as kids, we don't all laugh at the end.

When people read written instructions, they interpret them different-ly. If you find that a little hard to believe (it's in writing, after all!), then let me show you a few examples of instructions gone very, very wrong.

This is the cover of Jen Yates's book *Cake Wrecks* (Andrews McMeel Publishing). (Thanks to Jen and John Yates for supplying these.) The book sprang from her wildly entertaining website, *cakewrecks.com*. Please don't go there if you don't have at least an hour to waste. The site shows photos of oddly decorated cakes that defy explanation—but Jen explains them in spite of that. Now, one of the recurring themes in both the site and the book is misinterpreted requirements. But of course she doesn't refer to them as *requirements* because it's such a nerdy word. She calls them *literals* because the reader read and literally interpreted what was written. Looking at the photos, I can imagine someone listening to a customer and writing down what he wants, then handing that to someone else who'll decorate a cake.

Customer: Hello, I'd like to order a cake.

Employee: Sure, what would you like written on it?

Customer: Could you write "So long, Alicia" in purple?

Employee: Sure.

Customer: And put stars around it?

Employee: No problem. I've written this up, and will hand it to my cake decorator right away. We'll have it for you in the morning.

This is the result:

Here's another. In software development, we call these *nonfunctional requirements*:

These are funny examples, and we can laugh about wasting twenty bucks on a cake. But sometimes the stakes are much greater than that.

You've probably heard the story about the 1999 crash of a $125 million NASA Mars Climate Orbiter.[1] OK, maybe you haven't. But here's the punch line. If any project is sunk up to its eyeballs in requirements and written documentation, it's a NASA project. However, despite all the filing cabinets full of requirements and documentation, the orbiter crashed because while NASA used the metric system for its measurements, members of the Lockheed Martin engineering team used the old imperial measurement system to develop navigation commands for the vehicle's thrusters. While no one knows exactly where the orbiter ended up, some think it has found its happy place orbiting the sun somewhere past Mars.

Ironically, we put stuff in writing to communicate more clearly and to avoid risk of misunderstanding. But, way too often, the opposite is true.

Shared documents aren't shared understanding.

Stop for a minute and write that down. Write it on a sticky note and put it in your pocket. Consider getting it tattooed somewhere on your body so you can see it when you're getting ready for work in the morning. When you read it, it'll help you remember the stories I'm telling you now.

Shared understanding is when we both understand what the other person is imagining and why. Obviously, there wasn't shared understanding between several cake decorators and the people who gave them instructions in writing. And, at NASA, someone important didn't share understanding with others working on the guidance system. I'm sure if you've been involved in software development for a while, you don't have to reach back far in your memory to recall a situation where two people believed they were in agreement on a feature they wanted to add to the software, but later found out that the way one imagined it was wildly different from the other.

---

1. There are a lot of articles that try to describe what went wrong with the Mars Orbiter. Here's one of them: *http://www.cnn.com/TECH/space/9909/30/mars.metric.02/*.

Building Shared Understanding Is Disruptively Simple

A former coworker of mine, Luke Barrett, first drew this cartoon to describe this problem. I asked him where he first saw it, but he didn't remember. So someone out there isn't getting the credit he or she deserves. For years I saw Luke step through these four frames as slides in a PowerPoint deck while I casually dismissed them as interesting but obvious. Apparently I've got a thick head. It's taken me many years to understand how this cartoon illustrates the most important thing about using stories in software development.

The idea is that if I have an idea in my head and I describe it in writing, when *you* read that document, you might quite possibly imagine something different. We could even ask everyone, "Do you all agree with what's written there?" and we might all say, "Yes! Yes, we do."

However, if we get together and talk, you can tell me what you think and I can ask questions. The talking goes better if we can externalize our thinking by drawing pictures or organizing our ideas using index cards or sticky notes. If we give each other time to explain our thoughts with words and pictures, we build shared understanding. It's at this point, though, that we realize that we all understood things differently. That sucks. But at least now we know.

It's not that one person is right or wrong, but that we all see different and important aspects. Through combining and refining our different ideas, we end up with a common understanding that includes all our best ideas. That's why externalizing our ideas is so important. We can redraw sketches or move sticky notes around, and the cool thing is that we're really moving ideas around. What we're really doing is evolving our shared understanding. That's super-hard with just words alone.

When we leave this conversation, we may still name the same feature or enhancement, it's just that now we actually mean the same thing. We feel aligned and confident we're moving forward together. That's the quality we're managing to. And, sadly, it's intangible. You can't see or touch "shared understanding," but you can feel it.

Stop Trying to Write Perfect Documents

There are a great number of people who believe that there's some ideal way to document—that, when people read documents and come away with different understandings, it's either the reader's fault or the document writer's. In reality, it's neither.

The answer is just to stop it.

Stop trying to write the perfect document.

Go ahead and write something, anything. Then use productive conversations with words and pictures to build shared understanding.

> *The real goal of using stories is shared understanding.*

Stories in Agile development get their name from how they should be used, not what you write down. If you're using stories in development and you're not talking together using words and pictures, you're doing it wrong.

If your goal in reading this book is to learn to write better stories, you've got the wrong goal.

Good Documents Are Like Vacation Photos

If I show you one of my vacation photos, you might see my kids on a beach and politely say, "That's cute," but when I look at my vacation photo, I remember a particular beach in Hawaii that we had to drive more than an hour on a deeply rutted four-wheel-drive trail, and then hike another half-hour over lava fields to get to. I remember my kids whining, saying nothing could possibly be worth this, and me wondering the same thing. But it was. We enjoyed a blissful day on an incredible beach where very few people were, which is why we took the trouble to get there. The turtles came up on the shore to bask on the sand, which was the icing on the cake of this fabulous day.

Of course, if you look at the picture you won't know all that because you weren't there. I remember all that because I was.

For better or worse, this is the way documents actually work.

If you participate in lots of discussions about what software to build, and then create a document to make sense of it, you might share it with someone else who was there. You might both agree it's good. But remember, your shared understanding is filling in details that aren't in the document. Another reader who wasn't there won't get the same things from it that you will. Even if she says she gets it, don't believe her. Get together and use the document to tell a story the same way I used my vacation photo to tell you my story.

Document to Help Remember

I've heard people joke, "We're using an Agile process because we've stopped writing documents." It's a joke for people who know, because a story-driven process needs lots of documents to work. But those documents don't always look at all like traditional requirements documents.

It takes talking and sketching and writing and working with sticky notes or index cards. It's pointing to documents we brought into the conversation and marking them up with highlighter and scribbled notes. It's interactive and high energy. If you're sitting at a conference table while a single person types what you say into a story management system, you're probably doing it wrong.

When you're telling stories, most anything can be used as a tool to communicate. And as we tell these stories, and write lots of notes, and draw lots of pictures, we need to keep them. We carry them around to look at later, photograph, and retype into more documents.

But, remember, what's most important isn't what's written down—it's what we remember when we read it. That's the vacation photo factor.

Talk, sketch, write, use sticky notes and cards, and then photograph your results. Even better, shoot a short video of you talking through what's on the board. You'll remember lots of details in a remarkable depth that you could never possibly document.

To help remember, photograph and shoot short videos of the results of your conversations.

Talking About the Right Thing

There are lots of people who believe their job is collecting and communicating requirements. But it's not.

The truth is, your job is to change the world.

Yes, I said that to get your attention. And, yes, I know that sounds like hyperbole. That's because that phrase is usually associated with world peace, eliminating poverty, or even more far-fetched goals like getting politicians to agree with one another. But I'm serious. Every great idea you turn into a product solution changes the world in some small, or not-so-small, way for the people who use it. In fact, if it doesn't, you've failed.

Now and Later

There's a simple, change-the-world model that I personally use and keep in my head all the time, and you need to keep it in your head too while you're having story conversation and building shared understanding.

I draw the model like this:

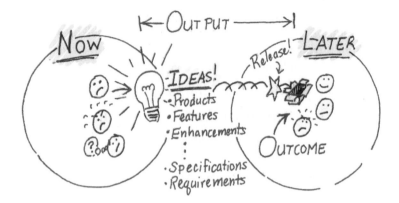

The model starts by looking at the world as it is now. When you look at the world as it is now, you're going to find people who are unhappy, mad, confused, or frustrated. Now, the world's a big place, so we'll focus mostly on the people who use the software we make, or the people we hope will use it. When you take a look at what they're doing—and the tools they use and how they're doing things—you're going to come up with ideas, and the ideas might be for:

- Entirely new products you can build
- Features to add to an existing product
- Enhancements to products that you've built

At some point in time, you'll have to communicate details about your ideas to some other people, and you might start to do some design and specification. If you're going to hand all this off to someone else, then you might indeed call all these details your *requirements*. But it's important to remember that requirements are just another name for the ideas we have that would help people.

Given those requirements, we go through some process that results in a delivery, and out comes some software that actually lands in the world, and it lands in the world *later*. And what we hope is true is that those people who were initially unhappy, mad, frustrated, or confused will become happy when that software lands. Now, they're not happy because they saw the pretty box it came in—software doesn't usually come in boxes these days anyway. They're not happy because they read the release notes, or downloaded the app to their mobile device. They're happy because when they use the software, or the website, or the mobile app, or whatever you've built, they do things differently— and that's what makes them happy.

Now, the truth is that you can't please everyone all of the time. Your mother should have told you that. Some people will be happier than others with whatever it is that you produce, and some might still be unhappy no matter how hard you've worked and how amazing your product might be.

Software Isn't the Point

Everything between the idea and the delivery is called *output*. It's what we build. People working in Agile software development will deliberately measure *velocity* of output and try to speed up their rate of output. As people are building software, they are, of course, concerned about the cost of what they're doing and the speed at which what they're doing gets done, as they should be.

But, while it's necessary, the output isn't the real point; it's not the output that we really wanted. It's what comes after as a result of that. It's called *outcome*. Outcome is what happens when things come out —that's why it's called that—and it's difficult because we don't get to measure outcome until things do come out. And we don't measure outcome by the number of features delivered, or what people have the capability to now do. We measure what people actually do differently to reach their goals as a consequence of what you've built, and most important, whether you've made their lives better.[2]

That's it. You've changed the world.

You've put something in it that changes the way people can reach their goals, and when they use it, the world is different for them.

If you remember, your goal isn't to just build a new product or feature. When you have conversations about that feature, you'll talk about who it's for, what they do now, and how things will change for them later. That positive change later is really why they'd want it.

---

2. The clean language and distinction between *output* and *outcome* was first made clear to me in a talk by Robert Fabricant called "Behavior Is Our Medium" (*http://vimeo.com/3730382*). Prior to that, I'd struggled with language that was clear in my head—and everyone else's too. Happily, it was clear in Robert's head.

Good story conversations are about who and why, not just what.

OK, It's Not Just About People

I care about people as much as the next guy, but truthfully, it's not just about making people happy. If you work for a company that pays you and others, you've got to focus on what ultimately helps your organization earn more, protect or expand its market, or operate more efficiently. Because, if your company isn't healthy, then you won't have the resources (or the job) to help anyone.

So I've got to revise this model a bit. It actually starts by looking inside your organization. There you'll find even more people who aren't happy. And it's usually because the business isn't performing as well as they'd hope. To fix this, they may have ideas to focus on specific customers or users and to make or improve the software products they're using. You see, it ultimately is about people, because:

Your company can't get what it wants unless your customers and users get something they want.

The flow continues by choosing the people to focus on, the problems to solve, and the ideas to turn into working software. And from there —if the customers buy, and the users use it, and people are happy— eventually the business that sponsored this development will see the benefit it's looking for. That'll be reflected in things like increased revenue, lower operational costs, happier customers, or expanded market share. This makes lots of people inside your company happy. It should make you happy, too, since you've just helped your company stay healthy while making real people's lives better in the process. It's a win-win.

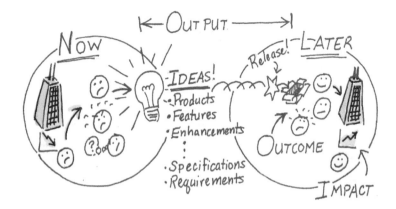

It's that longer-term stuff that happens as a consequence of good outcomes that's I'll label *impact*. Outcomes are often something you can observe right away after delivery. But impact takes longer.

Build Less

There's an uncomfortable truth about the software world, and I suspect it's true of lots of other places. But I know software. And what I know is that:

> *There's always more to build than we have*
> *time or resources to build—always.*

One of the common misconceptions in software development is that we're trying to get more output faster. Because it would make sense that if there was too much to do, doing it faster would help, right? But if you get the game right, you will realize that your job is not to build *more*—it's to build *less*.

> *Minimize output, and maximize outcome*
> *and impact.*

At the end of the day, your job is to *minimize* output, and *maximize* outcome and impact. The trick is that you've got to pay close attention to the people whose problems you're trying to solve. These include the people who will choose to buy the software to solve a problem in their organizations, the *choosers*, as well as the people who use it, the *users*. Sometimes they're the same people. Sometimes they're not.

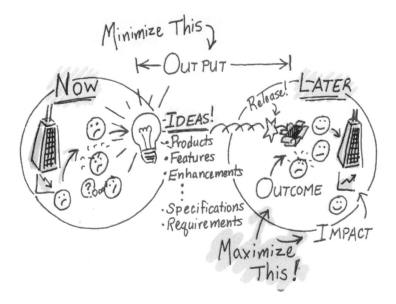

Your business has lots of possible users and customers it could focus on. Your businesses strategy should give you some guidance about who to focus on to get the impact you want. I promise you that no business has the resources to make *everyone* happy—it's just not possible.

Don't get me wrong here. Building more software faster is always a good idea. But it's never the solution.

More on the Dreaded "R" Word

For almost the entire first decade of my software career, which I spent building software for brick-and-mortar retailers, I got away without using the word *requirements*—at least, not much. It just wasn't a relevant term for what I was doing. I had lots of different customers who all had specific ideas about what would help them. I also knew I worked for a company that had to make money by selling my product. In fact, I'd spent long hours standing at trade shows helping my company sell its product to a wide variety of customers. I knew at the end of the day that I would have to continue to work with those customers after I shipped the products my team and I developed, and so I diligently worked to act in their best interest. This meant I couldn't give everyone everything they wanted, because they wanted different things. And my company and team didn't have infinite time, so I had to work hard to figure out the least I could build to make people happy. That may sound frustrating, but it's actually the fun part.

As the company grew, we added more traditional software people. At one point, the head of a different team came to me and said, "Jeff, I need you to make these changes to the product you're working on."

I said, "Great, no problem. Tell me who they're for and what problems this solves for them."

Her response? "They're the requirements."

I replied, "I get it. Just tell me a bit about who they're for, and how they're going to use this, and where it fits into the way they work."

She looked at me like I was stupid and said to me one last time with an air of finality, "They're *requirements*."

It was at that moment that I learned that the word *requirements* actually means *shut up*.

For a great many people, that's exactly what requirements do. They stop conversations about people and the problems we're solving. The truth is, if you build a fraction of what's required you can still make people very happy.[3]

Remember: at the end of the day, your job isn't to get the requirements right—your job is to change the world.

That's All There Is to It

If you get nothing else from this book, remember these things:

- Stories aren't a written form of requirements; telling stories through collaboration with words and pictures is a mechanism that builds shared understanding.
- Stories aren't the requirements; they're discussions about solving problems for our organization, our customers, and our users that lead to agreements on what to build.

---

3. Because I strongly agree with the sentiment, I'm paraphrasing the way Kent Beck cautions against the misuse of the term requirement in his book *Extreme Programming Explained* (Addison-Wesley).

- Your job isn't to build more software faster: it's to maximize the outcome and impact you get from what you choose to build.

Stories as they're intended are a completely different way of thinking about the challenges we face working together to create software—and lots of other things, for that matter. If you can work together effectively and create things that solve problems, you will rule the world. Or at least some small part of it inhabited by your products.

As you read this book, my hope is that you get back to the basics of using stories. I hope you work together with others, telling stories about your users and customers and how you can help them. I hope you draw pictures, and build big sticky-note models. I hope you feel engaged and creative. I hope you feel like you're making a difference. Because when you do it right, you are. And it's a lot more fun, too.

Now it's time to talk about the most fun you can possibly have telling stories, and that's when you're using a story map.

CHAPTER 1

The Big Picture

"I love Agile development! Every few weeks we see more working software. But it feels like I've lost the big picture."

If I had a dime for every time I heard something like that from an Agile team member, I'd have...well...a lot of dimes. I hear it a lot. You may have even said something like that yourself. Well, I've got good news for you. Using an Agile process and a story-driven approach doesn't mean you have to sacrifice the big picture. You can still have healthy discussions about your whole product and still see progress every few weeks.

Since you've patiently read the "Read This First" chapter, I'm going to bypass all the junk about stories and proceed directly to how story maps solve one of the biggest problems in Agile development. If you're already familiar with writing stories on Agile projects, this chapter may be enough to get you started.

The "A" Word

If you're reading this book, you likely know that story mapping is a way to work with user stories as they're used in Agile processes. Now, it's at this point that every other book that has something to do with Agile development reproduces the "Manifesto for Agile Software Development," that thing written in 2001 by 17 guys who were frustrated with some of the big counterproductive process trends going on at the time. I'm glad they wrote it. And I'm glad that the impact of their work has been felt by so many.

But I'm sorry to disappoint you—I'm not going to reprint the manifesto and gush about why it matters. I believe you already know why it does. And, if you haven't read the manifesto, then you should.

In the space that the manifesto would have taken up in this chapter, I am instead including a funny kitten photo.[1] Why? Because it has been proven time and time again that funny kitten photos on the Internet get far more attention than *any* manifesto could ever hope to.

So, you might wonder, what does this kitten have to do with Agile? Actually, nothing. But Agile definitely has something to do with this book, and with stories and the evolution of story mapping.

<Cue the flashback music…>

I was working at a startup in San Francisco in 2000, and the company had hired Kent Beck (the guy who created Extreme Programming and first described the idea of stories) as a consultant to get the software development process going. I'm rewinding way back, but the important thing is this story idea is an old one. If you're just starting out with using stories, you lost any early adopter status you could have had a decade or so ago. Kent and others who pioneered Extreme Programming knew that all those ways of doing requirements in the past didn't work out well. Kent's simple idea was that we should get together and

---

1. Photo taken by Piutus, found on Flickr (*https://flic.kr/p/4PifQX*) and licensed under the Creative Common Attribution license.

tell our stories; that by talking we could build shared understanding, and together we'd arrive at better solutions.

Telling Stories, Not Writing Stories

When I first heard the term *story*, it bugged me. I'll admit it. The idea that we'd trivialize the important things that people wanted by calling them stories didn't seem right. But I'm a slow learner—a point I brought up earlier when discussing shared understanding. It took me a while to really get that:

> *Stories get their name from how they should be used, not what should be written.*

Even before I'd really understood why stories had that name, I realized that I could write down a bunch of stories—a sentence or a short title —on sticky notes or cards. I could move them around and prioritize them to decide which one was more important. Once I decided that one was more important than another, then we could start having a discussion about it. This was super-cool. Why hadn't I ever written things on cards and organized them this way before?

The problem was that this one card could be something that might take a software developer just a couple hours to add to a product, or maybe a couple days or a couple weeks, or maybe a month—who knew? I didn't—at least not until we started talking about it.

I got into a nasty argument while working with stories on my very first Agile project when I began a story conversation and learned that my story was too big. I'd hoped to get this story done in the next iteration. The developers I spoke with informed me otherwise. I felt like I'd done something wrong. The developers identified a small part we could talk about that could be accomplished in our next iteration. But I left frustrated that we couldn't talk about the big picture. I really wanted to understand how much time the big thing I really needed would take. I'd hoped this discussion would accomplish that, and it didn't.

Telling the Whole Story

In 2001 I left the team I was on and started doing things differently. I, and my team, tried an approach to writing stories that focused on the big picture. We worked to understand the product we were building and to make tradeoffs together. We used that bunch of index cards with story titles to organize our thoughts and break down that big picture into the small parts we could build next. In 2004, I wrote my first article about this idea. I didn't coin the term *story mapping*, however, until 2007.

It turns out that the name you give something matters. It was after giving the practice a good name that I really saw it spread. I thought it was a great invention at the time—that is, until I started running into more people who were doing similar if not exactly the same things. I'd discovered a *pattern*.

I first heard this definition of a pattern from my friend Linda Rising: when you tell someone about a great idea and he says, "Yeah, we do something like that, too." It's not an invention, it's a pattern.

Story mapping is a pattern. It's what sensible people do to make sense of a whole product or whole feature. It's what they do to break down large stories into smaller ones. Don't feel bad if you didn't arrive at it on your own. You would have eventually. But reading this book will save you weeks or months of frustration.

Story maps are for breaking down big stories as you tell them.

Today, company after company has adopted the idea of story mapping. My friend Martina at SAP said in a message she sent in September 2013 that:

> ...at this point more than 120 USM [User Story Mapping] workshops have officially been recorded. A lot of POs just simply love it! It is simply a well-established approach at SAP.

Every week I hear from someone else from somewhere else telling me how mapping stories helped solve a problem for them. These days, I learn more from talking to others than I ever could on my own.

The original idea of stories was a simple one. It turned our focus away from shared documents and toward shared understanding. A common way to use stories is to build a list of them, prioritize them, and begin talking about them and then turning them into software one at a time. That sounds pretty reasonable when you hear about it. But it can create some big problems.

Gary and the Tragedy of the Flat Backlog

A few years ago I met Gary Levitt. Gary was a businessperson in the process of launching a new web product. The web product is out there right now, and it's called Mad Mimi, which when Gary conceived of his product, was short for *music industry marketing interface*.[2] Gary is a musician who had his own band. He managed his band, helped manage others, and was also a studio musician and created recordings for clients.

The day I met Gary he had an order from the Oprah Winfrey show for dozens of intros and outros, little bits of music that are used to go out to and come in from commercials and things like that. Producers of television shows buy those the way people laying out a newsletter buy clip art, so it's like audio clip art. Gary had an idea for a fairly big application that would help musicians like him and people he knew to collaborate with one another on projects like the one he was working on, along with lots of other things a band manager and musician would need to do to manage and promote his band.

Gary wanted to get the software built so he worked with somebody, and that somebody was working in an Agile way. That person told Gary to write down a list of all the things he wanted, prioritize the list, and then they would talk about the highest-valued things—the most important—and start building them one at a time. That list of things

---

2. Read about Gary in the *Business Insider* article "How This Guy Launched A Multi-Million Dollar Startup Without Any VC Money" (*http://read.bi/UtcIIE*).

is what Agile processes refer to as a *backlog*, and it seemed to make sense to Gary to create the list and start with the most important things first. So that's what he did.

Gary created his backlog and the development team started building things a bit at a time. In the meantime, Gary was hemorrhaging cash as he continued to pay for each piece of software that was built. The software was slowly taking shape, but Gary could tell it was going to take a lot longer for it to match his vision and he was going to run out of cash long before then.

I knew the person who was working with Gary. My friend knew Gary was stressing out and wanted to help him. The somebody I knew asked if I could have a conversation with Gary, to talk with him and help him get his ideas organized. I contacted Gary and made arrangements to meet him at his office in Manhattan.

Talk and Doc

Gary and I started talking. And as he talked, I wrote cards with key points from what he said. There's a mantra that I like when I build story maps. I'll say "talk and doc" (short for the verb *document*), which basically means don't let your words vaporize. Write them down on cards so you can refer back to them later. You'll notice how pointing to a few words on a card quickly helps everyone recall the conversation about it. We can slide them around the table where we can reorganize them. We start using useful words like *this* and *that* as we point to cards. It saves lots of time. Helping Gary externalize his thoughts was critical to getting shared understanding. It wasn't a habit for him, so it was easy for me to write the cards as he told the story.

> *Talk and doc: write cards or sticky notes to externalize your thinking as you tell stories.*

We started by placing cards on a tabletop, but quickly ran out of space. Gary was moving offices the day I visited with him, and much of the furniture in the New York City loft where he was located was off the floor. So we moved our growing map of cards onto the floor.

At the end of the day, the floor looked like this:

Think — Write — Explain — Place

When working with a team to build a story map, or having discussions about anything, create a simple visualization to support your discussion. One of the things that goes wrong is lots of ideas *vaporize*—that is, we say them, and people nod as if they've heard. The ideas are not written down or referred to. Then, later in the conversation, the ideas come up again and unfortunately need to be re-explained because people didn't really hear or forgot them.

Get in the habit of writing down a little about your idea before explaining it.

1. If you're using cards or sticky notes, *write* down a few words about your idea immediately *after thinking* it.

2. *Explain* your idea to others as you point to the sticky note or card. Use big gestures. Draw more pictures. Tell stories.

3. *Place* the card or sticky into a shared workspace where everyone can see, point to, add to, and move it around. Hopefully, there will be lots of other ideas from you and others in this growing pile.

I find that when I'm doing my best to listen to others, what they're saying causes me to think of other ideas. I used to try to hold those ideas in my head and wait for a moment to inject them into the conversation, resorting to outright interruption if the time didn't come soon enough. But then I realized I'd stopped listening to the person who was talking, as my limited brainpower was focused on recalling my great idea. Today, I simply scribble the idea on a sticky note and set it aside to wait for a better point in the conversation to inject it. Somehow writing it pops it out of my head so I can focus on what I'm hearing. And reading it from the sticky later helps me recall my idea and explain it.

I wasn't here to capture Gary's requirements. And the first thing we talked about wasn't that list of features. We had to back up a bit and start at the beginning.

Frame Your Idea

Our first conversation focused on framing his product idea. We talked about his business and what his goals were. *Why are you building this? Tell me about the benefits for you and for the people who will use this. What problems does it solve for those people and for you?* As you read this you might detect I've got that now-and-later model in my head. I'm trying to understand the outcomes Gary is looking for, not the output he wants to build.

If I put two cards down, one above the other, then people assume that the one above is more important. Without saying a word, if I simply slide a card above another, I've indicated something about importance. Try that with a list of goals. Purposely put them in the wrong order and watch the person you're working with reach out to adjust them. I did this with Gary and his goals, and it helped him express what was more important to him.

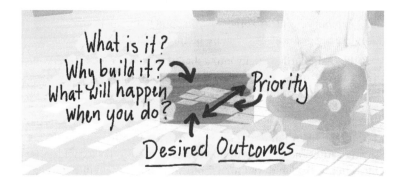

Describe Your Customers and Users

Gary and I continued to talk and doc. The next conversation Gary and I had was about the customers who would buy, and users who would use, his piece of software. We listed the different types of users. We talked about what benefits they would get, and asked why they would use the product and what we thought they would do with it. What was in it for them? We built a big pile of those. The cards naturally seemed to fall with most important users higher in the pile. Funny how it works out that way without an explicit decision.

Before we'd gone into any detail at all, I could already see that Gary's vision was big. One of the tough realities about software development is that there's always more to build than we have time and money for. So the goal should *never* be to build it all. The goal is to minimize the amount we build. So the first question I asked Gary was, "Of all these different users and the things they want to do, if we were to focus on thrilling just one of those users, who would it be?"

Gary chose one and we started to really tell stories.

Mad Mimi User Types

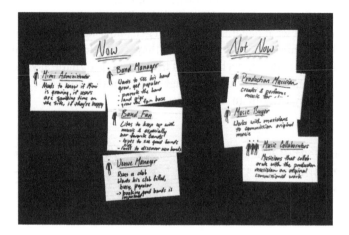

These are the different types of users Gary described for Mad Mimi. Just naming them and writing a little about what they want helped us both see that there was a lot here. Even before discussing features, we'd decided to defer creating software for some types of users.

Tell Your Users' Stories

I next said, "OK, let's imagine the future. Let's assume for a minute this product is live and let's talk about a day in the life of someone who uses it and start telling the story. First, they would do this, and then this, and so on and so on." And we told the story in a flow from left to right. Sometimes we backtracked and put things to the left of other things, and because they were on cards, we could easily rearrange them.

The other interesting thing that happens naturally when working with cards is if I put one to the left and another to the right, without saying a word I've indicated sequence. This is kind of magical for me—but I'm easily entertained. I marvel at how much we can communicate without saying a word.

Reorganizing cards together allows you to communicate without saying a word.

As we talk and doc, and as I write down our conversation, we're building something really important. No, it's not that pile of cards on the floor. The something that's really important is *shared understanding*. We're getting on the same page. This is something Gary had never done with anyone before about his product idea, at least not at this level of detail. He'd never even given it this much thought himself. The high points were in his head, sort of like the action scenes you'd see in a movie preview.

Before now, Gary had done what he was asked to do. He'd written a bunch of story titles, put them in a list, and talked about them one at a time. The conversations were more about the details of what to build and less about this big picture. And there were a lot of holes in Gary's big picture. You'll find that no matter how clear you are about your story, talking through it while you map will help you discover the holes in your own thinking.

Mapping your story helps you find holes in your thinking.

As we dug deeper, we realized that the story also wasn't just about one user. Gary's started with a band manager who wanted to promote his band and the work he was doing to create the promotion and email it to fans. Then we quickly had to talk about the fan of the band, and tell her story about seeing the promotion and then making plans to see a show.

Then, if we were promoting the band someplace, we'd need to tell the story of the venue's manager and the information he'd like to learn about the promotion. By this time, our map was wide enough that we bumped into the wall, so we had to continue the story in another layer below the first. That's why the map in the photograph has two layers.

During the story, sometimes Gary would get to a part where he was excited and he'd start describing lots of details. One card above another can indicate priority. But it can also mean *decomposition*, which is just a fancy word for smaller details that are part of a bigger thing. As Gary described the details, I'd record them on a card, and place them below the big user step above. For instance, when Gary described creating the flyer that band managers would use to promote their gigs, he was extra passionate and had lots of details to discuss.

Gary lived in New York City, and when bands are composing flyers he's imagining all these really cool things he sees stuck on walls and lampposts in New York. They might look like they were put together with glue and tape and then photocopied, but some were really elegant and artistic. After recording a handful of details, I said, "Let's come back and get to the details later. Let's continue on and move this story forward." It's easy to get lost in the details, especially the ones you're passionate about. But, when we're trying to get the big picture, it's important to get to the end of the story before catching all those details. Another mantra I use when mapping, at least at this stage, is "think mile wide, inch deep"—or for people in sane countries using the metric system: "kilometer wide, centimeter deep." Get to the end of the story before getting lost in the details.

Focus on the breadth of the story before diving into the depth.

Eventually we *did* get to the end of Gary's story. The band manager had successfully promoted a gig to thousands of fans who spread the word, and the show was a wild success. The product vision so far was clear in both our heads. I said, "Now let's go back and fill in the details and consider some of the alternatives."

Mimi's Big Story

If you read across the top of Gary's map, you'll see big activities like:

- Signing up
- Changing my service
- Viewing my band stats
- Working with my show calendar
- Working with my audience
- Publicizing a show
- Signing up for a band's email list
- Viewing promotions online

There were lots of other big things at the top of the map, but that's a good subset to give you an idea of what you'd write on a card. Notice how we can assume who does what. When Gary said, "Publicizing a show," he knew he was talking about the band manager. When I said, "signing up for the band's email list," Gary knew I was talking about the band's fan. Those cards were close by and easy to point to during our conversation.

"Publicizing a show" was a big thing. It broke down into these steps arranged left to right underneath the "Publicizing the show" card.

- Start a show promotion.
- Review the promo flyer Mimi created for me.
- Customize the promo flyer.
- Preview the promo flyer I created.

Notice how what we wrote on every card are short verb phrases that say what the specific type of user wants to do. Writing them this way helped us tell the story: "the band manager would then publicize the show. To do that he'd start a promotion, then review the flyer Mimi created, then customize it, and then…" Notice how when you put "and then" in between what's written on each card, you get a nice story.

Explore Details and Options

After we've got the breadth of the story map in place, it starts thickening up. The cards we put at the top of each of the columns in the map become big things, and then the details break down below them. We stop at each step in the user's story and ask:

- What are the specific things they'd do here?
- What are alternative things they could do?
- What would make it really cool?
- What about when things go wrong?

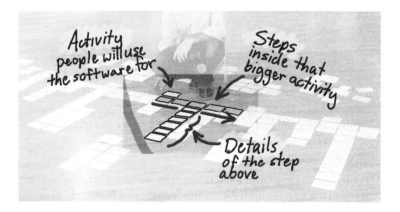

At the end of this we'd gone back and filled in a lot of details. The result was that we had told the story about a day in the life of a band manager, as well as the other people important to the band manager's success: fans and venue managers.

The Details

If you look inside a story step like "Customize the promo flyer," you'd see details like:

- Upload an image
- Attach an audio file
- Embed a video
- Add free text
- Change the layout
- Start with a promotion I've used before

You can see that even these smaller steps will need a lot more discussion to work out the details. But at least we could begin to name them all.

Notice how what's written on the cards are also those short verb phrases that help you tell stories. We can string this together with phrases like "or he might" like this: "to customize the flyer the band manager might upload an image, or he might attach an audio file or embed a video, or…" It's pretty cool, really.

I asked Gary, "Now what? We have all these other users with other things they want to do—do you want to talk about them? You can see that if we keep talking we'll need a bigger room. And, Gary, if you do all this stuff, it will take a lot of money to build this product. We could talk about the rest of this stuff, but if we built this much and you launched your product and just did this, that looks like it'd be a valuable product."

Gary agreed, and he said, "I'm going to stop there."

The sad part of this story is that I asked Gary, "You've been building a lot of software so far, but how much of the software you've built is on this map we've created?"

"Nearly none of it," Gary replied, "because when I built a list and prioritized things, I sort of assumed we needed to start somewhere else. I was thinking about the whole big vision of this thing, the vision that would have taken me years to reach, and now that we've had this discussion I wouldn't have started there at all."

Story mapping is all about having a good old-fashioned conversation and then organizing it in the form of a map. The part that most people look at is the map—that left-to-right shape with the steps people take to tell a big story. The top to bottom is about the details. But the critical parts that frame the product and give more context are often hung above and around the map. They're the product's goals, and information about its customers and users. If you keep a map on the wall, you'll find it's good idea to add user interface (UI) sketches and other notes around the map.

In just a day working together, Gary and I built shared understanding around the product he wanted to build. But there was a storm cloud forming above our heads, and we knew it. Inside each of those cards we wrote were lots of details and lots more discussions. And, for Gary, all those details and all those discussions equated to money he would need to spend to build software—money he didn't have. He'd learned one of the fundamental truths about software development: there's always more to build than you'll have time for.

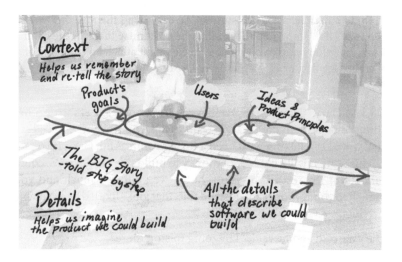

Now, there are a lot of other big assumptions Gary was making about the people who'd use his product, and if they really wanted to, or really could use it as he envisioned. But, right now, those things weren't his biggest concern. He needed to work harder to minimize his product idea to something that was feasible first.

Gary's story eventually has a very happy ending. But in the next chapter I'll tell the story of another organization that learned it had way too much to build, and how it used a map to find a viable solution.

Artgility—Creativity in Art Meets Creativity in IT

Ceedee (Clare) Doyle, Agile Project Manager and Coach,
Assurity Ltd, Wellington, NZ

Background

The Learning Connexion (TLC) is an art college in Wellington, New Zealand, that teaches art and creativity. TLC's programs are unique because they are based on "learning by doing"; that is, the practice is the theory. In conjunction with tutors, students develop briefs that connect with the ideas they choose to explore.

TLC was a typical small-to-medium-size organization that had developed ad hoc IT systems to support the needs it had at the time. Student information was collected in five different places and was different in each! TLC needed some way to manage students that would work for it and the way it teaches, which is quite different from most educational establishments.

TLC had no experience with IT projects. Each small application that had been built for it had been done by somebody's-brother's-friend's-flatmate's-dog using simple technologies like Microsoft Excel and Access. The sole commercial application (used for statutory reporting) double-handled data from the other four sources.

As a former student, I had kept in touch with the team and when they needed some help they contacted me. In 2009 I had been in IT for nine years and had wanted to do an Agile project for the last three, ever since I had heard about it. This was the right place, the right project, and the right time to do it!

Project Phoenix

The initial workshops were going to be two half-day sessions with key staff members. I was working with a large, diverse group, and my goal was to develop shared understanding. I started with an overview of how story mapping works and an overview of the big steps in the school's student management process.

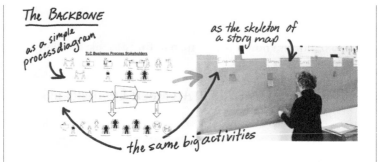

The BACKBONE

as a simple process diagram

as the skeleton of a story map

the same big activities

Up until I showed them this picture (the backbone of the story map), the team members each had an idea of what *they* did, but, as Alice the sponsor said, it was probably the first time they all had a clear picture of their own business process and how all the steps interacted.

From there we brainstormed what people wanted the system to do. The scope was *massive*, and the stories were *many*.

The map loaded with ideas

printed ideas we identified before the workshop

new ideas added during the workshop on sticky-notes

The beauty was that these were creative people and they were used to the "appreciative enquiry" method, so braindumping everything they could think of that the system needed to do was something they took to like a baker makes bread.

The main headings (from the diagram) were Enquiries → Admissions → Enrollments → Classes → Complete work → Completion → Graduation.

Using the story mapping guidelines, we then walked through each section to make sure that it made sense, and got the flow for a student through each step of the process. Several people had lights go on suddenly, as they realized where they fit into the overall process and *why* they had to do some of their activities, and others realized they were being left out of certain steps that would make a big difference to them. Stepping through the story map and my emphasis on having stories vertically—which happened together—showed places where they could work together better and steps that were doubled up. Until this point, the team had little view of what everyone else was doing, but they suddenly developed shared understanding of how the whole process worked and a common lexicon. In one example, *Classes* was renamed *Delivery* because not all students attend classes.

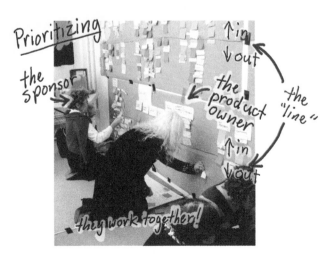

When it came to prioritizing, it wouldn't have worked to identify the must-haves, should-haves, and could-haves—it was either in or out. It was very simple: "we cannot go live without this" above the line, and everything else below it. After we'd walked through the Enquiries, the team got it and spent the remainder of the day doing the rest. I was able to step out of it! The staff took over and started adding subheadings to better describe that "these things all have to happen together, and then these things." So, by the end, they had created, as a group, a big picture of the steps a student follows to get from initial enquiry to graduation.

What started out as two half-day sessions turned into three full days of workshops in which people came and went as the need arose (they had to teach classes, and so forth). The flexibility of the workplace meant that nearly all the staff came through the Phoenix room and had their two cents' worth. They found the process really useful to get the big picture and for everyone to have their wants included. It also identified where there were gaps and made it easy to sift out what was really vital. At the end of it, we had a clear picture of what was to be in the first cut of the software.

CHAPTER 2

Plan to Build Less

*There's always more to build than you have
people, time, or money for. Always.*

Speaking in absolutes like "always" and "never" always gets me in trouble. But with the statement above, I honestly can't recall a situation where it wasn't true although I have no sciencey data to back this up. No one has ever once come to me saying, "We were asked to add this new feature, and happily we had lots more time than we needed."

But one of the coolest things about using a story map is that it gives you and other collaborators a space to think through alternatives and to find a way to get a great outcome in the time that you have.

Grab a cup of coffee and settle into your chair. It's time for a story.

This story is about my friends at Globo.com, the largest media company in Brazil. Globo.com owns television and radio stations, produces made-for-TV movies and original programming, and publishes newspapers. It is a media monster in Brazil, and the largest Portuguese-language media company in the world.

Globo.com knows better than most organizations on the planet what unmovable deadlines really are. For example, it produces a cool version of a fantasy football game that's revised and improved every year for World Cup soccer—the sport that most of the planet refers to as football. If Globo.com is late with development of that game, it doesn't have the luxury of changing the release date. Why not? Because the rest of the world won't reschedule the World Cup. Globo.com will produce features and content for the Olympics games that Brazil will host in 2016, and I can guarantee you that it'll get it done in time—it has to. And it'll produce features and content for the release of numerous new television programs and reality TV shows. None of these things can be rescheduled if Globo.com is late. Globo.com must *always* finish on time. And, since that's the reality of its business, Globo.com is good at it. That's not because the company is faster than everyone else—sure, it's fast, but it's not *that* fast. It's because it's smart about doing less.

Mapping Helps Big Groups Build Shared Understanding

Take a look at this:

That's just a portion of a pretty big map built by leaders of eight teams from three different groups at Globo.com working together. The teams from Sports, News, and Entertainment built this together to think through the work they needed to do to rebuild, revamp, and renovate their underlying content management system. This is the system that drives all those news websites, sports websites, soap opera websites, features that help publicize and recruit people for reality TV shows, and much, much more. This massive system needs to be able to handle large quantities of video feeds, real-time scores and election results, photographs, fast-breaking news stories, and much more. It has a lot to do, and it needs to look good doing it.

When I arrived at the Globo.com offices the day they built this map, the teams working together were about to fall into the *flat backlog trap*. Individual teams had prepared their respective prioritized backlogs. It was already clear there was a huge amount of work to do, and each team depended on the other. For instance, to get a good news site out would need not just the news team, but also all the other teams that built the foundational components that let the news website use photos, videos, real-time data, and lots of other things.

I sat down with them and reminded them of something they already knew: "I understand that you're different teams because you're focusing on different areas, but it's a major revision of *one* content management system. You'll have to release together. You can't plan a release until you can see it all together. You've got to visualize all these dependencies." They agreed and quickly went to work reorganizing their individual backlogs into a map. Within a few hours they built a map on the wall using sticky notes that told the story of their content management system.

I wasn't in the room while team members worked together to build the map. But when I returned later in the day, I was amazed at how quickly they'd built it. They were pleased with themselves, and had every right to be. They'd made sense of several complex backlogs, organizing them into one coherent product story. And now each team could see where its work fit into the big picture.

Map for a product release across multiple teams to visualize dependencies.

Anatomy of a Big Map

Globo's map is good example of what a typical map looks like *after* you've framed, mapped, and explored lots of details.

The Backbone Organizes the Map

At the top of the map is the *backbone*, which sometimes has a couple of different levels. You might start with the basic flow of the story, which is one level. But, when it gets really long, it's useful to go up one more level to summarize things further. Later, I'll add some language about what I like to put at each level, but I'm reminded of an old friend of mine who told me to stop trying to come up with precise language. "It's just big things and little things," he'd tell me. And he's right.

The whole thing kind of looks like you extracted the spine out of a weird, Seussian animal. You've got this long backbone at the top with ts of irregularly spaced vertebrae, and these long ribs of varying ngth hanging down from it.

Map in Whole Deliverable Releases

This map was built by multiple teams at Globo. There are development teams responsible for video, and teams charged with the task of building the stuff on the backend that editors use to create and manage content. There are teams responsible for some of the underlying metadata and associations between data—that semantic markup junk that I can never quite grok. And there are people who handle the external presentation and how good this stuff looks when users and/or consumers see it. And still more people are looking after specific features relevant to news, sports, or entertainment.

Multiple teams had to work together on this map because, for this major revision, no single team could release its part without the others. The teams built a single map because they needed to think through the release holistically.

Map in a Narrative Flow Across Many Users and Systems

The map started with people on the left, and the things they had to do to set up basic widgets for the screens that held news stories, pictures, and videos. There were other types of people who then combined those onto pages for soap opera or news websites. Then there were editors who added content to pages. This entire backbone tells the story of how lots of different people at Globo.com construct and manage content in its website.

When you read the backbone of the map from left to right, it tells a story about all the people who use the system and what they do in order to create and manage sites and content. The left-to-right order is what I call a *narrative flow*, which is an academic way of saying the order in which we'd tell the story. Of course, all these people are doing everything all at once, and sometimes things don't move in a perfect order, but we know that. We just put them in an order that helps us tell the story.

For this big system, that narrative flow has to *cut through many different users' and systems' stories*. I like to place stickies or simple persona thumbnails above the backbone so I can see who we're talking about at particular times in the story. And it's OK to anthropomorphize backend services or complex stuff the system does. My friends at SAP create fictitious personas for their systems and use pictures of R2D2 or C3PO from *Star Wars*.

Mapping Helps You Spot Holes in Your Story

When I talk with people who have built story maps, they'll tell me, "Every time we do this we find holes. We find things that we thought *another* team should be taking care of, but it didn't know. We find the necessary stuff in between the big important features that we'd forgot to talk about." By mapping together, Globo.com found some of that.

After you've envisioned the whole product or feature, it's easier to start to play the "What-About" game. That's where we start asking, "What about when this goes wrong?" Or "What about these other users?" Play What-About with any concern you have, and add stickies to the body of the map for feature ideas you'll need in order to address these things in your software. In Chapter 1, Gary played What-About to consider options and alternatives. When you do this with other teams, you'll find they're terrific at spotting problems that might arise where different systems connect to each other.

One of the criticisms people sometimes make about story mapping is that every time they sit down and create story maps, they end up with way too much. But it's my belief that we're just finding the stuff now that would have bitten us later on, and that's a good thing.

In the old-school approach to software development, when we'd find that new stuff later on—after we'd already estimated delivery time and committed to a delivery date—we'd call that new stuff *scope creep*. I personally believe that scope doesn't creep; understanding grows. And what happens when people build one of these story maps is that they find the holes in their understanding.

Scope doesn't creep; understanding grows.

There's Always Too Much

When I left the content management teams at Globo.com, everything was wonderful—understanding was rampant and the teams knew what to do. However, when I came back to check in with them a couple days later, they were struggling again because they realized that there was so much work to be done, that it would likely take more than a year to accomplish everything on the map. And, of course, as savvy readers can appreciate, when software developers say it's going to take a year to get something done, they really mean two years. It's not because they're incompetent, or that they are calendar-challenged, it's just that estimating the time to do something we've never done before is something we suck at. And, by nature, we're often optimistic animals.

They said to me, "There's way too much. We have a lot to do here and it's going to take a long time."

"Do you have to do it all?" I asked.

They, of course, replied, "Yes, because it's all part of one, big content management system."

"But projects don't run that long around here," I replied. "I know your CEO and he's going to want to see results much faster—right?"

"Yes," they confirmed, "he wants to see something live in time for the upcoming Brazilian election in a few months!"

"Do you need *all* of this to go live for the election?" I asked.

As soon as I asked the question, I could see light bulbs click on. Of course they didn't need *everything*. Up 'til now, they'd been focused on identifying sequence and dependency assuming they'd need to build everything. They did, but it was really a question of when. They shifted their thinking to focus on outcomes.

Focus on what you hope will happen outside the system to make decisions about what's inside the system.

Globo.com focused on Brazilian elections. The teams thought specifically about the great *outcome* of successfully impressing visitors, advertisers, and Globo's parent media company with newer, sexier styles of interactive content throughout the election. If they did that, they'd have a win.

This wasn't their first time facing down an impossible delivery date. They thought about it for a bit, and realized that they definitely needed to go live with the news website, and potentially some other things that supported it because that's where visitors and others would go to monitor Brazilian elections. Focusing on the news website meant paying attention to innovative ways to show real-time election data and breaking news stories faster. And, of course, there was a newer, up-to-date visual design overlaying everything.

Slice Out a Minimum Viable Product Release

The teams grabbed a roll of blue painter's tape and stretched lines across the map left to right to make horizontal slices. They then went to work moving cards up and down, above and below the blue lines to designate which things needed to be done in the first slice, and which could be done later.

The thought process worked a bit like this: *If we go live for the Brazilian elections, a lot of people in Brazil will see this thing. It's going to land with a splash. It's going to affect these websites of ours and we'll look good. Everything in this slice is what users will need to be able to do after the software is released so they can make that splash.*

> *Focus on outcomes—what users need to do and see when the system comes out—and slice out releases that will get you those outcomes.*

Slice Out a Release Roadmap

The map contained innovative things that would improve all Globo.com's web properties. But it really was going to take a long time to get all of it done. Hitting the market window that the elections created would be too big an opportunity to miss. Focusing on that helped Globo identify the first release.

The teams then went to work thinking about what kinds of web properties and market events should anchor the next releases. They posted sticky notes to the left of each slice with a few words describing their intention for each release slice—their target outcomes. Then they continued to move cards up and down into their correct slices.

In the end, they had an incremental release strategy that let them tackle all the work they needed to do to replace the whole content management system over time, and in such a way that they saw real benefit with each release. If they read down the left edge of the map, they had a list of named releases, each with specific target outcomes. This is a *release roadmap*.

Notice how the list isn't a bunch of features. It's a list of real-world benefits—because, remember, your job isn't to build software, it's to change the world. The hard part is choosing which people you want to change the world for, and how.

> *Focusing on specific target outcomes is the*
> *secret to prioritizing development work.*

And the opposite is true as well; that is, if you don't know what your target outcomes are—the specific benefits you're trying to get—then prioritization is close to impossible.

Don't Prioritize Features—Prioritize Outcomes

Notice also how the Globo teams started with a big goal of replacing their entire content management system. Replacing the content management system is the output, the stuff they were going to deliver. Doing that would result in lots of positive outcomes. The secret to breaking down that really big chunk of output was to focus on a smaller, specific outcome.

Remember: behind outcomes are specific behavior changes for specific people engaged in specific activities. By focusing on the upcoming Brazilian elections, Globo chose to focus on the people who follow the news, especially those looking for up-to-the-minute election details. But, in placing its focus on those people, it left out soap opera lovers, sports lovers, and lots of other types of users. Those other people would have to be satisfied with the current site for a while longer. Remember, you can't please everyone all the time.

This Is Magic—Really, It Is

I may be easily impressed, but slicing is one of the coolest things about organizing software ideas into a story map.

Many times I, and the teams I've worked with, have placed all our ideas about the perfect product into a map and been overwhelmed by the amount of work we'd have if we created it all. It *all* seems important. But then we step back and think about the specific people who will use our product, and what they'll need to accomplish to be successful. We distill that into a sentence or two. Then we carve away everything we don't need, and we're shocked at how small our viable solution really is. It's *magic*.

Gary from Chapter 1 went on to do something similar with his product. He eventually narrowed focus to the band manager, the fan, and Mimi's internal administrator—because you've got to keep the site running. Gary chose to leave out venue managers and production musicians. In the end, what he realized is that by focusing on just those few people and the activity of promoting, he ended up with a great email promotion platform. So, for those of you who are Mimi users today, that's the experience you know.

Externalizing our thinking in a big visible map makes all these steps easier. It makes it possible for lots of people to collaborate to accomplish it.

Finding a Smaller Viable Release

Chris Shinkle, SEP

FORUM Credit Union is one of the nation's largest and most technologically progressive credit unions. Although the company had a competent and creative development culture, it approached SEP to build a new online banking system that rivaled existing commercial off-the-shelf (COTS) solutions. Its goals included adding capabilities for its mobile banking, personal finance management, and text banking.

SEP kicked off the engagement with a two-day, collaborative story-mapping discovery session that included outcomes, personas, and story mapping. The session helped facilitate a structured conversation to prioritize a large set of feature ideas. The outcomes and personas were not enough, however, to prioritize the stories. By the end of two days, the story map covered nearly two walls in the 1,000+ square-foot development area!

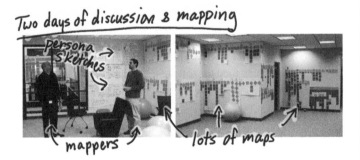

After the story map was constructed, SEP guided the FORUM stakeholders through a simple prioritization model:

Differentiator
    A feature that set them apart from their competition

Spoiler
    A feature that is moving in on someone else's differentiator

Cost reducer
    A feature that reduces the organization costs

Table stakes
    A feature necessary to compete in the marketplace

SEP indicated each story's category using different color sticky notes. Interesting discussions emerged—in fact, some stakeholders' differentiators were another stakeholder's table stakes. It was clear many of these conversations were happening for the first time! The story map with the prioritization model enabled conversations to happen that had not happened before. It helped guide the team to come to a shared understanding around priorities.

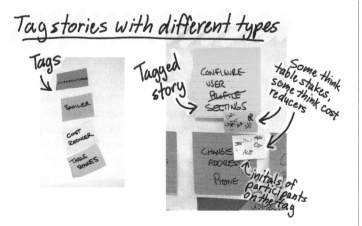

After labeling the stories, SEP used a voting system to help stakeholders converge the ideation and discussion into the most meaningful set of outcome-focused features. To everyone's surprise, several stories were deemed postpone-worthy or unnecessary. Rough calculations revealed several hundred thousand dollars in savings before one line of code was written.

When asked about using story mapping to kick off the project, Doug True, FORUM's CEO, said, "When we first kick-started this project with a story mapping process including the use of personas, I was skeptical. Specifically, I was concerned with the time invested to this softer side of the project. On the second day it clicked and the worthiness of the time materialized. In fact, now, I couldn't imagine pursuing a project of this scope and member-facing impact without such a process."

Why We Argue So Much About MVP

There's a term that's been kicking around in the software development industry for a long time: *minimum viable product*, or simply MVP.

Frank Robinson is credited with originally coining the term *MVP*, but these days definitions from Eric Ries and Steve Blank dominate. In spite of multiple smart people trying to define the term, everyone still seems confused—including me. Every organization I run into that uses that term means something slightly different. Even people in the same organization and the same conversation often mean different things.

Like most words in the dictionary, it has multiple meanings. I'm going to give you three definitions for the term: a bad one, and two good ones.

Here's the bad one:

> *Minimum viable product is not the crappiest product you could possibly release.*

And the MVP *isn't* the product that your users could use, but only in the simplest of circumstances, and only if they had a high threshold for pain. I commonly see organizations rationalizing their bad product decisions with the argument that someone could use the product, when it's clear to everyone involved that they probably wouldn't choose to.

If Globo.com had used this definition for slicing out its first release, it would have had a negative outcome. No one would have been impressed. The brand would have been hurt, and the company would have been worse off than if it had released nothing at all.

When we use the term *viable* when talking about a living organism, it means that an organism can survive in the world on its own without dying. And when we talk about software, we mean the same thing.

> *The minimum viable product is the smallest product release that successfully achieves its desired outcomes.*

I like this definition best. *Minimum* is a subjective term. So be specific about who it's subjective to—because it's not you. Be specific about who your customers and users are, and what they need to accomplish. What's *minimum* to them? I promise you, it'll help the conversation hugely. It's still a tough conversation. But the alternative is the "HiPPO" method—the "highest paid person's opinion." That one sucks worse.

The term I prefer these days is *minimum viable solution*. Most of the things I work with organizations on aren't whole, new products. They're new features or capabilities, or improvements on features already out there. So the term *solution* seems to make more sense. So let me revise my definition:

> *The minimum viable solution is the smallest solution release that successfully achieves its desired outcomes.*

Here comes the hard part…

We're just guessing.

When we slice out a bunch of software functionality and call it a minimum viable solution, we don't really know if it is.

The problem with outcomes is that you can't really observe them until things come out. When you slice out a release, you're forced to hypothesize what will happen. You might have to guess about what customers will buy your product, what users will choose to use it, if they can use it, and what's feasible to build in the time you have. You're forced to guess at how much will make them happy. That's a lot of guessing.

This sucks, because if you guess too low, well, that's less than minimal, and you've failed. If you guess too high, which many people do to hedge their bets, then you've spent too much money and often risk not getting things done at all. And worst of all, you could be just dead wrong, and no amount of what you ship will matter at all.

It's no wonder that the "crappiest product you could possibly release" definition still thrives. Because that's the one we don't need to guess about.

The New MVP Isn't a Product at All!

I know that some of you may have been feeling progressively twitchy over the last couple of chapters. You may have thought to yourself, *Jeff's overlooking the most important thing of all!* And you might be right. Some of the most important things you can discuss during story and story map conversations are:

- What are our biggest, riskiest assumptions? Where is the uncertainty?
- What could I do to learn something that would replace risks or assumptions with real information?

This leads me to my third definition of MVP, as popularized by Eric Ries in his book *The Lean Startup* (Crown Business). Eric learned the hard way, as most of us do, that we're just guessing. Eric worked for a company that released a product that it thought was viable, but it was wrong. Intelligently, he changed his strategy to focus on learning—to focus on validating all those assumptions the company had made in its first MVP release. Eric makes the important point that we need to create smaller experiments, prototypes that test our hypothesis about what's minimal and viable. And if you adopt Eric's way of thinking, which you should, your first product should really be an experiment —and the one after that, and the one after that, until you really prove that you've got the right product.

A minimal viable product is also the smallest thing you could create or do to prove or disprove an assumption.

While it was pretty cool that the folks at Globo.com were able to create a plan to build less, they weren't fooling themselves. They knew there was lots left to learn to prove their assumptions were good. From here they and everyone else need to create a plan to learn more. And that's where we'll pick up our story in the next chapter.

CHAPTER 3

Plan to Learn Faster

This is my friend Eric, standing in front of his backlog and task board in his team room. He's a product owner working hard with his team to build a successful product, but right now it's not. That doesn't worry Eric, though. He has a strategy for making his product successful. And so far it's working.

Eric works for a company called Liquidnet. Liquidnet is a global trading network for institutional investors. Long before Eric came to stand in front of the board in the picture, someone at his company identified a group of customers Liquidnet could serve better, along with a few ideas of how to do that. Eric is part of a team that took those ideas and ran with them. That's what product owners do. If you thought they were always acting on their own great ideas, well, you're wrong. One of the hard parts of being a product owner is taking ownership of someone else's idea and helping to make it successful, or proving that it isn't likely to be. The best product owners, like Eric, help their entire team take ownership of the product.

Start by Discussing Your Opportunity

Eric didn't start his work by building a backlog of user stories. He started with the big idea someone had, and treated it like an opportunity for his company—because it was. He had conversations with leadership in his company to understand more. They discussed:

- *What* is the big idea?
- *Who are the customers?* Who are the companies we think would buy the product?
- *Who are the users?* Who are the types of people inside those companies we think would use the product, and what would they be using it for?
- *Why would they want it?* What problems would it solve for customers and users that they couldn't solve today? What benefit would they get from buying and using it?
- *Why are we building it?* If we build this product and it's successful, how does that help us?

Eric needed to build shared understanding with others in his organization before he could take ownership of the opportunity. He knew he was going to need to tell the story of this product many times over the coming months, so he'd better get the big stuff right now.

Your first story discussion is for framing the opportunity.

Validate the Problem

Eric trusts his leadership's intuition, but he knows that this big idea is a hypothesis. He knows the only way to be sure the idea will succeed is when they actually see it succeed.

He first spent time talking to customers and users directly to really learn about them. Along the way he validated that there really were customers who had the problem, and they really were interested in buying a solution. Eric talked to the people who'd likely use the product. They didn't have the product today, and had only poor workarounds to address the problems the new product idea would solve.

*Validate that the problems you're solving
really exist.*

While Eric's been talking with customers and users, he's been building up a pool of people he thinks are good candidates to try his new software. Some companies refer to these people as *customer development partners*. Keep track of this detail, because it's going to come up later in the story.

Actually, during this stage, it wasn't just Eric. Eric was working with a small team of others who spent lots of time talking to their customers, and, in doing so, found that solving the problem wasn't so easy—and that there were other problems that needed to be solved first. The important thing for you to take away is that the more they learned, the more the original opportunity was changed—eventually, a lot. It's lucky they didn't just get to work building what they were told to. That wouldn't have served their customers or their organization.

By now Eric and his team, after talking to customers, had specific ideas for the type of solution they could build that users could use, and by doing so get the benefit their employers wanted. Now, here's where Eric and his team could have gone "all in"—where they could have bet it all. They could have built a backlog of stories that described their solution and set a team to work building it. Because they're smart people, they'd have used a story map to move from the big idea to the specific parts to build. But, because they're *really* smart, the last thing they're going to do at this point is to build software.

Prototype to Learn

It's around here that Eric began to act as the owner for this product. He moved to envision his solution first as a bunch of simple narrative stories—*user scenarios*. Then he moved to envisioning the idea as a simple wireframe sketch. And then he created a higher-fidelity prototype. This wasn't working software. It was a simple electronic prototype, created with a simple tool like Axure, or maybe even PowerPoint.

All of these are learning steps for Eric. They help him envision his solution. Ultimately, he wants to put his solution in front of his users to see what they think. But he knows he first needs to feel confident it solves their problems before he puts it in front of them.

Sketch and prototype so you can envision your solution.

Now, I've hidden an important detail from you. Eric was actually an interaction designer. He's the kind of designer who's used to spending time with customers and users, and used to building these simple prototypes. But, for this new product, he's also the product owner—the one ultimately responsible for the product's success. There are other product owners in Eric's company who don't have his design skills, and they very sensibly pair with designers to help with both interviewing users and envisioning solutions.

Eric did eventually bring prototypes back to users. And I wasn't there, so I don't know what really happened for Eric. But I've been in these situation lots of times, and I'm always surprised about what I learn from the people who'll really use my solution. All I can tell you is, be prepared for surprises and bad news. In fact, celebrate the bad news, because you could have received the same bad news months later, after you'd built the software. That's when it really sucks. Right now, it's cheap to make changes, and you should. And Eric did.

Prototype and test with users to learn whether your solution is valuable and usable.

After iterating his solution many times and showing it to his customers, Eric was confident he had a pretty good solution idea. Surely now he could get that backlog built, and get his team of developers to work turning that prototyped solution into real working software. But Eric's not going to do that. Well, not exactly that. That's a bigger bet than he's willing to take.

Watch Out for What People Say They Want

Eric has prototyped what he believes is a viable solution. But he's not really sure if it's minimal—because he showed people lots of cool ideas. And if you show people all the cool ideas, of course they'll love them. But Eric knows his job is to minimize the amount he builds and still keep people happy. How much could he take away and still have a viable solution?

Eric also knows something else that's a bit disturbing. He knows the people who said they'd like it and use it are just guessing, too.

Think back to when you've bought something yourself. You may have looked at the product. You might have watched a salesperson demonstrate the cool features. You may have tried out the cool features for yourself, and you could imagine really using and loving the product. But when you bought the product and actually started using it, you found the cool features didn't matter so much. What really mattered were features you hadn't thought about. And, worst of all, maybe you didn't really need the product that much after all. OK, maybe it's just me I'm talking about. But I've got lots of stuff in my garage that I wish I'd never bought.

Back to Eric. He knows his customers and users can imagine the product would be great to use, and knowing that gives him the conviction to up his bet. But the real proof is when those people actually *choose* to use it every day. That's the real outcome he's looking for—and the only outcome that'll get his company the benefit it really wants. And it's going to take more than a prototype to learn that.

Build to Learn

Now, here's where Eric gets to show how smart he really is.

Eric and his team actually do get to work building software. But their first goal isn't to build a minimum viable product. Actually, it's to build something less than minimal—just enough that potential users could do something useful with it. This is a product that wouldn't impress too many people, and they might even hate it. It's definitely not a product you'd want your marketing and sales people out there pitching. In fact, the only people you'd want to see this product are people who may one day use the product, and honestly care about finding a product that solves their problem.

It just so happens that Eric has a small group of people just like that. It's the customers and users he worked with earlier when he was learning about and validating the problem. They're his development partners. They're the ones who gave feedback on early prototypes. And there's a subset of them that Eric believes can best help him learn. They're the ones he'll put this first, less-than-minimum—and definitely not viable—product in front of. He hopes they'll become his early adopters.

And that's what he did.

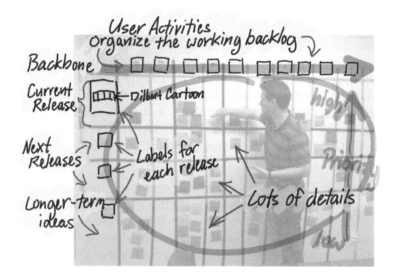

This is Eric pointing out a slice of his current backlog. When this picture was taken, he'd already released software to his development partners. After he did, he made a point of talking to them to get their feedback. His team also built in some simple metrics so they could measure whether people were really using the software, and what they did in the software specifically.

Eric knows that people are polite. They may say they like a product, but then never use it. The "using it" is the real outcome he wants, and polite isn't helping him. Eric also knows some people are demanding.

They may list all the problems the product has, or complain about bugs, but the metrics may be telling us that they use it every day anyway. And that's a good thing, in spite of all their complaining. The complaining is good, too, because it gives Eric ideas about where his next improvements should be.

Eric's backlog is organized as a story map with the backbone in yellow stickies across the top. Those yellow stickies have short verb phrases on them that tell the big story of what his users will do in the product, but at a high level. Below it are all the details—the specific things they'll do and need to really use the product. While the details he and his team work on change from release to release, the backbone stays pretty consistent.

The top slice, above the tapeline, is the one Eric and his team are working on right now. This release will take Eric two sprints. He's using a Scrum development process where his sprints are two-week timeboxes. So two sprints equate to basically a month. Below that are slices running down the board. The next slice contains what they think the next release might be, and so on. To the left of each slice, just as with the Globo.com team, hangs a sticky note with the release name and a few words about what they want to learn in this release. Except for the top release, which has a *Dilbert* cartoon posted over it. It's an inside joke in their team that I wasn't in on.

STORY-MAPPED BACKLOG   DEVELOPMENT TASK BOARD

If you look closely, the top of that current slice is sort of cleaned out. I've drawn in some sticky notes where they used to be. But they're not there anymore because those things that were on the top are the first things his team will build. As the team members worked together to plan their work, they removed those sticky notes and placed them on a task board to the right of the story-mapped backlog. That task board shows the stories they're working on now in this sprint, along with delivery task—the specific things that the developers and testers will need to do to turn the ideas in the story into working software.

One finer point of Eric's story-mapped backlog, and one that proves he's smart, is the thickness of that topmost slice. It's twice as thick as the slices below it. When Eric and his team finish a slice and deliver it to their development partners—what they call their *beta customers* —they'll move the sticky notes up from the slice below. When they do, they'll have lots more detailed discussion about this next sliced-out release. They'll play What About to find problems and fill in details. They'll talk about some of the ideas in the next release, and this discussion may result in their splitting the big idea into two or three smaller ideas. And then, they'll need the vertical height in that slice to prioritize—to make choices about what to build first.

See how smart they are?

Iterate Until Viable

Eric may have started this whole process with an idea about what the minimum viable product might be, but he's purposely built something less than minimal to start with. He's then adding a bit more every month. He's getting feedback from his development partners—both the subjective stuff from talking to them, and the more objective stuff he gets from looking at data.

He'll keep up this strategy, slowly growing and improving the product, until his development partners actually start using the product routinely. In fact, what Eric's hoping for is that they become people who'd recommend the product to other people—real reference customers. When they do, that's when he knows he's found minimum *and* viable. And that's when the product is safe to market and sell like crazy. If Eric and his team had tried to sell it before, they'd have ended up with lots of disappointed customers—people a lot less friendly than those with whom he built personal relationships throughout this process.

How to Do It the Wrong Way

What Eric could have done is to take his last, best prototype, break it down into all its constituent parts, and start building it part by part. Many months later, he'd have had something to release. And he'd have learned then if his big guess was right. You'll need to trust me on this, but it wouldn't have been—because it rarely is.

Not like this....

This is a simple visualization made by my friend Henrik Kniberg. It beautifully illustrates a broken release strategy where at every release I get something I can't use, until the last release when I get something I can.

Henrik suggests this alternative strategy:

Like this!

If I plan my releases this way, in each release I deliver something people can actually use. Now, in this silly transportation example, if my goal is to travel a long distance and carry some stuff with me, and you gave me a skateboard, I might feel a bit frustrated. I'd let you know how difficult it was to travel long distances with that thing—although it was fun to goof around with it in the driveway. If your goal was to leave me delighted, you might feel bad about that. But your real goal was to learn, which you did. So that's good. You learned I wanted to travel farther, and if you picked up on it, you also learned I valued having fun.

In Henrik's progression, things start picking up at around the bicycle release because I can actually use it as adequate transportation. And, at about motorcycle level, I can *really* see this working for me—and I'm having fun too. That could be minimum and viable for me. If I really love the motorcycle thing, maybe my next best step would be a bigger, faster Harley-Davidson, and not a sports car. I'm headed for a midlife crisis right now and that Harley is sounding pretty good. But it's after I try the motorcycle, and we both learn something from that, that we can best make that decision.

> *Treat every release as an experiment and be*
> *mindful of what you want to learn.*

But what about other folks who need to travel longer distance, and who have kids? For *that* target market, none of these would be good choices.

Always keep your target customers, users, and the outcomes you're hoping for in mind. It's really tough to get the same great outcome from all types of users. So focus.

Validated Learning

What my friend Eric did is apply a *validated learning strategy*—one of the important concepts in Lean Startup thinking. Eric knew that the problems he was solving, the customers and users he was solving them for, and the solutions he had in mind were all assumptions. Lots of them were pretty good assumptions. But they were assumptions just the same. Eric set out to understand the assumptions and then validate them, moving from the problems customers and users faced to the solutions he had for them. At each step he did or built something with the explicit goal of learning something.

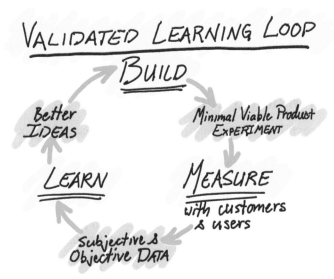

VALIDATED LEARNING LOOP

BUILD

Better
IDEAS

Minimal Viable Product
EXPERIMENT

LEARN

MEASURE
with customers
& users

Subjective &
Objective DATA

What Eric did is the heart of the build-measure-learn loop described by Eric Ries. And by Ries's definition, each release that Eric shipped was a minimum viable product. But you can see that it wasn't viable in the eyes of his target customers and users—at least, not yet. For that reason, I like referring to Ries's MVP as a *minimum viable product experiment*—or MVPe for short. It's the smallest thing I could build to learn something. And what I learn is driving toward understanding what's really viable in the eyes of my target customers and users.

Eric used lots of tools and techniques along the way. But telling stories using words and pictures was always part of the way he worked. Using a map to organize his stories helped him keep his customers, users, and their journey in mind as he iteratively improved his product to viable.

I like using the term *product discovery* to describe what we're really doing at this stage. Our goal isn't to get something built; rather, it is to learn if we're building the right thing. It just so happens that building something to put in front of customers is one of the best ways to learn if we're building the right thing. I borrow my definition of *discovery* from Marty Cagan.[1] And my definition of *discovery* includes Lean

---

1. Marty first described what he means by *product discovery* in this 2007 essay (*http:// www.svpg.com/product-discovery*). He later describes it in more detail in his book *Inspired: How to Create Products Customers Love* (SVPG Press).

Startup practice, Lean User Experience practice, Design Thinking practice, and loads of other ideas. And what I do during discovery continues to evolve. But the goal stays the same: to learn as fast as possible whether I'm building the right thing.

Really Minimize Your Experiments

If we recognize that our goal is to learn, then we can minimize what we build and focus on building only what we need to learn. If you're doing this well, it means that what you build early may not be production ready. In fact, if it is, you've likely done too much.

Here's an example: when I was a product owner for a company that built software for large, chain retailers, I knew my products needed to run on a big Oracle database on the backend. But the database guys were sometimes a pain for me to work with. They wanted to scrutinize every change I made. Sometimes simple changes would take a week or more. That slowed down my team and me too much. The database guys' concerns made sense, since all the other applications depended on that database. Breaking it was really risky for everyone. But they had a well-oiled process for evaluating and making database changes —it just took a long time.

The riskiest part for me was making sure my product was right. So we built early versions of software using simple, in-memory databases. Of course, they wouldn't scale, and we could never release our early versions to a large general audience. But our early minimum viable product experiments (we didn't call them that then) allowed us to test ideas with a small subset of customers and still use real data. After several iterations with customers, and after we found a solution we believed would work, we'd then make the database changes and switch our application off the in-memory database. The database guys liked us too, because they knew that when we made changes, we were confident they were the right ones.

Let's Recap

Gary used a map to get out of the flat-backlog trap and see the big picture of his product, and then to really start focusing on who it was for and what it should be.

The teams at Globo.com used a map to coordinate a big plan across multiple teams and slice out a subset of work they believed would be a viable solution.

Eric used a map to slice out less-than-viable releases into minimum viable product experiments that allowed him to iteratively find what would be viable.

There's one last challenge that seems to plague software development, and that's finishing on time. Suppose you're confident that you have something that should be built. And suppose others are depending on it going live on a specific date. There's a secret to finishing on time that's been known by artists for centuries. In the next chapter, we'll learn how to apply it to software.

CHAPTER 4

Plan to Finish on Time

This is Aaron and Mike. They work for a company called Workiva. Workiva makes a suite of products on a platform called Wdesk. It solves big problems for large companies, and it's one of the biggest software-as-a-service companies you've likely never heard of.

Aaron and Mike look happy, don't they? But that's typical for people who've worked together to solve tough problems. Or could it be because the guy on the right has a beer in his hand? Nah, that's not it. It's that feeling from having solved a tough problem that's making them happy. The beer is just a reward for solving the tough problem. If *you*

don't get beer, or an equivalent reward, for solving tough problems where you work, you should have a talk with someone about that.

Aaron and Mike have just completed several rounds of product discovery, and they're confident they have something that should be built and go into production.

For them, discovery started with framing the feature idea they were working with to really understand who it was for and why they were building it. Then they talked directly to customers to validate their guesses about how they were working today and what the real problems were. After that, they built simple prototypes. For Aaron and Mike, they were able to build simple electronic prototypes in Axure and test them with customers remotely—first to see if they valued the solution, and then to be confident that it was usable. For the feature they were working on, they didn't feel like they needed to prototype in working software to learn what they needed.

After multiple iterations with simple prototypes, they finally felt confident they had something worth building. That may sound like a lot of work, but they did it all in about three days. Their last step was to create a backlog and a plan for delivering the feature. That's their plan in the picture. It's a good plan. And that's why they're happy.

It's important to note that this map isn't about a whole product, it's just about a feature they're adding to an existing product. That's why it's smaller than Gary's in Chapter 1, or that of the Globo.com teams. I'm telling you this because some people mistakenly believe they need to map their whole product to make a small change, and they use that as a reason not to map.

> *Map only what you need to support your*
> *conversation.*

Tell It to the Team

To build this new feature, these two guys will need to build shared understanding with their team. Their team needs to be able to point out problems and possibilities for improvement, and to estimate how long it's going to take. That's what they built this final map for. They used it to tell the feature's story—step by step, from the user's perspective. Notice the printed screens injected into the map? They pointed at screens and highlighted details while walking through the map so those listening could better envision the solution. The people at Disney who walk through movies using a storyboard have nothing on these guys.

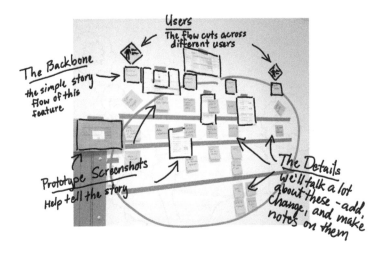

When team members asked why the screen behaves as it does, they had stories to tell about variations they'd tried, and how users behaved. When the team asked detailed questions about exactly what happens when data is entered, or information submitted, these guys had given it thought and could answer. Or, when they didn't know, they discussed ideas with the team, and made notes on the prototypes or sticky notes in the model. They even added a couple of sticky notes for details they hadn't thought of, but the team did. Aaron told me that the team spotted several technical dependencies that he and Mike would never have found.

The Secret to Good Estimation

Anyone who's been in the software development game for any length of time knows that one of the biggest challenges is estimating how long development will actually take. I'm going to let you in on one of the best-kept secrets of good estimation:

The best estimates come from developers who really understand what they're estimating.

There are lots of methods that promise to give more accurate estimates. I'm not going to cover any of those here. But I *will* tell you none of them work if the people building the software don't have shared understanding with one another, and with those who envisioned it.

Building shared understanding shouldn't be a well-kept secret about estimation. So you should go tell someone else right now.

Plan to Build Piece by Piece

The team at Workiva can't really get away with building less at this point. They can't do what Globo.com did in Chapter 2 and cut things away, because they've already validated that they need it all. When they were prototyping, they were able to cut away a lot and validate that their solution was still valuable to customers. But, when you look at their map, it's cut into three slices.

"Why would they care?" you might ask. A third of what the customers want is sort of like delivering a third of a sports car. No one could drive it. But Mike is the product owner. He doesn't get to walk away after he's identified a good solution. His role changes now, and he's a bit more like a director in a movie. He's got to be there as every scene is shot. And he's got to decide which scenes should be shot first, and which scenes get shot last. He knows that in the end the entire movie needs to come together and look like one coherent whole.

So Mike worked with his team to create a development plan. This is what they did: they sliced their map into three, crosscutting slices.

The first slice cuts all the way through the functionality. Once they build all those pieces, they can see the functionality working from end to end. It wouldn't work in all the situations it needs to, and if they shipped to users this way, those users would howl. But Mike and his team will be able to see the software running end to end. They'll be able to put real data in it to see how well it performs, and they could apply some automated testing tools to it to see how well it scales. They can learn a lot about the technical risks that might cause them trouble later on. They can be more confident going forward that they will be able to release on time. Or, at least they'll spot the unforeseen challenges that would slow them down. I call this first slice a *functional walking skeleton*—a term I borrowed from Alistair Cockburn. I've heard others call this a "steel thread" or a "tracer bullet."

They'll layer on the second slice to build up the functionality—to get it closer to releasable. Along the way, they're likely to learn some things they couldn't predict. They may have overlooked some characteristics this feature should have—finer points that weren't explored in the prototype. They may have found that the system just doesn't perform the way they expected and some extra work will need to be done to get the speed they want out of it. These are the "predictably unpredictables"—a concept closely related to Donald Rumsfeld's "unknown unknowns." Don't pretend they don't exist. You know they do.

Finally, they'll layer on the third slice to refine the feature, to make it as polished as it can be. They'll also add in some of those unpredictable things.

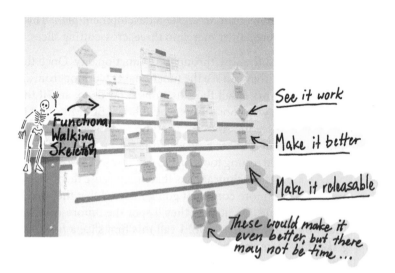

Don't Release Each Slice

Each of these slices isn't a release to customers and users: it's a milestone the team members will use to stop and take stock of where they are. From a user and customer perspective it's incomplete, so save yourselves the embarrassment.

Mike and Aaron's team estimated this feature to be about two months' worth of work. Like Eric, they used two-week sprints, so it would take them four sprints. I guess they could have made four slices, one for each sprint, but they weren't thinking of it that way. And you shouldn't, either. Think of these slices as three different buckets with different learning goals for each. Decide which sprints or iterations they'll go into when the time comes.

The Other Secret to Good Estimation

One thing that seems to be a secret, but really shouldn't be, is that estimates are…estimated. Hit the Web and find any list of oxymorons. I'm confident you'll find this term there: *accurate estimate*. If we knew exactly how long things would take, then we wouldn't have called it an *estimate*, would we?

But if you build little bits of software, one thing you can be pretty sure of is how long they took to build. That's called *measurement*, and that's quite a bit more accurate.

Ok, so here's the other secret: the more frequently you measure, the better you get at predicting. If you commute to work every day, I suspect you're pretty good at predicting how long it'll take. If I asked you how long it'd take to get to a different address in roughly the same area, I'll bet you could predict how long commuting there would take within plus or minus about 10 minutes. That's the way estimation works.

By slicing large things into small things, we get more opportunities to measure. Of course, there's some subtlety to this, but as a general principle, you'll get better predictions if you've got more examples of how long similar things have taken to build.

As a product owner, Mike is ultimately on the hook for getting this feature released on time. He's a good product owner, so he helps everyone in his small team take some ownership of that goal too. He treats these early estimates as his delivery budget.

Manage Your Budget

Mike and Aaron worked together with developers they trust early on to get an initial time estimate. They treat it as a *budget*. And they actively manage it.

With every small piece the team builds, they can measure how long that piece took to build. They treat what they've built as spending against their budget. They may find that they're halfway through their budgeted time, but only a third of the way through building the feature. Certainly they didn't expect that, but now they're aware and they can do something about it. They could borrow some budget from other features they're working on. Or there may be small changes they could make to the feature that won't substantially change the benefit users get. Or they could just face the music and see what they can do to change expectations with the people they've promised delivery to.

Depending on how bad it is, they may all need more beer.

When slicing out a development strategy, they'll look to tackle the things that may blow their budget as early as possible. Those are the risky things. And it's conversations with the whole team that help spot them.

Exposing Risk in the Story Map

Chris Shinkle, SEP

A large security company set out to build a mid-price-point, wireless, access control system for medium-size buildings (e.g., schools, doctors' offices, retail, etc.). The company hired SEP to develop the firmware within the locks as well as the wireless ZigBee gateway with which they communicated.

The project was technically exciting, but had all the ingredients for failure, including skimpy budget, tight timeline, midstream leadership changes, untested technology, and tons of scope bloat.

Of course, things quickly began to unravel. The project team had missed several milestones. The client was unhappy and team morale was low. During a retrospective, the team discovered the biggest driver for missing dates was unplanned work, mostly due to uncertainties and realized risks. Something needed to change.

Like any group of smart engineers, the team tackled the problem head on. Their solution? Modify the story map.

At a high level, they increased the frequency and fidelity of their story map. By increasing the frequency of story mapping at each interim release, they suspected they would increase the likelihood of identifying more risks. By increasing the fidelity of the map to include "Risk

Stories" (in addition to normal Activities, Tasks, and Details), they suspected they would be able to visualize, discuss, and better manage the risks.

The results were astounding.

The team knew that the width and depth of a typical story map gave a sense of the project size. They also knew the number of paths through the map was a good indicator of complexity. But, since uncertainty and risk weren't previously reflected in the story map, the map didn't depict the actual amount of work (including learning) to be done.

The new map, with Risk Stories, gave a better picture for the size and complexity of the road ahead. Project size and complexity were better represented, because they were composed of both the original known stories as well as the new "unknown stories"—the risks, or the knowledge the team needed to gain to confidently move ahead with the known stories.

As you'd expect, the story map became much more useful for planning. It now highlighted risks and uncertainties that would need time from the team. The ability to incorporate that time into planning made the team much more predictable and reliable.

Side benefits included a tangible way to measure and update stakeholders on learning. In conjunction with the traditional feature burn-down chart, the team included a risk burn-down chart. It was particularly helpful for the customer to see the risk burn-down data when the feature burn-down didn't look great.

At the end of the day, the team learned that increasing the frequency of story map creation and adding new Risk Stories are powerful ways to make your maps better reflect reality.

What Would da Vinci Do?

I often ask myself that. OK, I don't really. But maybe I should.

What Mike and Aaron have done is to follow a strategy used by artists to finish in time. It's one I've used for years with software. And, when I first met my friends at Globo.com, I found it's one they use, because as I mentioned before, if they're late with cool, new interactive stuff for the Olympics, the Olympic committee won't reschedule the Olympics. I'll guess this strategy is one you even use routinely, without thinking.

Let me first explain what da Vinci *doesn't* do. But, unfortunately, it's too often what people building software do try to do.

Suppose you were da Vinci, and you wanted to create a painting and were working the way a naïve software team does.[1] You might start with what you believe is a clear vision of the painting in your mind. Then you break up the painting into its parts. Let's say you had five days to paint this painting. Every day you'd paint more parts. At the end of day five, huzzah!—you're done! What could be simpler?

Only, it doesn't work like that—at least not for artists. This way of creating things assumes our vision is correct and accurate. It also assumes something about the skill of the creator and her ability to precisely define parts without seeing them in context. If you do this in software development, it's called an *incremental strategy*. It's the way a bricklayer might build a wall. And it works if each piece is as regularly sized and well defined as a brick.

When I used to draw as a kid, I fell into this trap. I'd often be drawing some sort of animal and start with the head. I'd work on that 'til it was perfect, then continue to draw the rest of the body—legs, tail, and so

---

1. I got the idea for this simple visualization from John Armitage's 2004 paper "Are Agile Methods Good for Design?" John describes approaching user experience design this way. I'm suggesting we carry the metaphor into the way we build as well.

---

on. By the time I got close to done, I could see that the proportions of my animal had gotten a bit off. The head was too big, or too small for the rest of the body. The legs seem to be twisted at an odd angle. And the pose of the creature just seemed a bit stiff. At least, that was my perspective as a talented six-year-old—and all six-year-olds are talented artists.

It was later in life that I learned I'd benefit from sketching the whole composition first. From there I could get proportions right, and make changes to the pose of the creature. I'd maybe even reconsider what I was going to draw.

I wasn't there with da Vinci, but I expect he did something much the same.

Even da Vinci would probably acknowledge that his vision wasn't perfect, and that he'd learn something as he was creating the painting. On day one, I imagine he first sketched the composition, or maybe did a light underpainting. I can imagine him at this point making changes to the composition. "Hey, I think the smile is going to be an important part. I'll move her hand away from her mouth. And those mountains in the background…too much."

By midweek, da Vinci is adding lots of color and form to the painting, but he's still making changes as he goes. By the end of the week, he knows he's running out of time, so all his effort shifts to refining the painting. One wonders if the *Mona Lisa* missing her eyebrows was a deliberate choice, or if da Vinci simply ran out of time to add a new, fully refined feature.

> *Great art is never finished, only abandoned.*
> *— Leonardo da Vinci*

That quote is attributed to da Vinci, and it speaks to the notion that we could continue to add and refine forever, but that, at some point, we need to deliver the product. And, if da Vinci's work and that of lots of other artists are good examples, we—the people who appreciate the work—have no idea it was abandoned. To us, it looks finished.

Iterative AND Incremental

An artist or author works this way. In fact, the people who put together the morning paper or evening news work this way. The people who create live theater work this way. Anyone who must deliver on a deadline, and learn as he goes, recognizes this strategy.

> *Use iterative thinking to evaluate and make changes to what you've already made.*

In software development, *iterate* has two meanings. From a process perspective, it means to repeat the same process over and over. That's why the development time-box used in Agile development is often called an *iteration*. But when you use this term to describe what you're doing with the software you build, it means to evaluate and change it. And changing software after it's built is too often seen as a failure. It's where terms like bad requirements or scope creep get used to reprimand the people who made decisions about what to build. But we all know that change is a necessary result of learning.

> *Use incremental thinking to make additions.*

Unfortunately, we can easily get trapped in the whirling eddies of iteration. So we've got to keep our eye on the calendar and keep incrementally adding more. The artist adds more not only by adding whole new things to a painting, but also by building up things that were already added.

You might do the same things in software by first creating a simple version of functionality without any extras. You might think of this as your sketch. After using the simple version, you'd build it up by adding more functionality to it. Over time, it builds up to be the finished version you and others may have originally envisioned. If things go really well, it builds up to something different than you originally envisioned, but better because it benefits from what you've learned.

Opening-, Mid-, and Endgame Strategy

This may hurt your head a bit, but I'm going to mix some metaphors here. I personally rely on a strategy based on a chess metaphor when creating software. I'm a crap chess player who barely knows how to play the game, so if I'm misusing the metaphor, you're not allowed to write me and correct me. No matter how small the product or feature release, I prefer to slice my release backlog into three groups:

Opening game

Focus on the essential features or user steps that cross through the entire product. Focus on things that are technically challenging or risky. Skip the optional things users might do. Skip the sophisticated business rules you know you'll need before you can release. Build *just* enough to see the product working end-to-end.

Midgame

Fill in and round out features. Add in stuff that supports optional steps users might take. Implement those tough business rules. If you've done your opening game stuff right, you'll be able to start testing the product end-to-end for things like performance, scalability, and usability. Those are all the quality concerns that are hard to bake in. We need to be aware of them, and constantly test them.

Endgame

Refine your release. Make it sexier, and more efficient to use. Since you can use it now with real data and at scale, here's where you'll find improvement opportunities that were hard to see from a prototype. It's here that you'll have feedback from users you'll be able to apply.

Slice Out Your Development Strategy in a Map

If you've discovered what you believe is a viable first release to customers and users, work together as a team to slice that first public release again into opening game, mid game, and endgame stories. The team creating the product is best at identifying where the risks and opportunities to learn are. They'll feel the strongest ownership over the plan they create together.

That's what Aaron and Mike did with the help of their whole development team. Look again at how happy they are.

It's All About Risk

In Chapter 3, Eric had to deal with the risk of identifying the wrong product. He used a strategy of slicing out releases that allowed him to put whole products in front of customers.

In this chapter, Aaron and Mike are focused on technical risk, the things that might blow their delivery schedule or cause the feature to cost much more than they expected. They won't show what they end up with at the end of every cycle to customers and users because they already know it's not sufficient. But they'll take a good, hard look at it themselves and with their team, and use what they learn to safely steer the development of this feature.

It's subtle, but you might have caught in Chapter 2 that Eric was taking two two-week sprints to build his next minimum viable product experiment. And he had to decide which things to build in the first sprint, and which to build in the second sprint. He used this kind of thinking to make those decisions. He and his team put the risky bits first—the parts that Eric or his team wanted to see working sooner so that they could course-correct before they put it in front of their customers.

Now What?

You've seen four pretty good examples of building and using maps for different purposes. There are a lot more ways to use maps that we'll explore in later chapters. But before you get too far, I want to show you my favorite trick for teaching others how to map. I promise if you try it, you'll map like an expert from that moment on.

Let's pick up there in Chapter 5.

CHAPTER 5

You Already Know How

If you think that creating a story map is complicated, or mystical, or in any way hard to do, let me assure you right now that it's not. In fact, you're already wired to understand all the basic concepts used to create a map. Let's work through an example right now, taken from everyday life. And, to make it simple, we'll use *your* life. Along the way I'll give some names to those important concepts you already understand.

Grab a pad of sticky notes and a pen, and follow along with me. Don't worry—take your time. I'll wait.

Ready?

1. Write Out Your Story a Step at a Time

Close your eyes, and think back to the moment you woke up this morning. You *did* wake up this morning, right? What's the first thing you recall doing? Now, open your eyes, and write it down on a sticky note. I'll write along with you. My first sticky note says, "Hit snooze." Unfortunately, it usually does. On bad mornings I may have to hit it two or three times.

Now, peel off that sticky and put it on the table in front of you. Then, think of the next thing you did. Got it? Now, write it on the next sticky, peel it off, and place it next to the first one. Then keep going. My next couple of stickies say, "Turn off alarm" and "Stumble to the bathroom."

Keep writing sticky notes until you've gotten ready for work, or whatever you're doing today. I usually end with "Get into my car" to start my drive for work. I expect it'll take you three or four minutes to write all your stickies.

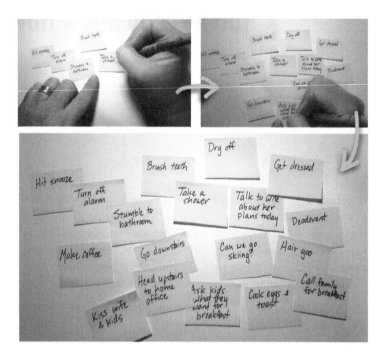

Tasks Are What We Do

Take a look at all the sticky notes you wrote. Notice how all of them start with a verb? Well, almost all of them. These short verb phrases like "Take a shower" and "Brush teeth" are *tasks*, which just means something we do in order to reach a goal. When we describe the tasks people using our software do in order to reach their goals, we'll call them *user tasks*. It's the most important concept to building good story maps—not to mention writing and telling good stories. You'll find that almost all the sticky notes in story maps about what people do using your software use these short verb phrases.

Now stop here for a minute and think about how easy that was. I asked you to write down what you did, and naturally out of your brain tasks came out. I think it's pretty cool that the most important concept is the most natural.

Don't get too hung up on that word *task*. If you're a project manager, you've noticed project plans are full of tasks. If you've been using stories in Agile development, you know that planning work involves writing a bunch of development and testing tasks. If you're neither a project manager nor a software developer, watch out when you use the word *task* because those other people might think you mean the kind of tasks *they* usually think about, and they'll tell you you're using it wrong.

> *User tasks are the basic building blocks of a*
> *story map.*

Now, count the number of tasks you wrote down.

Most people write somewhere between 15 and 25. If you wrote more, that's fabulous. If you wrote less, man, you've got a simple life. I wish I could get ready in the morning that quickly. But you may want to look back at your list and see if there's anything you skipped writing down.

My Tasks Are Different Than Yours

I'm sure this doesn't come as a surprise to you, but people are different from one another. You'll see these differences expressed in the way they choose to do things.

For instance, some people have both the motivation and self-discipline to exercise almost every morning. If you wrote a couple of tasks related to exercise, you rock! I'm still working on that myself.

Some people simply have more responsibilities because of the household they live in. If you've got kids, I promise you wrote down several tasks that people without kids didn't. If you have a dog, you may have a task or two dedicated to taking care of the dog.

Keep that in mind when you're thinking about people using your software. They may have different goals when using it. They may use it in different contexts that force them to take into account other people or things.

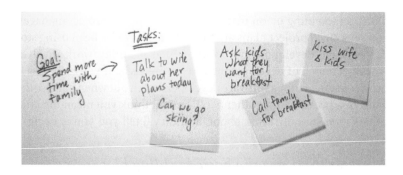

I'm Just More Detail-Oriented

In this exercise, some people just write a lot more details than others. They might take something like "Make breakfast" and instead write "Put bread in the toaster," "Pour a glass of juice," or, if you're my wife, "Add kale to the smoothie," which is one of the tasks I really hate her doing.

Tasks are like rocks. If you take a big rock and hit it with a hammer, it'll break into a bunch of smaller ones. Those smaller rocks are still rocks. It's the same thing with tasks. Now I don't know when a rock is big enough to be called a boulder, or small enough to be called a pebble, but there's a cool way to tell a big task from a small task.

My friend Alistair Cockburn described the *goal level* concept in his book *Writing Effective Use Cases* (Addison-Wesley Professional). Don't worry, we're not going to start writing use cases. It's just that the concept is really useful when we're talking about human behavior.

Alistair uses an altitude metaphor where sea level is in the middle, and everything else is either above or below sea level. A sea-level task is one we'd expect to complete before intentionally stopping to do something else. Did you write "Take a shower" in your list of tasks? That's a sea-level task because you don't get halfway through your shower and think, *Man, this shower is dragging on. I think I'll grab a cup of coffee and finish this shower later.* Alistair calls these *functional-level tasks* and annotates them with a little ocean wave. But I'll just call them tasks.

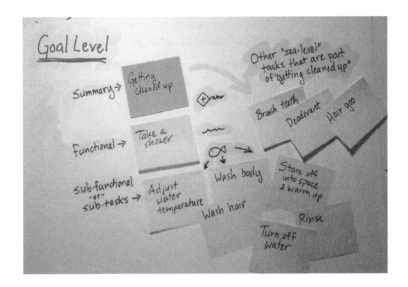

Tasks like "Take a shower" break down into lots of smaller *subtasks* like "Adjust water temperature" and "Wash hair," and, if you're my wife, something involving an exfoliating loofah thing. Remember, people are different, and you'll see behavior differences in the way they approach tasks. Alistair annotates these with a little fish because they're below the ocean.

Finally, we could roll up a bunch of tasks into a *summary-level task*. Taking a shower, shaving, brushing teeth, and all that other stuff you do in the morning after you get out of bed could roll up into a summary task. I'm not sure what I'd call it, though. "Getting cleaned up?" "Morning ablutions?" *Ablutions* is a silly word. Don't use that.

> *Use the goal-level concept to help you aggregate small tasks or decompose large tasks.*

2. Organize Your Story

If you haven't done this already, organize your tasks in a left-to-right flow with what you did first on the left, and what you did later on the right.

Try telling a story by pointing at the first sticky note and saying, "First I did this," and then pointing to the next sticky and saying, "then, I did this." Now keep going moving from left to right and telling your story.

You can see that each sticky note is a step, and hidden in between each sticky note is the nifty little conjunction phrase "…and then I…"

I'll call this left-to-right order the *narrative flow*, which is a fancy way of saying "storytelling order." We'll call this whole thing a *map* and that narrative flow is its left-to-right axis.

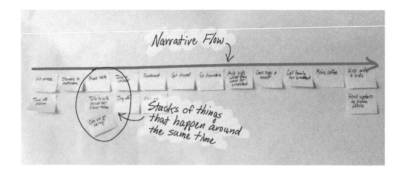

Wow, my flow got pretty wide. I started stacking things that happen in and around the same time. As I lay out the flow, I see I already missed a few details, and I'm trying to decide if they matter.

> *Maps are organized left-to-right using a narrative flow: the order in which you'd tell the story.*

Fill in Missing Details

The cool thing about this arrangement of sticky notes is that it allows us to see the whole big story. Seeing the story organized in a narrative flow allows you to more easily see the parts of the story that are missing.

Look back at your growing map and look for steps you might have missed.

I added just a few more. There's lots of details that are below sea level that I've decided to not write down. If I did, there'd be hundreds of stickies.

3. Explore Alternative Stories

So far this is dead obvious, right? Learning this was hardly worth the paper you're wasting. But wait, it's about to get interesting.

Take a minute and think about what you did *yesterday* morning. If there are different things you did yesterday morning than you did this morning, write them down and add them to your map.

Think of mornings when things went wrong. What if there was no hot water? What did you do then? What if you were out of milk or cereal or whatever you normally eat for breakfast? What if your daughter flew into a panic because she forgot to do her homework that's due today, which is what happens in my house every once in a while. Then what? Write tasks for what you'd do and add them to the map.

Now, think about your ideal morning. What would make your morning perfect? For me, it would be getting some exercise and enjoying a long breakfast while I catch up on some reading. But then I'd have to get up a lot earlier and stop hitting snooze.

Notice also that you'll want to put some tasks in a column, both to save space and because they seem similar to other tasks you might normally do. For example, you might find that you've got tasks for making a really great breakfast that you can put in a column along with the tasks for making the quick breakfast you normally make.

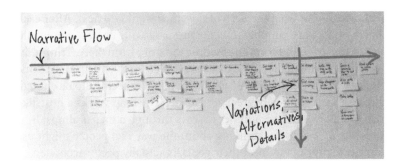

My friend David Hussman calls this "playing What-About," a phrase you might remember from Chapter 2 and Chapter 3. Unfortunately, we could play What-About for a long time and make this map huge. I added a few more things to my map specifically for things I wish I'd done, like exercising or doing a bit of relaxing reading during breakfast. I also added a few more common alternatives that often happen in the morning.

Details, alternatives, variations, and excep-
tions fill in the body of a map.

Keep the Flow

Notice that when you start to add these new tasks, you'll likely have to reorganize your narrative flow. I know *I* did. For instance, I'd need to slip that exercise thing in between getting up and taking a shower. And I'd have to add in "Put on exercise clothes," which isn't the same as the "Get dressed" step after taking a shower.

If you relax and put things where it seems natural, you'll find a narrative flow that feels right. When you tell your story now, you'll find that you can tell it a bunch of different ways. You can tell the *typical* day story, the *fabulous* day story, and the story that has an *emergency* or two—all by pointing at different stickies as you talk through it from left to right. Try using some other conjunctions to glue your tasks together. You might say, "I usually do this, but sometimes I do this" or "I do this, or this, and then this." (I'm expecting you to fill in the word *this* with what you actually do, because I can't see what you're pointing at from here.)

When I was a kid, there was a popular series of children's books called *Choose Your Own Adventure*. Maybe you remember them. The idea was that you'd read to the end of a section and then be given a couple of choices about what the hero of the story would do next. After each choice was a page number. Once you made your choice, you would turn to that page and continue reading the story from there. Truthfully, I was never a fan of those books. I always seemed to end up at the same place no matter what choice I made; there never seemed to be enough choices to make a really great adventure. The map works a little like that, except better. The number of ways through a map is almost limitless—which, if you're thinking about the way real people might use a software product to meet their goals, is actually pretty accurate.

If you want to make things *really* challenging, do this exercise with a couple of people you work with. You'll learn more than you ever wanted to know about the people you work with, and you'll have a bit of fun finding a narrative flow everyone agrees on. By "fun," I mean "argument." There are always people who eat breakfast before showering, and some who eat after. There's the great tooth-brushing debate—do you brush before or after breakfast, or both?

Relax.

If you're arguing, it likely means that it doesn't matter. For instance, putting breakfast before or after taking a shower is a matter of preference. Go with what's most common for the group you're working with. You'll find people won't argue about things that *do* matter. For example, putting "Get dressed" after "Take a shower" isn't just a matter of preference. Doing it the other way around results in showing up to work wearing wet clothes.

4. Distill Your Map to Make a Backbone

By now, your map should be looking pretty wide, and if you've explored lots of options, maybe a little deep. It'll likely have 30 or more tasks. It should look like the spine and ribs of a weird animal.

If you step back a bit and look across your map from left to right, you'll find there are bunches of stories that seem to go together—for instance, all those things you do in the bathroom to get ready, or all those things in the kitchen to make breakfast, or that junk you do to check the weather, grab a coat, and load your bag with your laptop or other stuff you'll need before leaving the house. Can you see those clusters of tasks that seem to go together to help you reach a bigger goal?

Above each of these clusters of similar stickies, put a different colored sticky note. Write a short verb phrase on it that distills all the tasks underneath it.

If you don't have a different color of sticky note, I'll let you in on a secret. Every package of sticky notes comes with two shapes! Rotate a sticky note 45 degrees and, poof, you've got a cool diamond shape. Use that if you want to make a sticky look different.

These sticky notes with a higher goal-level task are called *activities*. Activities organize a bunch of tasks done by similar people at similar times in order to reach a particular goal. When you read the activities across the top of the map, they're in a narrative flow, too. The row of stickies is the backbone of the map. If you've got a map with lots of stickies in it and you wanted to share it, a good way to start is by telling a high-level story. Just read the backbone of the map, with the "…and then they…" conjunction between each activity.

Activities aggregate tasks directed at a common goal.

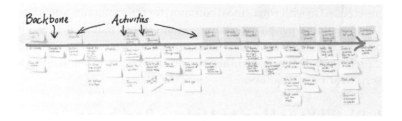

Here's my growing map with activities added to give the map a backbone. It makes it easier to read and find things, at least for me. And it makes it easier to really get the big picture of what's going on in my morning.

> *Activities and high-level tasks form the backbone of a story map.*

Activities don't seem to have common language the way tasks do. For instance, what do you call that thing you do before leaving the house? That thing where you gather up your bag, find a shopping list, check the weather, and grab an umbrella if you need it? I could call it "gathering up my junk." You might call it something different.

When you build these for your products and your customers, you'll want to call it what *they* call it.

5. Slice Out Tasks That Help You Reach a Specific Outcome

Now, here's the really cool part—the part where you get to use the map to help you imagine something that didn't happen.

If you look at the map you've built, you'll probably see "Hit snooze" or "Turn off alarm" somewhere on the left edge. Imagine that this morning you can skip that one. You can skip it because last night you forgot to set your alarm. Your eyes shot open and looked at your clock and you saw you needed to be somewhere in just a few minutes. You're really late! Don't panic—we're just pretending.

Write "Get out the door in a few minutes" on a sticky and place it to the left of the map near the top. Now, imagine a line slicing through the middle of the map left to right—kinda like a belt. Now, move all the tasks below that line if you wouldn't do them to reach the goal of getting out in a few minutes. Don't move the activities down, even if there are no tasks left under them. Having the activity with no tasks in it lets you show that you aren't going to hit that goal this morning.

You'll likely be left with just a few tasks in the top slice. Now go back through the flow and fill in tasks that are missing and that you would do if you were late. For example, you might normally take a shower, but when you're late you instead add in tasks like "Splash water on face" or "Use a washcloth to wash the particularly stinky parts of my body." When doing this activity with a group of developers, I often see the task "Apply extra deodorant." I'm not judging. I'm just saying.

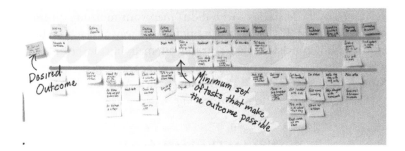

Here's my map sliced to find the tasks I'll need to get out the door in a few minutes.

You can try this trick by thinking of different goals to hang on the left side. Like "Have the most luxurious morning ever" or "Leave for a two-week vacation." You'll find the narrative flow stays pretty durable, but that you'll need to add or remove tasks to help you reach that different goal.

Use slices to identify all the tasks and details relevant to a specific outcome.

That's It! You've Learned All the Important Concepts

That was really easy, wasn't it? As you built this map you learned that:

- *Tasks* are short verb phrases that describe what people do.
- Tasks have different *goal levels*.
- Tasks in a map are arranged in a left-to-right *narrative flow*.

- The *depth* of a map contains variations and alternative tasks.
- Tasks are organized by *activities* across the top of the map.
- Activities form the *backbone* of the map.
- You can *slice the map* to identify the tasks you'll need to reach a specific *outcome*.

Do Try This at Home, or at Work

Now, I'm pretty sure a great number of you were just reading along and not really mapping as you read. Don't think I didn't notice. But if you're one of those slackers who didn't map your morning, promise me you will try it. It's hands down my favorite way of teaching these basic mapping concepts. If you're trying out mapping for the first time in your organization, get a small group of people together and run through this exercise. You'll all learn the basics. And you'll be well on your way to being able to map *anything*.

Do You Need to Shower Before Work?

Rick Cusick, Reading Plus, Winooski, Vermont

We ran the morning map exercise with four developers, the product owner, a tester, a UX lead, and two of our product trainers. Split into two teams, we captured each person's morning rapidly, and then sorted and resorted our respective mornings into a single representation of what "an average morning" looked like. People enjoyed the work of building the map, even though they had never done it before or considered it in terms of building our own product's experience.

My goals in approaching the exercise were to promote the efficiency of visualizing our work, demonstrate how putting the map together created shared understanding, and leverage the value of seeing the experience in an accessible format. The unexpected benefits were the effects of close collaboration—working as a team on a project where the goal was revealed through the work itself—and the moments of empathy for one another. "I didn't realize you dropped your kids off at school every day." "You do yoga in the morning before work?" "I can't go without breakfast—I'll be useless!"

There was some confusion around events that happened simultaneously, or with causality. "If I read the paper while I'm drinking coffee, is that one or two sticky notes?" "On Fridays, my wife takes the kids to school, so how do I represent that?" The other challenge was a concern that the linear nature of time in a left-to-right story map wasn't able to capture all possibilities. As the facilitator, I found it gratifying to see that kind of thinking in progress during the exercise, even if I didn't have all the answers right then.

As we prioritized activities, some hard choices were made to comic effect. "Do we *need* to shower before work?" is a funny if somewhat odiferous joke that popped out. "No matter what else we cut out, we have to wake up, get dressed, and drive to work," observed one participant, with another quickly piping up, "Unless you are working from home!"

Soon after this exercise, story maps became our preferred way to communicate an experience, prioritize user stories, and schedule iterations and releases. It had entered the company's vernacular and the development culture, and continues through the present day.

One lesson I learned, having run this same exercise now for multiple teams in our organization, is to use an icebreaker to prime the mindset of the participants. Start the session by having each person write just one thing he or she did between waking up and getting to work. Then ask each person to answer the question: "Why did you take that action?" I found that this starts a background mental thread that shows up in later planning sessions: "What is the value of this user story? Why would our users do this?"

It's a Now Map, Not a Later Map

I suspect a few of you caught this, but the map you just created has a fundamental difference from the maps created in the first four chapters. The maps Gary, Globo.com, Eric, and Mike and Aaron created all imagine how users will use their products in the future—*later*, after the product is delivered. They wrote tasks and activities that they imagined people doing in the product. But the map you created is a map about the way you do things *now*—this morning, as a matter of fact. And, as it turns out, the concepts are the same in both. So be relieved I haven't wasted your time.

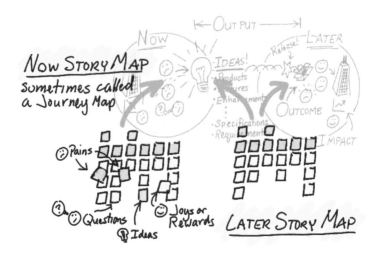

One of the cool things about "now story maps" is that you can build them to better understand how people work today. You just did this to learn how you got ready this morning. You can learn even more if you go back and add other things to the map. The easy things to add are:

Pains
> Things that don't work, parts people hate

Joys or rewards
> The fun things, the things that make it worth doing

Questions
> Why do people do this? What's going on when they do?

Ideas
> Things people could do, or that we could build that would take away pain, or make the joys even better

Lots of people in the user experience community have been building these for years to better understand their users. Sometimes they're called *journey maps*, but they're the same basic idea.

Try This for Real

In the early 2000s, I led a team at a small product company called Tomax. We built software for brick-and-mortar retailers—those shopping places we used to go to before spending all our time online. We'd taken on a new customer that ran a large chain of paint and interior decoration stores. Now, we knew quite a bit about retail—and about the users who sold things at point of sale and managed inventory—but there were some things we didn't know that were specific to paint and decor stores. For instance, we didn't know how to sell custom-tinted paint or custom blinds. And we had to learn fast.

To help us learn, we asked for the help of these three ladies. They're not software people. They're interior decorators working for the company that wanted our software. From them we learned the ins and outs of selling custom blinds. So that we could learn quickly, we asked them to think back to the last time they sold custom blinds. We asked them to write down everything they did—from the moment a customer contacted them, until the moment the blinds were installed and their customer was happy. Now that should sound familiar, because we asked them to do the same thing you just did to map your morning—and it went pretty much the same way. They could name what *they* did to sell custom blinds as easily as you could name what *you* did to get ready in the morning. And, when we organized their tasks, we all learned that there wasn't any one way to do things, that they each did things differently or in a different order. You'll see the same thing if you try the getting-up-in-the-morning map with a small group of different people.

From this simple storytelling and mapping activity, we all built *shared understanding* of how they worked *now*. It was from here that we could begin to translate this map into the things they'd need to do in the software we'd create *later*.

With Software It's Harder

I won't lie to you. If you're a software professional, it may take you a while to stop talking about features and screens, and to start writing short verb phrases that say what people are really trying to do. Keep practicing. You'll get it.

This will be really hard if you don't know exactly who your user is, what she's trying to accomplish, or how she goes about it. Sadly, trying to build a map in this situation will just point out what you don't know. If that's where you are, then you'll need to learn more about people and what they do. Better yet, work with them directly to create a map.

Six Simple Steps to Story Mapping

I can boil down the last four chapters into just six steps. You might be thinking, *Why didn't he do that in the first place?* But then I'd have skipped telling you the stories, and just given you the requirements. And that just doesn't work.

While I know there are lots of right ways to build up and use a story map, I have found that the following six-step process works well for me:

1. *Frame the problem.* Who is it for, and why are we building it?

2. *Map the big picture.* Focus on breadth, not depth. Go a mile wide and an inch deep (or a kilometer wide and a centimeter deep, for my friends in the rest of the world). If you don't have a clear solution in mind, or even if you think you do, try mapping the world as it is today, including pains and joys your users have.

3. *Explore.* Go deep and talk about other types of users and people, how else they might do things, and the kinds of things that can (and likely will) go wrong. For extra credit, sketch, prototype, test, and refine solution ideas—changing and refining the map as you go.

4. *Slice out a release strategy.* Remember: there's always too much to build. Focus on what you're trying to achieve for your business, and on the people your product will serve. Slice away what's not needed to reveal minimum solutions that both delight people and help your organization reach its goals.

5. *Slice out a learning strategy.* You may have identified what you think is a minimum viable solution, but remember that it's a hypothesis until you prove otherwise. Use the map and discussion to help you find your biggest risks. Slice the map into even smaller minimum viable product experiments that you can place in front of a subset of your users to learn what's really valuable to them.

6. *Slice out a development strategy.* If you've sliced away everything you *don't* need to deliver, you'll be left with what you *do* need. Now slice your minimum viable solution into the parts you'd like to build earlier and later. Focus on building things early that help you learn to spot technical issues and development risks sooner.

The Map Is Just the Beginning

Building a map helps you see the big picture, to see the forest for the trees. That's one of the biggest benefits of story mapping. But if you're the one responsible for building the forest, you'll need to do it one tree at a time. You've already learned the two most important things that make stories work:

- Use storytelling with words and pictures to build shared understanding.
- Don't just talk about what to build: talk about who will use it and why so you can minimize output and maximize outcome.

Keep these things in mind, and everything will fall into place as you go forward.

It's time we talked about some of the tactics for using stories "tree by tree," because a lot can go wrong, and there are a few more things you need to know to use stories well.

User Story Mapping at SAP—It's All About Scaling

Andrea Schmieden

When Jeff first presented his concept of user story mapping, it immediately made sense to us at SAP. It seemed to be a simple yet powerful method to turn a product vision into a backlog, and understand what we were going to develop, for whom, and why. So we decided to give it a try.

Yet, as we soon were to discover, what might be a simple thing for a lone entrepreneur or an individual Scrum team is a completely different beast for product development teams consisting of *several* Scrum teams. At SAP, with its large development organization of about 20,000 developers, large product development teams with dependencies on other teams are generally the norm, not the exception. We needed to come up with a reliable way to scale user story mapping for a large organization.

The Challenge

So, the challenge for us was two-fold:

- How can we map complex products without getting lost in stickies?

- How can we popularize the method within the development organization and enable people to use it?

1. User Story Mapping for Large Products

To find answers to the first question, we decided it was best to run a few pilot workshops with actual projects. We started out with a small team of enthusiastic coaches and approximately 10 pilot projects, the largest consisting of 14(!) Scrum teams. In this pilot phase, we varied the method in several aspects, such as workshop formats, contents, project phases, map formats, and more. After several feedback rounds and iterations, we arrived at a set of good practices that for now seem to work pretty well in our large-scale development context.

Key Good Practices

When a team first uses user story mapping, we recommend the involvement of an experienced coach. The coach sets up a meeting with the requestor and discusses the workshop goals, whom to invite, agenda, relevant inputs, and so forth. Typically, we do a facilitated one-day workshop with the whole team and smaller follow-up sessions as required.

On the day of the workshop, we typically start with a product vision exercise such as the well-known Elevator Pitch or the Cover Story (*http://gamestorming.com/?s=cover+story*)[1] format where the team describes what they would like to read about their product in a trade journal article a year from now. This shows whether the team has a common understanding about the general direction, or whether they might need to invest in some additional research (e.g., additional interviews, prototype testing, etc.).

The next step is to look at the typical users of the product. If the workshop goal is to specify a detailed backlog, the user roles or personas should result from the user research phase. If the project is in an early phase, the team writes down their assumptions. These can then be tested in user research phases. This has proven to be a good way to prepare the user research. This is also an aspect where design thinking practices and user story mapping work very well together.

We next use a three-tier approach to defining user stories: (1) starting with high-level usage steps, these are broken down into (2) finer activities per user role, which in turn are broken down into (3) con-

---

1. Cover Story is one of the many great practices found in the book *Gamestorming* (*http://gamestorming.com/?s=cover+stor*) by Dave Gray, et al. (O'Reilly).

crete user stories in the format *"as <role>, I want <functionality>, so that <value>."* These user stories add up to a first product backlog. This three-tier approach is especially useful for bigger projects. On each tier, the team can decide where it makes sense to drill down into the details and where dependencies to other teams need to be considered. This approach helps focus on the key development tasks at hand while keeping the big picture in mind.

To make the map easier to grasp, we use color-coded stickies for activities and user stories related to an individual persona or role, as you can see in the following graphic.

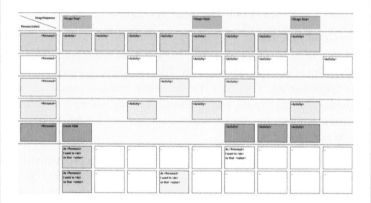

Often, while the team is creating the map, additional aspects come up, such as "white spots" where the team needs to do more research, or open questions, dependencies, or gaps. To highlight these issues, we use stickies in different colors or different sizes. At first it might seem awkward to put all these open issues on the map. However, in our experience, this is one of the most useful aspects of the mapping process: you get an honest and tangible impression of the things that need further clarification. After the issues are on the table, it's a lot easier to tackle them.

When the team has reached a reasonable level of detail, we prioritize the user stories in the backlog. Depending on the size of the project and the project phase, this is sometimes done even on the activities level rather than the user stories level. We typically use simple voting techniques, such as dot voting. Sometimes, we use a simplified Kano model for the voting, which means that the teams tag user stories as "Must haves," "Delighters," or "Satisfiers." These simple voting results are again a good basis for further alignment and validation with stakeholders, end users, and customers.

As one of our product owners put it, "As a product owner, you often have the challenge to fit lots of requirements into a very tight timeline. We invited our customers to a one-day user story mapping workshop, and it proved to be a very efficient and effective way to get to a common understanding of their priorities."

Further details, detailed effort estimations, and so forth are usually not part of the workshop, but rather are discussed in smaller groups afterward.

2. Scaling User Story Mapping

To scale and roll out this approach, the initial team of coaches provided materials such as an Excel-based template for maps, templates for personas, a standard workshop agenda, wiki articles, and method description "cheat sheets." In addition, an internal tool for user story mapping is being developed.

However, materials are one thing, and running a workshop is another. So, again, we strongly recommend involving an experienced coach in the process. To be able to provide enough coaches, the initial coaching team trained more coaches. These "junior coaches" attended a workshop with a senior coach, facilitated individual sessions, and then ran workshops on their own. We also ran workshops and "train the trainer" sessions in SAP's main development locations worldwide. To make sure we learn from one another, and from the various experiences, we implemented a global network call where coaches can share questions and good practices backed up by wiki pages and communities of practice. And, last but not least, we learned a lot from numerous great exchanges with Jeff.

Our efforts at scaling user story mapping were successful. We ran more than 200 facilitated workshops in various units and locations, and now most teams are able to use user story mapping successfully on their own.

CHAPTER 6

The Real Story About Stories

Story mapping is a remarkably simple idea. Using a simple map, you can work with others to tell a product's story and see the big picture form as you do. Then, you carve up that big picture to make good planning decisions. Underneath all that is the simple concept of Agile stories.

Kent's Disruptively Simple Idea

The idea of stories originated with a very smart guy by the name of Kent Beck. Kent was working with other people on software development in the late '90s, and he noticed that one of the biggest problems in software development sprang from the traditional process approach of using documents to describe precisely what we want—that is, the requirements. By now you know the problem with that. Different people can read the same document and imagine different things. They can even "sign off" on the document believing they're in agreement.

I'm glad we all agree.

It's later, when we get into the thick of developing software—or even later than that, after it's delivered—that we realize we weren't thinking of the same things. Lots of people call this lack of shared understanding "bad requirements."

Let me vent a minute here. I have the pleasure of working with lots of teams. And we often start work together by talking about their biggest challenges. And, hands down, the one I hear most is "bad requirements." And then everyone points at that document. The document writer feels bad—as if he should have written more, or less, or used some cool requirements technique. Those who signed off feel bad at first, and then indignant. "Surely you didn't expect I'd read every detail! After all, we talked about this for days. I just expected you'd understood what I said. I can't understand your silly requirements document anyway." And the people building the software feel blindsided. They muddled their way through those cryptic documents and what they built was still wrong. Everyone hates the document in the end. Yet we still keep trying to write a better one.

We can both read the same document, but have a different understanding of it.

But misunderstanding the document is only half the problem. We waste lots of time and money building what the document describes, only to find out later that what actually solves the intended problem is something very different. You heard me right. Those documents often accurately describe the wrong thing. Documents usually describe *what* we need, but not *why* we need it. If the person building software could simply speak with someone who understood the users who will be using the software and why they'll be using it, there's often a more cost-effective way to delight those users. Without talking, we just never know about it.

> *The best solutions come from collaboration between the people with the problems to solve and the people who can solve them.*

Kent's simple idea was to *stop it*—to stop working so hard on writing the perfect document, and to get together to *tell stories*. Stories get their name not from how they're supposed to be written, but from how they're supposed to be used. Let me repeat that with more emotion. Right now you should stop whatever you're doing and say this out loud:

> *Stories get their name from how they're supposed to be used, not from what you're trying to write down.*

Kent's idea was simple. If we get together and talk about the problem we're solving with software, who'll use it, and why, then together we can arrive at a solution, and build shared understanding along the way.

Simple Isn't Easy

A while back I began to notice that this entire story thing had gone a bit sideways; that is, lots of the people writing books, teaching, and using them focused on the activity of writing stories. If I had a dime for every time I've been asked how to write good stories, I'd have even more dimes than I collected a few chapters ago.

With all the focus on writing stories, I went back to Kent to make sure I wasn't missing something here. Over the course of an email conversation, Kent explained where the idea came from:

What I was thinking of was the way users sometimes tell stories about the cool new things the software they use does. [For example,] if I type in the zip code and it automatically fills in the city and state without me having to touch a button.

I think that was the example that triggered the idea. If you can tell stories about what the software does and generate interest and vision in the listener's mind, then why not tell stories before the software does it?

— Kent Beck via personal email, Aug 2010

So the idea is *telling*, and you know you're doing it right if you're generating energy, interest, and vision in the listener's mind. That's big. And it sounds a lot more fun than reading a typical requirements document.[1]

But folks who start using stories for software development—and who still have a traditional process model in their heads—tend to focus on the writing part. I've seen teams replace their traditional requirements process with story writing, and then get frustrated trying to write stories to precisely communicate what should be built. If you're doing that now, stop it.

If you're not getting together to have rich discussions about your stories, then you're not really using stories.

Ron Jeffries and the 3 Cs

In the book *Extreme Programming Installed*, Ron Jeffries et al. (Addison-Wesley Longman Publishing) describe the story process best:

Card
> Write what you'd like to see in the software on a bunch of index cards.

Conversation
> Get together and have a rich conversation about what software to build.

---

1. There's some evidence that a fact wrapped in a story is much more memorable than the fact presented alone—22 times more memorable, according to psychologist Jerome Bruner.

Confirmation

Together agree on how you'll confirm that the software is done.

If it sounds simple, it's because it is. Just remember, simple isn't easy.

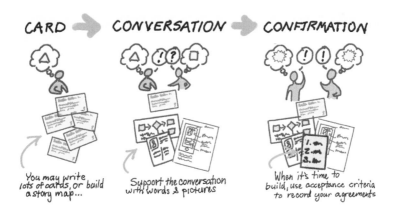

1. Card

Imagine you're responsible for working with a team to get some software built. Imagine that software as best you can. Then, for each thing users want to do with the product, write a card. You'll end up with a bunch of them. Kent's original idea was to write them on index cards because it's easy to organize a bunch of cards on a tabletop. It's easier to prioritize them, or organize them into a structure that helps you see the big picture—a structure like a story map, of course.

The bunch of cards that describes the whole product, or all the changes we'd like to make to a product we have, is called a *product backlog*. That term originated with the Agile process Scrum. Someone I know once said, "I hate that term *backlog*. We haven't even started to build software, and it already sounds like we're behind!" I'm not sure I have a better name for that bunch of stories, but if you can think of a good one, please use it, and let me know what it is.

2. Conversation

The conversation might start with you describing what you're thinking, and the person listening might form an idea in her head based upon what she heard. Because it's hard to explain things perfectly, and because it's easy to imagine different things based on our past experience, the listener likely imagined something different than you. But that's where the magic comes in.

Because this is a conversation, the listener can ask questions and it's the back and forth that will correct that understanding and help everyone arrive at some shared understanding.

In a traditional software process, the goal for the person who had the requirements is to get them written down correctly; and for the person who's going to build the software, it's to understand them correctly. Because this is a story-driven process, you each have a different shared goal. Your goal is to work together to understand the problem being solved by building software, and solve it as best you can. Eventually, you'll need to agree on what you should build that you both believe will help the users of the product.

Let me say this again, because it's an important point:

> *Story conversations are about working together to arrive at a best solution to a problem we both understand.*

3. Confirmation

All this talking is cool, but we've eventually got to build some software —right? So, when we feel like we're converging on a good solution, we'll need to start focusing on the answer to these questions:

If we build what we agree to, what will we check to see that we're done?

> The answer to this question is usually a short list of things to check. This list is often called *acceptance criteria*, or *story tests*.

When it comes time to demonstrate this later at a product review, how will we do that?

> The answer to this question often reveals some holes. For example, you could make the software work, but to demonstrate it you'll need to get your hands on some realistic data. Discussing demonstration may add a few more bullets to your list of acceptance criteria.

Words and Pictures

The path to get to this agreement isn't just a single card and lots of hand waving. The conversation goes best if it includes lots of things such as simple personas, workflow diagrams, UI sketches, and any other traditional software model that'll help explain things. That way, you don't have to just wave hands—you can point a lot, too. Whatever we bring into the conversation we'll mark up, write on, correct, and change. We'll even create a lot of things on the spot during that conversation. Use a whiteboard or flipchart paper. And don't forget to take some "vacation photos" before you leave. Photos of what you've created will help you recall all the details of the conversation that would be difficult to write down.

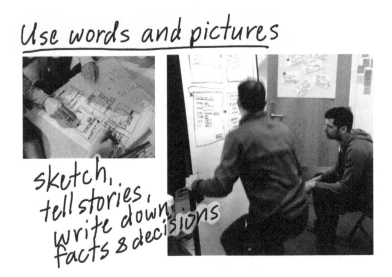

Good story conversations have lots of words and pictures.

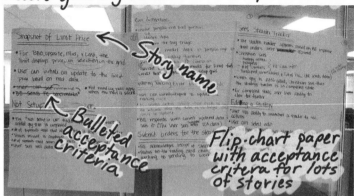

Keep the acceptance criteria you decide on big and visible during the conversation. This team uses flipchart paper to record as they go.

That's It

That's all there is. That's Kent's disruptively simple idea. And, if you do it, I promise you it'll change everything.

Unless it doesn't.

For people used to working the old-fashioned way, this conversation can go really badly. They fall back into their old patterns of the person bringing in stuff, trying to work hard to communicate exactly what he wants to the other person, and the other person working hard to try to understand and then punch holes in what the other person is saying. If this goes on too long, they often feel like punching holes in each other, which is not conducive to getting things done.

There are some things to keep in mind to help these conversations go better. Happily, that's what the next chapter is about.

CHAPTER 7

Telling Better Stories

The idea of stories is simple. Maybe too simple. For lots of people in software development, conversations like these feel very foreign…and a little uncomfortable. And people often revert to talking about requirements like they always used to.

When Kent Beck originally described the idea of stories, he didn't call them *user stories*, he just called them *stories*—because that's what he hoped you'd be telling. But very soon after the first books on Extreme Programming were published, *stories* picked up the more descriptive prefix *user* so that we'd remember to have conversations from the perspective of the people outside the software. Changing the name wasn't enough, however.

Connextra's Cool Template

This is my friend Rachel Davies. And she's holding a story card.

In the late 1990s she worked for a company called Connextra. Connextra was one of the earliest adopters of Extreme Programming, the Agile process where stories came from. When the Connextra folks started using stories, they found they ran into some common problems. Most of the people who wrote the stories at Connextra were from sales and marketing. They tended to write down the feature they needed. But, when it came time for developers to have conversations, they needed to find that original stakeholder and get a good conversation started—one that included who and why. Just having the name of the feature wasn't helping the team find the right people to talk to, or to start the right discussions. And, back then, there wasn't much guidance about what could or should be on a card. The template evolved over time at Connextra. It wasn't Rachel's invention specifically. Rather, it was the entire organization's desire to build things that mattered.

After using the template for a while, the folks at Connextra wanted to show off their cool new trick. They printed a bunch of example cards to show off at XPDay 2001, a small conference in London. That's what Rachel is holding. It's her last card, and might very well be the last card in existence, so that makes it a historical artifact.

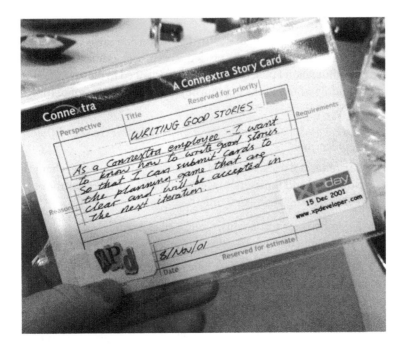

The template goes like this:

> As a [type of user]
>
> I want to [do something]
>
> So that I can [get some benefit]

The folks at Connextra used this simple template to write the *descriptions* of their stories. Note that their stories still have short, useful titles. They found that writing this little extra bit to start to tell the story forced them to pause and think about: who, what, and why. And, if they didn't know, they might question whether they should be writing the story at all.

When they sat down to have the story conversation, they'd pick up that card and then read that description. That description started the conversation.

Use the simple story template to start conversations.

If you're picking up an individual card outside of a story map, the template is a good way to boot up the conversation. Remember in Chapter 1 that one of the cards in the body of Gary's map said, "Upload an image." And that card was one of the details under the card "Customize my promo flyer." What I write on the cards in a map are those short verb phrases—the tasks the users are performing with my software. But when I pick one up by itself, I'll need to pick up the story in the middle of the user's big journey described in the map. I might say:

> "As a *band manager*, I want to *upload an image* so that I can *customize my promo flyer.*"

That's a pretty cool trick. I can find the cards for different users hanging above the map, and the users' bigger goal is often in the card above the one you're viewing at any one time.

But remember—it's just a conversation starter. And, in fact, the conversation might continue like this:

> "Why would the band manager want to customize the flyer?"
>
> "Well, because it won't have his band's photo on it automatically, and he'd want it to be there. And he cares a lot about being original—he wouldn't want it to look like everyone else's."
>
> "That makes sense. Where do people like band managers keep those photos?"
>
> "Well, they're all over the place, really. They may be on their local hard drives, in Flickr accounts, or in other places on the Web."
>
> "Hmm…that's different than I was originally thinking. I assumed they'd just be on their hard drives."
>
> "No, lots of the people we've talked to have them spread all over the place. It's kind of a problem."

In fact, a lot of the conversation I had with Gary went like that. As we were talking, we'd write something down on a whiteboard or on the card itself. Before too long we'd be sketching ideas.

You can see that the very short template isn't nearly enough to be the specification. But when we start a conversation using that template, we end up in a much richer conversation than if we'd just talked about a file uploader.

Rediscovering the Small Conversation

Mat Cropper, ThoughtWorks

I was working as a business analyst on a ThoughtWorks project for a UK government agency. We were responsible for delivery, but also for giving the client team some practical experience around Agile methodologies. That being the case, we were quite a big team of some 25 or so technologists and businesspeople. One room, 25 different air conditioning setting preferences—you get the idea!

To start off, the product owner and I would write stories, and then at the beginning of every two-week iteration, the entire team got together for planning. It was a necessarily big meeting, and it was a car crash. "Why are we doing it this way?" "These stories are way too big/small." "It doesn't make sense." "I have this strong preference for a particular technical implementation." These were common (and frustrating) discussions. To be honest, I left those meetings feeling pretty dejected. It felt like a personal failure.

Something had to be done to fix this, so we decided that rather than have one meeting with everybody to discuss everything, we would move to conversations with a tighter focus. Backlog grooming, for example, took place in week one of the iteration with a small group (project owner, project manager, business analyst, technical architect) who kicked the tires of the various stories so that when we did a grooming session as a full team later there would be much fewer distractions. The conversation was about tweaking and improving our stories, and we ignored things like prioritization, story points, and so forth. It worked.

We also made sure that we were much more constructively creating stories. I'd have an idea of the stories I was working on that week, and they'd be up on the card wall in the "In Analysis" column. Each day in our team's standup, I'd call out that I was working on a particular story, and could use some time from a developer pair to pull it together. We'd sit down, discuss what we were aiming for, usually touch on the technical aspects, and then get it all down on paper. We ignored Trello, which we were using for our digital card wall at the time, and focused instead on the face-to-face conversations, sometimes standing at a whiteboard. Working as a group, down in the detail, is actually pretty rewarding, and as it took only about 20 minutes each time, it wasn't too much of an overhead either. People were genuinely happy to pair and contribute.

As a happy consequence, our large backlog grooming sessions were a breeze, and we also found that story sizes were becoming more and more uniform. Iteration planning became less of a pain as a result. The quality of the conversations leading to the documenting of a story had improved, and so had the work we were producing.

Template Zombies and the Snowplow

The term *template zombies* comes from the book *Adrenaline Junkies and Template Zombies: Understanding Patterns of Project Behavior* by Tom DeMarco et al. (Dorset House). The name says it all, but I'll give you the authors' definition:

Template Zombie:

The project team allows its work to be driven by templates instead of by the thought process necessary to deliver products.

As simple as that template is, it gets abused quite a bit. I see people really struggle to force ideas into the template when they just don't fit. Stories about backend services or security issues can be challenging. I see people writing and thinking about things from their own perspective, not that of the people who ultimately benefit: "as a product owner, I want you to build a file uploader so that the customer requirements are met." Nasty things like that.

Even worse, the template has become so ubiquitous, and so commonly taught, that there are those who believe that it's not a story if it's not written in that form. Many people have even quit using titles on stories and write only that long sentence on every single card. Imagine trying to read through a list of stories written that way. Imagine trying to tell someone a story using a story map where every sticky is written that way. It's tough on the brain.

All of this makes me sad. Because the real value of stories isn't what's written down on the card. It comes from what we learn when we tell the story.

It doesn't need to be written in a template to be considered a story.

The person in this picture is learning to ski.[1] If you've ever learned to ski, and someone helpful is teaching you, you'll do what this person is doing. It's called a snowplow. It's where you put the tips of your skis together and lean on the inside edges of your skis. It's the easiest way to control your speed and stay upright when you've got two slippery boards clamped to your feet. It's the way I'd recommend learning to ski. But it's not best practice—it's a best *learning* practice. There's no Olympic snowplow event. You won't impress anyone on the slopes with your cool snowplow stance. It's nothing to be embarrassed of, though. If people see you skiing that way, they'll know you're learning.

For me, the story template works a bit like learning the snowplow. Use it to write the descriptions of your first stories. Say it aloud to start your story conversations. But don't get too concerned if you find that

---

1. This photo was taken by Ruth Hartnup, found on Flickr, and licensed under the Creative Commons Attribution License.

it doesn't always work. Just like the snowplow technique for skiers, it's not the best choice for difficult terrain.

My favorite template: if I'm writing stories on sticky notes or cards, and they won't be sitting inside a bigger story map, I'll first give them a short, simple title, and then under it I'll write:

Who:

What:

Why:

And I'll give a couple of lines in between each, because I'll want to specifically name all the different whos, say a little about the what, and make notes about the different reasons why. I'll want to leave room on the card to add extra information when we start talking about the stories. It's actually a pet peeve of mine when people write the title in the middle of the card, because it doesn't leave me any room to make notes when we start talking. But I'm nitpicky that way.

A Checklist of What to Really Talk About

☐ *Really talk about who*
Please don't just talk about "the user." Be specific. Talk about which user you mean. For Gary, he could talk about the band manager or the music fan.

Talk about different types of users. For many pieces of software, especially consumer software, there are very diverse types of users using the same functionality. Talk about the functionality from different users' perspectives.

Talk about the customers. For consumer products, the customer (or chooser) may be the same person as the user. But for enterprise products, we'll need to talk about the people who make buying decisions, their organization as a whole, and how they benefit.

Talk about other stakeholders. Talk about the people sponsoring the software's purchase. Talk about others who might collaborate with users.

There's rarely just one user who matters.

☐ *Really talk about what*
I like my stories to start with user tasks—the things people want to do with my software. But what about services like the kind way

beneath the user interface that authorizes your credit card for a purchase, or authenticates you on an insurance website? Your users didn't make a deliberate choice to get their credit cards pass: [authorized] or have their credentials verified. It's OK to talk about the services and the different systems that call them. It's OK to talk about specific UI components and how the screen behaves. Just don't lose sight of who cares, and why.

○ *Really talk about why*
Talk about why the specific user cares. And dig deeply into the "whys," because there are often a few, and they're layered. You can keep "poking it with the why stick" for a long time to really get at the underlying reasons why.

Talk about why other users care. Talk about why the user's company cares. Talk about why business stakeholders care. There are lots of great things hidden inside why.

○ *Talk about what's going on outside the software*
Talk about where people using your product are when they use it. Talk about when they'd use the product, and how often. Talk about who else is there when they do. All those things give clues about what a good solution might be.

○ *Talk about what goes wrong*
What happens when things go wrong? What happens when the system is down? How else could users accomplish this? How do they meet their needs today?

○ *Talk about questions and assumptions*
If you talk about all those things, you've likely stumbled across something you don't know. Identify your questions and discuss how important they are to get answered before you build software. Decide who'll do the legwork to get those questions answered, and bring them back to your next conversation. You'll find it takes lots of conversations to think through some stories.

Take time to question your assumptions. Do you really understand your users? Is this really what they want? Do they really have these problems? Will they really use this solution?

Question your technical assumptions. What underlying systems do we rely on? Do they really work the way we think? Are there technical risks we need to consider?

All these questions and assumptions may require deliberate work to resolve or learn. Make a plan to do just that.

○ *Talk about better solutions*

The really big win comes when those in a story conversation discard some original assumptions about what the solution should be, go back to the problem they're trying to solve, and then together arrive at a solution that's more effective and more economical to build.

○ *Talk about how*

When sitting in a story conversation, I often hear someone anxiously say, "We should be talking about the what, not the how!" By that they mean we should be talking about what users need to do, not how the code should be written. And I feel the same anxiousness when we talk about the "what" without talking about the "why." But the truth is, we're trying to optimize for all three in a good story conversation. What goes wrong is when either party assumes that a particular solution or the way it's implemented is a "requirement." Without explicitly talking about how (and if you're a developer, I know you're thinking about it), it's difficult to think about the cost of the solution. Because, if a solution is too expensive, then it may not be a good option.

Be respectful of the expertise of others in the conversation. Don't tell a highly trained technical person how to do her work. Don't tell someone intimately familiar with users and their work that he doesn't understand. Ask questions, and genuinely try to learn from each other.

○ *Talk about how long*

Ultimately, we need to make some decisions to go forward with building something or not. And it's tough to make this sort of buying decision without a price tag.

For software, that usually means how long it'll take to write the code. In early conversations, that might be expressed as "a really long time" or "a few days." Even better is comparing it to something already built—"about the same as that feature for commenting we built last month." As we get closer to building something, and we've had more conversations and made more decisions, we'll be able to be a bit more precise. But we always know we're talking about estimates here, not commitments.

Create Vacation Photos

Because there's a lot to talk about, and you won't want to forget it, make sure you're recording specific things that help you remember the decisions you made, or the questions and assumptions you'll need to look into. Don't forget to externalize your thinking so that others in the discussion see what's recorded.

If you write it down, you can pick it up and refer to it later. If it's posted on the wall, you can just point at it. And, if you're talking together as a team, you'll find you won't have to repeat everything so often, because people will remember—especially if you anchored your conversations with simple drawings and documents...those vacation photos.

This small group is having a story discussion. As they talk, they visualize their ideas and make notes about what they decide.

My favorite approach is to do exactly what they're doing. I record on flipchart paper or a whiteboard as we talk. I like making a note of who was in the conversation directly on the board, and then photographing the board when I'm done. I'll share the photo using a wiki or other tool. I know I can extract details or write them up more formally when I need them later. If I can't remember exactly what was said, one of those people in the conversation might. It's a good thing I wrote their names down.

It's a Lot to Worry About

It's daunting to think about how much there is you could be talking about in stories. At this point, you may want to go back to the good old days when all you needed to do was worry about understanding the "requirements." Back when it wasn't your job to really solve problems. Back when you just needed to build what you were told to, and it was someone else's problem to make sure it was the right thing to build. But I believe that you, and most people out there, really like solving problems. So now's your chance.

It may have occurred to you that with all these things to talk about, there will be a lot of information to keep track of. And all that stuff isn't going to fit on a sticky note or an index card. You're right. It won't. So let's talk next about what really does go on that card, and what doesn't.

CHAPTER 8

It's Not All on the Card

Yes, the big idea was that short story titles on cards would help us plan and facilitate lots of conversations between the people who could build software and the people who understood the problems that needed to be solved with it. But, sadly, it takes more than a couple of people to get a finished piece of software out the door.

On a typical team you'll find project managers, product managers, business analysts, testers, user experience designers, technical writers, and some other roles I'm probably forgetting. They're all looking at the same cards, but the conversations they have are going to be different because they've all got different concerns to look after.

Different People, Different Conversations

If I'm a product manager or product owner, and I'm responsible for the success of this product, then I have to know a little more about my target market. I need to form some hypothesis about how many people will buy or use this product, or how it's going to affect the profitability of my company. I'll want to talk about those things.

If I'm a business analyst, I might be diving into a lot of details, so I need to understand what's going on in the user interface, and the business rules in the system that are behind the user interface.

If I'm a tester, I need to think about where the software is likely to fail. I need to have some conversations to help me put together a good test plan.

If I'm a UI designer, I don't want to be told what the UI looks like any more than a developer wants to be told the way the code should be written. I'll want to know who's using it, and why and what they're doing, so I can design a useful and usable user interface.

Finally, if I'm a project manager responsible for coordinating this group of people, I'll have to pay attention when all of them are talking to make decisions about all these details. I'll need to pay attention to dependencies, schedules, and the status of development when it gets started.

That's a lot of conversations. And some of them have to happen before others. And many of them happen more than once. So, to make it accurate, we'd probably have to add another dozen Cs to the 3 Cs. But happily, if you're really having conversations and building shared understanding along the way, you'll avoid lots of misunderstandings and course corrections.

> *There are many different kinds of conversations with different people for every story.*

We're Gonna Need a Bigger Card

When you say the words in that heading, I hope you're thinking of the old movie *Jaws* when, after seeing the huge shark up close and personal for the first time, Police Chief Brody says to Quint, "You're gonna need a bigger boat."

You see, the original idea was also that I could pick up a card and write the title on the front, and then as we had conversations, I could flip it over on the back and write the details of all the things we agreed to that came up. I could sketch the user interface and write a lot of other information on the card. On some projects, it can really work this way. It's cool when it can, and it's usually a side effect of small teams working closely together with a lot of tacit knowledge. Those are the teams that don't have to write much to remember.

But I don't think even Kent and the folks who perfected the concept of stories actually thought that all these conversations between all these different people could be contained on just a single card, and in fact, they usually aren't.

The metaphor that works for me is a card in a library card catalog, for people who are old enough to remember when libraries actually *had* card catalogs. Stories written on cards work a bit like those.

This is a card catalog

In it are cards like this one...

But the real information is out there in a book.

If I pick up a card from a card catalog, it's going to have just enough information for me to identify the book. It likely has a title, the author name, a description, the page count of the book, the category of the book—like "nonfiction"—and a code (remember Mr. Dewey's decimals?) to a location where I can actually find a copy of the book in the library. The card's just a token that's easy to find and organize. No one confuses the cards with a book. The card catalog is handy because it takes a lot less space than thousands of books would. And I can organize cards in different ways—by author, for example, or by subject.

Your stories will work the same way; that is, you may write them on cards, keep them in a list in a spreadsheet, enter them into your favorite tracking tool, or enter them in the tracking tool your company makes you use—you know, the one everyone grumbles about. In a library, you know there's a book out there somewhere, and if you have identified the right card filed away in the card catalog, it's easy to find it. Similarly, with a story, you know there's a growing amount of information out there somewhere. It grows and evolves with each conversation. And, hopefully, however your company chooses to keep track of the information, it's easy to find, too.

If you want to go really old school, keep the details of all those discussions taped onto big sheets of flipchart paper on the wall so you can keep talking about them whenever you want. But remember: you'll want to take them down when you've completed the work or else you'll run out of wall space. And you'll want to photograph them and keep those photos somewhere for posterity.

This is my friend Sherif, who's a product manager at a company called Atlassian. Atlassian makes Confluence, a popular wiki used in a huge variety of organizations to keep track of the knowledge those organizations accumulate, among other things. They also make JIRA, one of the more popular tools for managing work in Agile development. You'd think a company that focuses on building tools used for keeping and sharing information electronically would use its own tools— "eat their own dog food," so to speak—and you'd be right that Atlassian does. But it also understands how to have good face-to-face conversations.

When I walk around the Atlassian office in Sydney, I see the walls covered with sticky notes, whiteboard drawings, and screen wireframes. If you look closely, you'll see that the sticky notes reference ticket numbers in those tools the team relies on. They nimbly move back and forth from tools to physical space. When Sherif shows me what they keep in Confluence, I'm amazed at the combination of photographs, short videos, and back-and-forth discussions.

Radiators and Ice Boxes

In his book *Agile Software Development: The Cooperative Game* (Addison-Wesley Professional), Alistair Cockburn coined the term *information radiator* to describe how big, visible information on the wall radiates useful stuff into the room. People walking by look at it and engage with it. When the information is alive and useful, lots of conversations end up at the wall, where people can point to and add to the information accumulating there.

When I walk into environments where the walls are clear, or even covered with pleasant artwork—or worst of all, motivational posters —it makes me sad. There's so much great collaboration that could be happening every day with those useful walls. If what's on the wall is an information radiator, some refer to the tools people use as an *information icebox*—because that's where information goes to be preserved —and potentially be crusted over with that thin layer of ice like that stuff in the back of your freezer. (I'm always shocked by what I find back there.)

That's what's really remarkable to me about Atlassian. They keep information alive and useful, both in and out of the tools they use.

What's Really on a Story Card?

Imagine a card from a library's card catalog. That card's got useful information on it to help you organize it and confirm you're talking about the right book. A good story card is a bit like that.

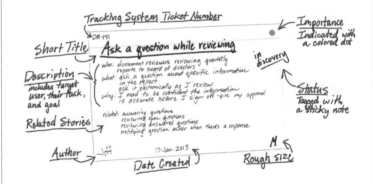

Common things you'd expect to find on a card are:

Short title

> One that's easy to insert into a conversation when you're talking about it. A good title is the most valuable part of your story. Don't be afraid to rewrite it if it's confusing people.

Description

A sentence or two that describes what we're imagining. It's a good idea to describe who, what, and why—who uses or needs it, what they'll do with it, and what benefit they hope to get from it.

As you begin to discuss stories, you'll add information that summarizes some of your discussions. That'll include stuff like:

Story number

When you get a bunch of these or put them into a tracking system, this will help you find them—sort of like the Dewey Decimal System in a library. But, whatever you do, *please* don't start referring to your stories by their number. If you do, it's a sure signal you haven't chosen a very good title. And even librarians don't refer to books by their Dewey Decimal numbers.

Estimate, size, or budget

As you begin to discuss the story, you'll want a prediction on how long it might take to build the software. There are lots of terms for this, like *estimate*, *size*, or *budget*. Use the term your company uses.

Value

You might have lengthy discussions about the relative value of one thing over another. Some might use a numeric scale. Some might annotate cards with *high*, *medium*, or *low*.

Metrics

If you really care about results, identify specific metrics you'll track after the software is released to determine whether the software was successful.

Dependencies

Other stories that this one might depend on or go with.

Status

Is it planned for a particular release? Is it started? In progress? Done?

Dates

Just as a book's card has the date it was published, you might keep the date this story was added, started, and finished.

You could scribble any other notes you like on the card. Or flip it to the back and write notes or bulleted acceptance criteria.

The only thing that's required on your card is a good title. All those other bits of information could be helpful, but you and your team get to decide which you'd like to use.

Not too much fits on the card, and that's good. Remember, it's just a token you'll use to plan with. You could use cards, or sticky notes, too. Having the physical cards lets you use handy words like *this* and *that* in conversations as you point to cards on a wall or tabletop. You can't do that with a thick document. With cards, you can shuffle them around a desk, rank them by importance, tape them to the wall, and wave them around while you're talking to make your point more emphatically. If you were doing that with a thick document, you could hurt someone—perhaps yourself. And, of course, you'll want to arrange bunches of cards into story maps to tell even bigger stories.

That's Not What That Tool Is For

A lumberjack comes across a man in the forest. The man is working hard trying to chop down a tree by hitting it with a hammer. The lumberjack stops the man and says, "Hey, you're using the wrong tool! Try this…" and hands the man a saw. The man thanks him, and the lumberjack continues on his way, happily knowing that he's helped. The man then begins striking the tree with the saw the same way he was with the hammer.

This joke reminds me that we can use the *wrong tool* for the job, and we can also use the *tool wrong*.

When I tell people how companies like Atlassian use tools, they're usually surprised. They're often surprised because they've been trying to use tools as a replacement for whiteboards and sticky notes. And, predictably, they've been struggling with that. It may be that they're using the wrong tool for the wrong job, or using the right tool wrong. To figure out what might be going wrong, it's best to look at the job first, and not the tool.

Building Shared Understanding

When we're working together to tell stories and make decisions about solutions to build, our first goal is to build shared understanding. This is where externalizing and organizing your thoughts is critical. And nothing beats face-to-face work in front of a whiteboard, armed with sticky notes. But, if you've got to accomplish this task with others working remotely, this is tough. Video conference tools that let you see one another's faces don't help much, since it's not their faces you need to see—it's the ideas you'll be placing on the wall or tabletop.

> *Use a document camera or web camera during a video conference to let remote people see what's being created on the wall.*

I've worked with teams that have video cameras at both ends of a video conference, and the call focuses on the growing models on the wall, not the team members' faces.

If you use a tool to visualize, it's ideal if people on both sides of the conversation can add and move things around, just like they could if they were working together at a whiteboard. This is a screen from a tool called Cardboard.

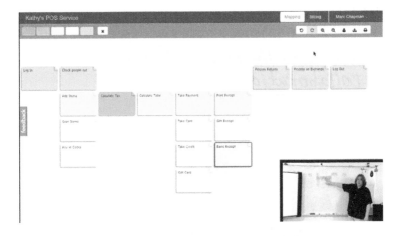

The person using Cardboard is creating a map at the same time as David Hussman, one of Cardboard's creators, maps on a wall. Others who are sharing the same map from other locations see it come together in real time. They can add, remove, and change cards, and everyone can see what everyone else is doing. You can virtually "step back" and look at the entire wall at once, which is handy because computer screens are just a tiny portal on what you could see if you were working at a wall.

When collaborating remotely, use tools that allow everyone to see, add to, and organize the model concurrently.

Happily, I'm seeing a lot more tools enter the market that understand and support working together to build shared understanding. This is a good thing.

Remembering

When we've worked hard together to get on the same page, we should be keeping copies of whatever models or examples we've created to use as vacation photos—to help us remember all the details we've discussed. Tools like Atlassian's Confluence offer a rich wiki for storing not just words, but also pictures and video. Taking and keeping pictures and videos after working together is one of fastest ways to document.

These folks at Atlassian are doing just that. They've snapped a picture after working at a wall, and uploaded it to their wiki for safekeeping.

Use tools to post pictures, videos, and text to help you retain and remember your conversations.

I personally like staying lo-fi and keeping information on the wall, but if I worry at all about a cleaning person taking it down at night, I'll photograph and keep it just in case. If I'm sharing information with people who couldn't be in the room, even virtually, I'll shoot a short video stepping through the model on the wall and post that where others can see it.

Tracking

One of the things that tools most excel at is taking all the work we've planned on doing, and letting us track its progress. Tools are great at keeping track of the numbers that are tedious for us—things like exactly when we started, when we finished, and how much we've got left to do. The better tools will generate useful insights for us as we routinely track what we're doing.

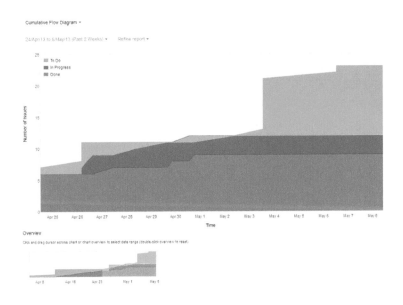

This is a cumulative flow diagram generated by Atlassian's JIRA product. It's a chart that shows the work we're doing and its state over time. And it's a chart I would hate to produce by hand.

For single, collocated teams and small projects, the wall will do just fine. But, if you've got larger teams working from different physical locations, and longer-running projects, use a tool to keep track of all the details.

Use tools to sequence, track, and analyze progress.

The trick is using the right tool for the right job. Don't try to use a really great tracking tool to build shared understanding. And don't struggle to do complex analysis on a whiteboard.

It's been an Agile ideal to keep things simple and fast, to stay working on index cards and whiteboards as much as possible. And I promise you if you can stay small and fast and avoid unnecessary tools, you'll be happier. But remember: those tools are just a means to an end. Next, we'll need to talk about what happens after the card.

CHAPTER 9

The Card Is Just the Beginning

The three *C* s are just the beginning.

I know I said earlier that I don't feel obligated to quote the Agile Manifesto, but I'm going to anyway—well, at least a small part of it. One of the value statements in the manifesto reads "Working software over comprehensive documentation." I could rephrase that as "working software over comprehensive conversation," and the meaning would be the same. All those conversations—and the documentation that helps us recall them—are just a means to an end. Eventually we'll need to build something.

If we finish the cycle, the model looks like this:

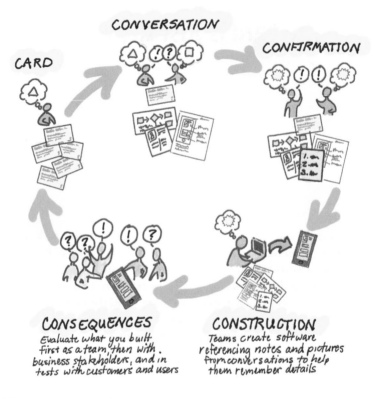

There are some gotchas that always manage to sneak in here after we've got shared understanding and agreement on what we'll build. Keep an eye out for them.

Construct with a Clear Picture in Your Head

After having conversations, and writing down details that'll help us remember those conversations, and writing down confirmation—that is, our agreement about the things we'll check to confirm we're done —we're finally ready to make something:

- Software developers can get started building the software.
- Testers can create test plans and test.

- UI designers can create detailed UI design and digital assets, if they haven't already done so as part of arriving at a shared understanding.
- Technical writers can write or update help files or other documents.

The most important thing here is that all these people are armed with *the same picture in their heads: the picture they built while talking together.*

I'm going to pause here for effect.

Now, I'm going to say this next part slowly, so you should read it slowly.

> *Handing off all the details about the story to someone else to build doesn't work.*
> *Don't do that.*

If you and a group of people have worked together to understand what should be built, and if you've documented all the important things someone needs to know to build it, you may be very tempted here to hand it off to someone else. After all, when you look at the information, it's crystal clear to you. But don't fool yourself. It's clear to you because your really smart brain is filling in all the details that aren't written down. Your brain is so good at it that it's hard for you to detect what could be missing. Remember, those details are *your* vacation photos, not *theirs*.

Build an Oral Tradition of Storytelling

Sharing stories is reasonably simple. Someone who does understand the story, and the information collected that helps tell the story, needs only spend a little time retelling the story to the next person who needs to learn. Now, this should go lots faster than early conversations where you worked together to make tough decisions, since hopefully you won't need to remake them. Use what's written to help tell the story. Talk and point to pictures. Let your listener ask questions and make changes to the pictures that help her remember. Help her turn the information associated with the story into her own vacation photos.

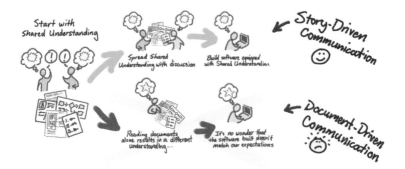

There's a nasty anti-pattern I often see here. Some think that since anyone in a team might pick up the story and do work on it, everyone on the team should be involved in every conversation. Perhaps you work at this company. You'll know it because you'll hear lots of people complaining that there are way too many meetings. By the way, "meeting" is often the euphemism we use for unproductive collaboration.

Effective discussion and decision making goes best with small groups of two to five. It's dinner conversation sized. You know that if you have a group of friends sharing a meal, it's easy to hold a single conversation when there are just a few of you. But any more than about five people is where it becomes a real effort.

Let small groups work together to make decisions, and then use continued conversations to share the results with everyone else.

Inspect the Results of Your Work

If you're on the team, you'll all work together armed with shared understanding about what you're building, and why. As you work together, you'll keep having conversations because you never think of everything. But when the software is done, you'll all come back together and talk about it.

This is a good time to congratulate yourselves on a job well done. It's pretty cool to see real progress. In traditional software development, the opportunities to see the results of your hard work can come a lot less frequently, and they're rarely shared as a team. In a typical Agile process like Scrum, you'll be sharing every couple of weeks at an end-of-sprint product review. In the healthiest of teams, team members get together frequently to inspect their work as it's done. But you'll need to go beyond show and tell. After congratulating yourselves, take time for a short but serious reflection on the quality of the work you did.

When talking about quality, I start with discussions of these three aspects:

User experience quality
Review the work from the perspective of its target user. Is it straightforward to use? Is it *fun* to use? Does it look good? Is it consistent with your brand and other functionality?

Functional quality
Does the software do what you agreed it would without bugs or errors? Testers and other team members have hopefully spent time testing and you've fixed any bugs already. But good testers can often tell you that there are likely more bugs lurking in your product that may emerge later. Or hopefully they can say that it feels rock solid.

Code quality
Is the software we wrote high quality? Consistent with our standards? We may own this stuff for a while, so it'd be good to know if we think it'll be easy to extend and maintain, or if we've just added a pile of technical debt we'll need to address later.

I have some bad news for you here. You're likely to find things you believe should change about what you've done.

It'll help everyone's sanity to separate out two concerns. First: *did we build what we agreed to build?* And then: *if it's what we agreed to build, now that we see it, should we make some changes?*

Everyone will have worked hard together at the outset to figure out what to build that would solve users' problems and be economical to build. You'll have done your best to identify the things to check to confirm that it's done. Check all those things, and congratulate yourselves if you've accomplished that much. You got exactly what you agreed you wanted to get.

Now, here's where some old Rolling Stones song lyrics play in my head. If you know the song, hum along: "You can't always get what you want. But, if you try sometime, you just might find, you get what you need." The irony with software is that it's exactly the opposite.

You'll work together to agree on what you want. And, if you're working with a competent team, you'll see that you can get pretty good at getting it. It's only after seeing it, though, that you can better evaluate if it's what you need. This sucks. But don't blame yourselves—that's just the way it works.

You do, however, have a way of fixing it. And it starts by writing a card with your ideas about what to change in the software to fix it. This, of course, sucks if you'd planned on being right the first time. Maybe Mick Jagger was right after all. Maybe what you really needed was to learn that being right the first time is a risky strategy—especially in software.

It's Not for You

I'm sorry. I've got even more bad news.

In reality, the person who originally wrote the card and who started this entire cycle is likely not the person who will use the software every day. The person who originally wrote the card, and the entire team who worked together, may believe they've nailed it—that they've built the perfect solution to the challenges their target users have.

Don't fool yourself.

If we're on this team together and we're smart, we'll take the software out to users and test it with them. This isn't show and tell, either. We'll test by watching them use the software to reach a real goal they'll normally need to accomplish using the software.

Have you ever sat with someone as she uses software you've helped build? Think back to the first time you did. How did it go? I wasn't in the room with you at the time, but I'm willing to bet that it didn't go the way you expected.

If you've ever sat next to a user as she uses your product, you know what I mean. If you've never done this, then do it.

You'll need to test with the people who'll actually buy, adopt, and use your product at some regular frequency. I often wait until I've built up a bit of software—enough that they could use it to accomplish something they couldn't before. Whatever frequency you adopt, don't let more than a couple weeks go by without seeing a genuine user interact with the software.

Everyone on the team doesn't need to be there with users. In fact, it'll kind of creep the users out if everyone is. But being there builds empathy that you won't get any other way. It's a powerful motivator to see people struggling to use your product, especially when you were so confident they wouldn't need to. If you were there, share what you saw with others by telling stories back to them.

After testing with users, you'll identify problems to fix and obvious ways to improve the software. And for each one of those things, you should write a story card with your ideas for improving the software.

Build to Learn

If you'd labored under the belief that using stories would stop your team from writing bad software, you were at least half right. In fact, all the conversations between smart people focused on understanding the problem—and how what we're building solves it—go a long way toward making a much better product. But we need to acknowledge that building software isn't the same as working on an assembly line. You're not just building one more widget like the one you built a few minutes ago. Each new story we create software to support is something new.

One of the luminaries in the Agile development community is my aforementioned friend, Alistair Cockburn, who once told me, "For every story you write, you need to put three into your backlog of stories."

I asked him why, and he said, "You just do."

I asked, "What should I write on the other two?"

"It doesn't matter what you write."

"What do you mean?" I asked, "I have to write *something* on them!"

Alistair replied, "Well, if you have to write something on them, then write what you want on the first card, and on the second card write 'Fix the first card.' Then on the third card, write 'Fix the second one.' If you aren't going around this cycle three times for each story, you're not learning."

In a traditional process, learning gets referred to as *scope creep* or *bad requirements*. In an Agile process, learning is the purpose. You'll need to plan on learning from everything you build. And you'll need to plan on being wrong a fair bit of the time.

Eric's strategy used in Chapter 3 helped him build smaller solutions and continue to iterate them until they were viable. Eric counted on learning from every release.

The *Mona Lisa* strategy used by Mike and Aaron in Chapter 4 helped them slice every story down into smaller, thinner, undeliverable bits so they could learn sooner and manage their delivery budget wisely to finish on time.

These are both great learning strategies. Try those. Invent your own. But please don't assume you're always right. I promise you'll be disappointed.

It's Not Always Software

In 2011, Kent Beck—the creator of the story—opened one of the first Lean Startup conferences with his revision of the Agile Manifesto. If I'd done it, it might have been blasphemy. But he's one of its creators, so he should know. He revised the value about working software to read:

> *Validated learning* over working software (or comprehensive documentation)

If you remember from Chapter 3, validated learning is the super-valuable concept that comes from the Lean Startup process. The key word there is learning. What makes it *validated learning* is discussing what we want to learn as part of making something, and then going back and considering the *consequences*—reflecting on what we learned or didn't learn. And one of the things we're realizing is that we don't always need to build software to learn. But we do usually need to make or do something.

I like using stories to drive the work we do to build simple prototypes, or to plan the work we're doing to interview or observe users. I like talking about the who, what, and why for those things, too. I like agreeing on what we'll make before we make it. And I look back at the consequences of having done it to consider what we've learned.

Try using stories to drive the making of anything, whether it's software or not.

Plan to Learn, and Learn to Plan

Story maps are useful for breaking up our big product or feature ideas into smaller parts. Chapter 3 and Chapter 4 were about slicing up those smaller parts into buildable chunks where each chunk was focused on learning something. But there's a different way to break things down that you need to be aware of, and to keep separate in your head. It's the work we do to break down a story into our plan to make something. That's what we'll talk about in the next chapter.

CHAPTER 10

Bake Stories Like Cake

Two weeks ago it was my daughter's birthday and we wanted a cake. Our family has our own baker—a person we call to make our cakes. Now, we're not rich or afraid to make cakes ourselves. It's just that Sydnie, our baker, makes incredibly fantastic-tasting cakes. We don't know exactly what culinary magic she wields to pull it off, but whenever we ask our kids what kind of cake they want for their birthday, the shout "We want a Sydnie cake!" seals the deal for our baker.

To get a cake, I call Sydnie on the phone. She'll ask who the cake is for and what the occasion is. Two weeks ago I told her Grace was turning 12. "What's Grace into?" she asks. We talk a bit about what Grace likes and what she was thinking of. We also talk about what shapes of cake pans Sydnie has, and what kind of cake design is feasible for her to have ready in time. We agree on a bird-shaped cake this time.

That's how telling a story works. Sydnie asked lots of who, what, and why questions. She asked about the context—where and when we'd be serving the cake, and how many people would be there. During the conversations, we considered a few different options. We talked long enough to build shared understanding. And, because we've gotten lots of cakes from Sydnie, we already have some shared understanding about how they'll look and taste when we get them. If we didn't, we'd have wanted to see some pictures or taste some cake, and the phone wouldn't have worked well for that.

Create a Recipe

During our discussion, Sydnie is thinking about how she'll make the cake. She has to so she can figure out if she can make it in time. When it comes time to make the cake, she'll have a list of things she'll need to do—things like measuring flour, sugar, butter, eggs, and milk. She'll need to mix, bake, decorate, and likely perform some other top-secret steps I don't know about. I suspect she has different recipes for different kinds of cakes, and a checklist of things she has to do for every cake before it's stuck in a box and ready to pick up. If Sydnie wrote down the list of all the things she has to do, she'd have a work plan full of specific cake-baking tasks.

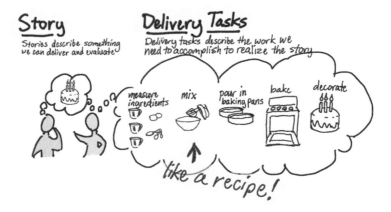

The same thing happens when someone brings a story to a development team. Together they make decisions on specifically what to build, and the development team creates their work plan, composed of lots of development tasks. The development team includes testers, UI designers, technical writers, or whatever people and skills are necessary to create the software, so the tasks aren't all about coding. And, just like Sydnie didn't create her plan while she talked with me on the phone, the development team won't likely create their plan during the story conversation. But they will listen, take notes, draw pictures, and gather lots of the details they'll need to create their plan. At least, that's the way we hope it goes.

Story
Stories describe something we can deliver and evaluate

Delivery Tasks
Delivery tasks describe the work we need to accomplish to realize the story

Design User Interface
Identify Business Rules
Write Domain Object Code
Persist Data
Test Manually
Automate Regression Tests

like a recipe!

When talking with Sydnie, I don't tell stories about cups of sugar and flour. I wouldn't tell a story about baking unless my goal was to build an oven. When you tell stories about software, and collect a list of story names as you do, you tell the story imagining the software you'll have in the end. And you don't just *imagine* the software—you think and talk about who uses it and why. Sydnie didn't just stick to details about the cake, she asked me who it was for, what my daughter liked, how many people would be at the party, and lots of information that helped us decide together what the best cake should be. Sydnie wasn't just asking for cake requirements, we were working together to decide on the best way to create a cake we'd all love. That's the real spirit behind a story conversation.

Breaking Down a Big Cake

But there's just one thing. Often what goes wrong here is that, when we start telling the story to people who are really capable of turning our vision into reality, we quickly figure out that the software our story describes is *really* big. Well, the card it's written on is the same size as all the others. And the goal our users are trying to reach with it may be no more important to them than others, but it's when we talk about it that we realize it'll take a lot of time to write the software necessary to reach that goal.

The same thing could have happened when I was talking with Sydnie about my cake. I could have imagined an elaborate cake that calls for cake pans Sydnie doesn't have, or cake-building and decorating techniques she's not mastered. The result would be a cake I can't afford, and one that Sydnie couldn't predictably deliver before my daughter's birthday.

In Chapter 7, I pointed out that when the solution we're thinking of is too expensive, we need to step back and really look at the problems we're trying to solve, and the outcomes we're trying to achieve. And we'll need to consider other alternatives. That's one way to get a smaller cake—or maybe a pie?

> *If the story describes a solution that's too expensive, consider a different solution that helps you reach the goal.*

But, if it's really big, and we can afford it, then there's no reason to break it down any smaller, right? Well, actually, there is. With software, especially, by building things in smaller parts, we can see and measure progress sooner. This helps the people spending money feel a bit less nervous. And, as in Chapter 4's *Mona Lisa* strategy, it helps the people making the product evaluate parts to make sure we're on the right track.

> *If the story describes a solution that's affordable but big, break it into smaller parts that allow you to evaluate and see progress sooner.*

There's a trick to breaking down large stories, and it helps me to keep the cake metaphor in my head. If you like cake, by now you might be getting hungry—especially if the cake you're imagining is a particularly tasty one. Sorry about that.

Let's say our story describes a need for a lot bigger cake, like a super-giant wedding cake that will feed hundreds of people. If so, then it isn't just cups of flour and sugar anymore, it's *sacks* of flour and sugar. Most people break down software the same way. Instead of just a little user interface, a little business logic, and a little database interaction, there's lots of each. But remember that software isn't cake. It doesn't take that much more time to measure two pounds of flour than it does to measure two cups of flour. But building the user interface for 20 screens takes a lot more time than for just 2 screens. So, if teams use the simple breakdown structure that seems logical, they get tempted to break software down into weeks of frontend development, weeks of business logic development, and so on. When we use that strategy, it takes a long time before we can "taste *any* cake," so to speak. So don't do that.

> ## *Don't break down big things into big plans. Break big things into small things with small plans.*

Now the metaphor is really going to break down here, but stick with me for just one more minute. The way you approach a big software cake is to break it down into lots of little *cupcakes*. Each one is deliverable, and each one still has a similar recipe, with a little sugar, a little flour, an egg or two, and so on.

OK, now let's get a little more serious again. Software *isn't* cake. It can get huge, horrendously expensive, and horribly risky. As I write this text, I've just heard yet another story on the morning television news of the US government's failed website to sign people up for healthcare. It's easy to criticize after the fact. But it's also easy to see that no one tasted that cake before it was served at the metaphoric wedding—at least no one with any taste. And that half-baked cake ruined the party.

If you've worked in more traditional software development for a while, you likely learned to break down big software into big plans. I know I did. It'll seems counterintuitive to break down something big into smaller pieces that may not quite look like the finished product you're trying to deliver. You'll know that as you combine these pieces of software, you'll have to do a bit of rewriting and adjusting of each piece to combine them. But remember—you're thinking this way for lots of good reasons. One of the biggest is to avoid the risks involved with not seeing, using, or "tasting" the software too late. You're breaking big things down to small, evaluable parts so you can learn sooner.

If I were breaking down a cake with the goal of tasting it sooner or seeing the decoration sooner, I'd do well to bake small cupcakes that help me learn sooner. I'd bake some in a number of different flavors so I could taste them all, choose the one I liked best, and be confident I'd made the right choice. If I were concerned about colors and decoration, I'd want to look at different cupcakes decorated in different styles, and choose the one that was best.

With software, the cupcakes are portions of working software that allow users to evaluate if they can effectively complete a user task. They may be portions of software that help expose a technical risk. But each piece helps us learn something.

But a pile of cupcakes isn't a wedding cake—or is it?[1]

Software isn't cake. And every piece of software we build *does* combine into one larger working product in a way that cake can't.

One of the silly mantras that comes from my friend Luke Hohman is that you can deliver "half a baked cake, not a half-baked cake." Half a baked cake may not be enough to feed a wedding party, but it's enough to taste and leave everyone looking forward to the rest of the cake.

1. Mary's wedding cake (photo courtesy of Mary Treseler).

CHAPTER 11

Rock Breaking

The original idea of stories was pretty simple—write something on a card, talk about it, and agree on what to build. Then, complete the cycle by building it and learning from what you've built. That's it— pretty straightforward, right? If you've been involved in software development for even a small amount of time, you know nothing is that simple. Stories go through a long journey with lots of conversations involving lots of people to move an idea for a product, feature, or enhancement into your product, and then move that product out to market. The good news is you can use stories and storytelling all the way through. And I promise that relying on stories and storytelling *will* help you all the way through.

Size Always Matters

I ended the last chapter by talking about Sydnie's cake and the idea of breaking big cakes into little cakes. But software is a lot less tangible, and size can't be measured in inches, centimeters, ounces, or grams like it can with a cake.

The original idea was that a user or a person who needs something could write what he needed on a card and then we could have a conversation about that. The person who needed it didn't figure out how to express his need as something that would take only a short time to develop. It was *need* sized.

A right-sized story from a user's perspective is one that fulfills a need.

When it comes time to write software, there's big benefit in writing, testing, and integrating software in small parts. If I can see and test small parts sooner, I can measure how fast we're building and what kind of quality we're getting. If I can divide something big into lots of smaller parts, it makes it a little easier for my team to pick up and build parts concurrently. A good rule of thumb is to break down stories to something that takes a couple of days to build and test.

> *A right-sized story from a development team's perspective is one that takes just a few days to build and test.*

But, from a business perspective, it may make the most sense to release software to customers and users in bundles of multiple features. If you're releasing a whole new product, that first bundle can be pretty large. This is the bundle I called a *minimum viable solution* earlier, and it's focused on reaching specific outcomes for a target group of users. Ideally, businesses should be striving to release more of these more frequently—to push them closer to matching users' need size, or a smaller and more specific business outcome. But, if you've got a large, diverse group of customers using your product, and you don't have an infrastructure or business model that supports a more continuous release process, then your business's releases may be bigger.

> *A right-sized story from a business perspective is one that helps a business achieve a business outcome.*

I could say there's no "right size" for stories, but that's not true. The right size is the size that's relevant to the conversation you're having.

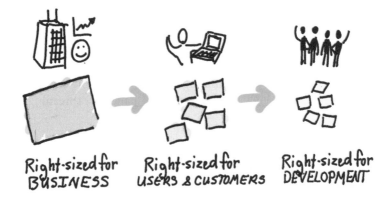

Right-sized for **BUSINESS**   Right-sized for **USERS & CUSTOMERS**   Right-sized for **DEVELOPMENT**

Those big stories contain lots of smaller stories, which in turn contain lots more smaller stories. Depending on who you're talking to, you might have to "roll up" your conversation to a higher level.

Stories Are Like Rocks

Think of stories like rocks. If I were to take a really big rock and put it in the middle of the floor and hit it with a mallet where it broke into 30 pieces, we'd call those 30 pieces rocks. If you took one of those smaller rocks and hit it with a mallet, it would break into smaller pieces. We'd call those pieces rocks, too. Now, we might get creative about the names we give these rocks, like *boulder* or *pebble*. But I'm never sure when something stops being a boulder and starts being just a plain old rock. It looks like a rock until it's dropped on your foot. Then it feels like a boulder.

Boulder?   Rock?   Pebble?
they're all rocks, no matter how precise we are in our naming

My rock-breaking tool is a big mallet. And that works pretty well.

Big stories break down into smaller stories, and those smaller stories can be broken down to even smaller stories. Just like rocks. And, at every size—no matter how small—they're still a story. But what's the best tool we use for breaking down stories? That's right: it's conversation. Sometimes just a little thinking will do it, but if you use conversation and collaboration with someone else, then you're spreading the shared understanding.

> *Conversations are one of the best tools for*
> *breaking down big stories.*

Now software people, and I'm one of them, are uncomfortable with the lack of precision here. In most organizations I've worked with, language will emerge to classify stories by size. But it starts to raise the "boulders versus pebbles" question again. The precision about size matters most when you're the one being hit with the rock, which could explain why software people get wrapped up in classifying their stories.

If you create language in your organization, don't try to be too precise. The wiggliness about what's in a story and how big it should be is intentional. It gives us the flexibility we need to use this simple idea throughout the development cycle.

Epics Are Big Rocks Sometimes Used to Hit People

Epic is a common term (I'm not sure who coined it originally) used to describe big user stories, sort of like *boulder* is a good term for a big rock. Now I'll be honest with you that it took me years to get comfortable referring to the important stuff we were building as *stories*, but I understand now why they're called that. I'm still struggling with the term *epic*. I hear my English Literature teacher describing an epic as a story about a hero battling evil—like Beowulf or Achilles or Frodo —usually with some sort of magic weapon or the assistance of the gods. But, I digress…

> *An epic is a story that we expect is large, and know needs to be broken down.*

It's OK to have a term for a large story, but watch out. The term *epic* sometimes gets used as a weapon. I've often seen a development team member tell someone who is a businessperson, a product manager, a user, or someone who's asking for something, that his story is an *epic*, not a story. This is usually said in a tone that indicates the storywriter has done something wrong, causing her to seriously consider sucker-punching the development team member. So, please, if you are a team member, don't use the term *epic* as a stick to reprimand someone else. It's a bad start (and, possibly, a premature ending) to what should be a productive conversation.

Remember, epics are big stories that may be the right size from a business, customer, or user perspective—just not from a development perspective. Work together to break them down. But keep the epic around because you'll need to speak to people about it, and all the detailed stories it broke down into.

If you're using an electronic tool that supports Agile development, it'll likely use the concept of an epic as a big parent story that can be split up into lots of smaller child stories.

Themes Organize Groups of Stories

Use the term *theme* to describe a group of stories that it's useful to group together. As you start rock breaking—breaking down those big stories and organizing them into products that people want, can use, and can afford to build—you'll end up with lots of smaller stories. I think of a theme as a sack I can use to collect a pile of stories that are related. I could use a theme to collect a bunch of stories that are needed for a next release, part of the same feature, relevant to a particular type of user, or related in some other way. But my metaphor is slightly broken since the same story can be in two different themes, but the same rock can't be in two different sacks.

If you use one of the available tools that help organize groups of Agile stories, it may support the concept of bundling stories up into a theme. You might simply refer to the theme by what it really is: your next release, the feature, or the stories relevant to a particular type of user.

Forget Those Terms and Focus on Storytelling

The terms *epic* and *theme* have found their way into Agile lifecycle management tools, into some specific named Agile approaches, and into the common language used to discuss stories. For that reason, you'll need to know and understand them.

Now, let's set aside those terms; forget I even mentioned them. At least for a little while. Let's step back and take a look at the whole rock-breaking lifecycle. In that cycle we'll start with big ideas, which you can think of as the big rocks, and move them all the way through to small pieces of working software. And then reassemble those small pieces of working software into features, products, and releases that customers and users want.

From a distance, that rock-breaking cycle looks like this:

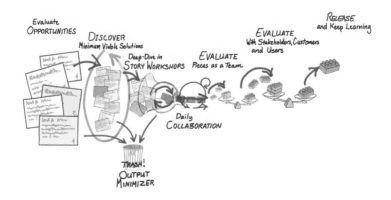

Now, let's dig into the details.

Start with Opportunities

The story's journey starts as an idea. It may be an idea for a new feature, or a whole new product. It could be a change we'd like that would improve a feature we already have. It could be a problem we need to solve. But I'll use the term *opportunity*, because it's an opportunity for us to make something that we'll benefit from. I suggest you name and build a list of these opportunities. I call them an *opportunity backlog*.

Our first good story conversation is a higher-level, who-what-why discussion. And our big goal is to make a go/no-go decision. Go doesn't mean we'll build it. It means we'll go forward with deeper-dive discussions to really understand the story. But I don't want to move forward with spending lots of time doing this if we can detect that it's a bad idea from the outset. No-go is a polite way of saying "trash." So, let's call this a go-forward/trash decision. Remember, there's always too much to build, and killing a mediocre opportunity before it wastes too much of everyone's time should be celebrated.

> *Use opportunity discussions to agree the problem is worth solving—to make a go-forward or trash decision.*

Discover a Minimum Viable Solution

Now that you've chosen to go forward, it's time to dig much deeper. Use discovery to find a solution worth building. And don't forget to really minimize that solution. Seek to make it as small and valuable as you can.

During discovery you'll really dig deep into:

- Who the customers and users are you believe will use your solution
- How they meet their needs today without your solution
- How the world would change for them with your solution
- How your solution might look and behave
- How long your solution might take to build

There are a huge number of practices that can be helpful during discovery, especially story mapping. Story mapping can help you understand how people work today, and then map your ideas about how things will change for them after your solution is created.

Discovery is where it's critical to look hard at our assumptions and to do work to validate them. This may take the form of deeper analysis to understand business rules or outside regulations. It should take the form of spending time directly with customers and users to understand how they work. It should involve building prototypes of your solution and validating them with your target audience. And it should include building technical prototypes to chase out technical risks.

Use discovery conversations and exploration
to find a small, viable solution.

Celebrate every part of that solution that you can safely trash, or push back to a backlog of opportunities to deal with elsewhere. Our opportunities may have been big rocks. But inside those rocks were diamonds and precious metals. Break down those rocks and separate those really valuable parts from the stuff that's just rock. And celebrate trashing that stuff.

Throughout discovery, you may choose to build small things that help you learn—specifically, UI or architectural prototypes.

Spike is a term used for bits of development or research we do with the explicit goal of learning. It's a term that came from the Extreme Programming community to describe work that may not yield software we choose to ship. Use stories to describe spikes that get your team building something to learn.

After you're confident you've got that small subset of stories you should build and release to customers and users, then it's time to move them forward into delivery. That subset of stories that leads to a valuable product release is what I refer to as a *release backlog*.

Dive into the Details of Each Story During Delivery

Our opportunities may have started as big rocks. Discovery conversations broke them down and separated the rock from the precious metals. But delivery will move fastest and most effectively if we can keep breaking down those pieces into the smallest parts possible—keeping in mind that every part still needs to be something we can build and learn from. It's going to take a lot more conversations that dive into a lot more depth to do that.

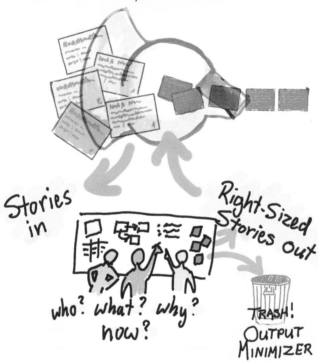

Deep-Dive in STORY WORKSHOPS

Stories in

Right-Sized Stories Out

who? what? why? now?

TRASH! OUTPUT MINIMIZER

I picture a cool rock-breaking machine: on one side I load these big, rough rocks that contain all those precious metals, and then the other side spits out small, just-right-sized rocks ready to go into the next development cycle. I'm going to label this machine the *story workshop machine*, and its name describes exactly what we'll do.

We'll use deep-dive discussions with developers and testers, and everyone else on the team who'll build the software, to really dig into the details. These are our "last best conversations"—the conversations where we really need to agree on *confirmation*, or the acceptance criteria for the small parts of software we build—because the next step is building them. Since we know that it's conversations that break up software, we'll use these conversations to get our stories into the right size and shape to put into the next development sprint, or iteration.

Use deep-dive story workshops to discuss the details, break down stories, and really agree on specifically what we'll build.

I like to call these last best story conversations *story workshops* because everyone knows that meetings are unproductive, but workshops are for getting work done. They can happen as needed, almost every day. Sometimes they happen all at once during a planning session. In the Agile process Scrum, they may happen during what's called a *backlog grooming* or *backlog refinement* session. Whatever you call these discussions, have them.

Keep Talking as You Build

The story workshop machine feeds the next in line—the Agile delivery machine. And here's where I picture the Agile delivery machine really kicking in. In one side we put these small, regular-sized stories, and out the other side comes a polished, working bit of software—or whatever it is that your story described making.

No matter how hard you try, even your last best story conversations won't have predicted everything you'll learn once you start to build. Plan to have lots of frequent, ad hoc story conversations every day. Bring up the need for them in your daily standup meetings.

Daily
COLLABORATION

If you're a developer and the details you trapped in story discussions aren't enough to answer questions you have now, jump up and find someone to talk with to continue your discussion. You can't blame bad requirements here. Remember that, before you started, you worked with others to identify all you'd need to know to build. But we're all human. It's OK to miss some things.

If you're a product owner, UX designer, business analyst, or one of the other folks who helped decide what to build, don't be afraid to get up from your desk to see how development is going. I promise that once you see something working, you'll see something useful. And, more than likely, the person getting it working could use a little feedback.

Use conversations as you build to fill in details and give feedback on what's being built.

Evaluate Each Piece

When those finished bits of working software roll out of the Agile delivery machine, it's time for the people who helped describe what to build, and the people who build it, to pause and look closely at what we built.

Remember, these aren't really machines. And you and the people you work with aren't cogs in a machine. And all those pieces you just turned out aren't exactly the same widget. They're all different.

EVALUATE
Pieces as a Team

Product
Quality   Plan   Process
UX?   Done?   Working?
Functional? Velocity? Not working?
Technical?   Change?

Stories
to improve
or change
the product   Stories with
work remaining

Stop and really look at the quality of the solution built. Reflect on how effectively you planned. Did you really finish what you expected? Did it take a lot longer? Shorter? Or about what you imagined? And really talk about how well the "machine" is working. It's time to make adjustments or changes to the way you work to get better-quality stuff out more predictably.

> *Frequently reflect on product quality, your*
> *plans, and the way you work.*

This first pass at evaluation in Scrum is called a *sprint review and retrospective*. Whatever you call these times to stop, review, and reflect, make sure you have them.

Evaluate with Users and Customers

Remember that what you're building wasn't for you—at least not usually. You'll need to get it in front of users and customers to see how they feel about it. For some of these folks, all they'll have seen is a prototype, or a wireframe, or a textual description. Seeing and touching something working really lets them evaluate whether or not they've got the right thing.

But each of these little pieces that came out of the Agile delivery machine may not be enough for them to tell. In my mental model I picture each of those pieces piling up on a scale. It's one of those old-style scales with a counterweight on the other side. On my counterweight is the word *Enough*; that is, enough to test with users and customers and for them and us to learn something.

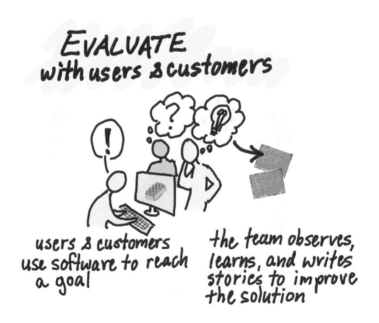

EVALUATE
with users & customers

users & customers use software to reach a goal

the team observes, learns, and writes stories to improve the solution

Usually *enough* means a whole screen, or a flow of screens, that allows users to complete a task or reach a meaningful goal. And I don't want to do a show and tell with users. I'm not looking for them to say, "That's great." I'm looking to learn—and learning usually takes the form of "That's not quite right" and "Now that I really use it, it would be better if..."

Learn by testing meaningful chunks of working software with customers and users.

Evaluate with Business Stakeholders

There are likely others in your organization who have a vested interest in the software you're building. They may not be the people who'll use it every day, but they're concerned that the software is going to be delivered to those people as soon as possible—or at least when you said it would be.

Use a review to show them the product so far. Use the review to talk about where you are in relationship to your bigger plan. Remember: they likely aren't interested in whether you meet your plan for the bunch of single, small parts you built. What they're interested in is progress on the minimum viable solution—because that's the smallest part we could release and really get some value from in the outside world. So speak to that. Share with them the results from tests you've done with users or customers. They'll be interested in learning that, too.

Keep your progress and quality visible to stakeholders inside your organization.

Release and Keep Evaluating

I picture one last scale at the end of all this. On this scale I pile up the parts we've reviewed together, tested with customers and users, and made visible to stakeholders in my company. Coincidentally, this scale is very similar to the one that we used a couple of steps ago—evaluate with users and customers. As with this other scale, on the counterweight it says *Enough*—but this time it means enough to release to those customers and users to produce the outcome I'm looking for. When that scale balances, release it to customers and users.

But don't stop there. You've still got something to learn. If you were like Eric in Chapter 3, learning was your primary goal, so you'll need to use metrics to learn if and how people use your product. You'll need to use face-to-face conversations to learn why they do or don't use it. If you predicted that people would be using your product, and they and your company would be benefiting from it, don't just assume that. Use metrics and conversations to really learn what's happening.

*Use metrics and face time with users to really
learn if your target outcomes were met.*

If this were a project, you'd be done—because you shipped it. But you just made something. It's a product. And a product's life *starts* when it's delivered. When you start paying attention to what people are doing with your product, I promise you'll find opportunities to improve it. Write those down, and feed them back into the beginning of this model.

That's the *real* circle of life—or at least, the life of a story.

And that's a lot of rock breaking. So exactly who is supposed to do all that rock breaking? I'm glad you asked, because that's what the next chapter is about.

CHAPTER 12

Rock Breakers

There's a nasty misassumption in common Agile practice: that there's a single person responsible for writing stories and conducting all these story conversations. In the Agile process Scrum, that person is called the product owner. There are two big reasons, however, why this logic doesn't work, and probably a lot of smaller reasons, too.

Big reason #1

> There are too many conversations to have to move a story along its journey from vague idea to small, specific things to build. One person isn't enough to cover all these conversations. And, if you set up your process so that one person has to be there, you'll quickly see what a bottleneck that person can be, and likely will become.

Big reason #2

> One person can't come into the conversation with the expertise and diverse viewpoints it takes to arrive at a best solution. It takes the collaboration of people with different skills to really arrive at best solutions.

Requiring a single product owner to write all of the stories and be present for all story conversations doesn't work.

Don't get me wrong here. In my vision of good product development, the product owner is a critical leader. He keeps the product and whole team focused on moving the same direction.

The alternative is design by committee—a seriously bad anti-pattern where everyone gets an equal say in what we do. In a committee, when we only have time and resources to do one thing, we compromise. My ex-wife and I would often do this when choosing a restaurant. She wanted seafood, and I wanted Mexican food, and we'd settle on something neither of us liked. When a committee isn't constrained by time and resources, we do it all. You've used software products like this: the product with more features than anyone can count, and where your biggest problem is finding the feature or remembering how to use it.

Effective product owners surround themselves with the people they need to make good decisions. They incorporate the expertise and opinions of many. But, in the end, when resources are constrained or the success of the product is at stake, they must make decisions. And there's always someone who'll be unhappy with that decision. My friend Leisa Reichelt puts it well: "Design by community is not design by committee…design is never democratic."[1]

Valuable-Usable-Feasible

In his book *Inspired: How to Create Products Customers Love* (SVPG Press), Marty Cagan describes the responsibility of a product manager to identify a product that's valuable, usable, and feasible. When I first read these words, I pictured in my head a simple Venn diagram where the solution we want is an intersection of what's valuable to our company and our customers, usable by its users, and feasible to build given the time and the tools we have.

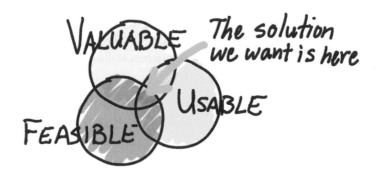

1. Leisa Reichelt originally included this gem of a comment in a 2009 IXDA talk. See her later essay here: *http://www.disambiguity.com/designbycommunity/*.

But what may not be dead obvious here is that, to really identify the solution in the center of that sweet spot will take collaboration between people who understand our business, our customers, our users, and the technology we use—and not just understand those things, but take responsibility for the success of the solution. These people actually speak with stakeholders, customers, and users; they actually design and test user interfaces; they actually design and test the code that makes the product work.

Remember that misconception in Agile development where a single product owner or product manager decides what to build? It's rare if not impossible for a single person to possess the business, user interface design, and engineering skills necessary to find that valuable-usable-feasible sweet spot. That's why the most effective organizations use small, cross-functional discovery teams that work together to find that right solution. As we discussed in the preceding chapter, think of discovery as rock-breaking work. It's the work we do to move a story from a big vague idea to something small and specific we can build.

A small, cross-functional team led by a product owner orchestrates product discovery work.

The ideal size for the team is two to four people—dinner-conversation-sized so the members can quickly build shared understanding.

This team should be led by a product owner or product manager who has deep understanding of her business's vision and strategy, and of the market her product serves. This core team includes someone who understands users, is comfortable working with them to learn about the way they work, and can sketch and create simple UI prototypes. It also includes a senior engineer from the team who'll build the product. This person needs to understand the current architecture of the system and have insight into newer engineering approaches that could be used to solve tough problems. The real secret here is that the most innovative solutions often come from the engineer supplied with insight about the business problem and the users' problems.

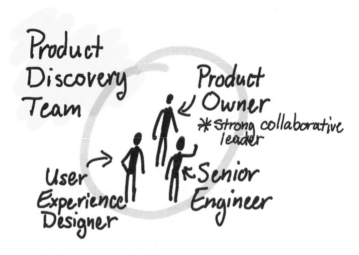

A cohesive discovery team is a powerful, fast-moving group of experts who can find problems and validate solutions quickly. I often hear the term *triad* used to describe this core team. On my recent visit to Sydney-based Atlassian, Sherif, whom you met in Chapter 8, pointed to three seats close together. He explained, "This is where the triad sits." The area around the triad was filled with desks and computers where the rest of the team sat. I hear the term *triad* used when there are two people, four people, or even more on the discovery team, since it's the three concerns—valuable, usable, and feasible—we're talking about, not three bodies.

Support product owners with a core team that includes user experience, design expertise, and technical expertise.

A Discovery Team Needs Lots of Others to Succeed

An effective discovery coordinates collaboration with not only the development team, but also business stakeholders, subject matter experts, customers, and end users. It's tough work that requires top-notch communication and facilitation skills, in addition to the specific expertise each team member brings in.

Discovery Teams are the hub of collaboration

Experts

Customers & Users

Discovery Team

Business Stakeholders

Delivery Team

Now, here's the real secret. For a product of any significance, it'll take a team to get it built. To keep the vision of the product clear, ensure the solution the team builds is cohesive, and help keep everyone moving in the same direction, a good product leader is critical. The best of these leaders focus on helping everyone take ownership. In a healthy story-driven environment, you'll see lots of story conversations going on all the time. And many of them won't need the product leader there.

The Three Amigos

¡Three Amigos! is the name of a mediocre 1986 western comedy starring Steve Martin, Chevy Chase, and Martin Short. What does this film have to do with Agile software development and stories? There's a more tactical triad of collaborators that's valuable during story workshops. And I'm not sure who originally gave them the moniker "the three amigos," but it appears to have stuck.[2] (I'm sure if more people had seen the movie, it wouldn't have.)

---

2. This article on the Scrum Alliance website by Ryan Thomas Hewitt explains a three amigos–style story workshop: *http://bit.ly/Utg8er.*

You might recall that *story workshops* is the term I give to that last best conversation where we decide specifically what to build. It's here where the three amigos come in.

During this last best conversation, we really need to consider lots of details and alternatives for implementation, so we'll need a developer from the team who'll build the software—ideally, one of the developers who will actually work on it.

For this small piece of software to be considered done, it'll need to be tested, so we'll need a tester in the conversation. A tester—the *first* amigo—will often bring a critical eye into the discussion, spotting things that might go wrong sooner than most. The tester is often the best at playing the "What-About" game.

And, of course, we'll need someone who understands what we're building, who it's for, and why we're building it, so we'll need a member of that core product discovery team. That person is the *second* amigo.

At this stage we're often not introducing a new feature idea. We likely already did that back in discovery. Now we've more or less committed to build something, so it's important to understand specifically how that software should look and behave. So often the person involved in this conversation is a user experience designer or business analyst who's worked through those details. This is your *third* amigo.

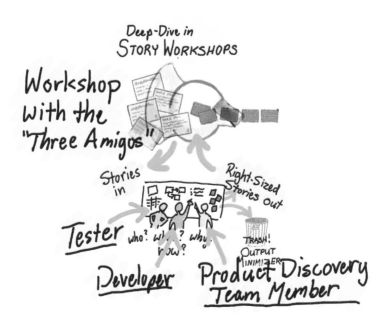

Deep-Dive in STORY WORKSHOPS

Workshop with the "Three Amigos"

Stories in

Right-Sized Stories Out

Tester who? what? why? how?

Developer

TRASH! OUTPUT MINIMIZER

Product Discovery Team Member

This group will work through the details and agree on specific acceptance criteria for the story. It's out of this conversation that we'll have our best estimate of how long it will take to build and test the software. And it's often in this conversation that we'll make decisions to split the story into smaller, "right-sized" development stories—those stories that take one to three days to build and test.

Story conversations happen continuously as we move ideas through software development. In every conversation, keep what's valuable, what's usable, and what's feasible in the discussion. Include people who can speak to those things. Avoid design by committee by holding a product owner responsible for a successful, cohesive product.

The Client-Vendor Anti-Pattern

There's a nasty anti-pattern that gets in the way of using stories well. In fact, it can get in the way of people working together to do *anything* well. It's the dreaded client-vendor anti-pattern.

In this anti-pattern, one person in a conversation takes the client role, while the other takes the vendor role. It's the client's job to know what he wants, and to explain the details to the vendor. That's what we call "requirements." It's the vendor's job to listen, understand, and then think through a technical approach for delivering what the client asked for. The vendor then gives her estimate—which in software lingo actually means "commitment," and is the reason why developers often fear giving estimates without thorough investigation.

The rest of the story is sadly predictable.

Every once in a while, the estimate is deadly accurate, and the client gets what he wanted, and what he wanted actually turns out to be what he needs.

But, most of the time, constructing a solution takes longer than the vendor predicted. The person in the vendor role can cite all sorts of excuses for the delay, including lack of details in the requirements she was given, or just "bad requirements." The client can blame inaccurate estimation—which no one seems to notice is an oxymoron. When the solution is delivered, and the person in the client role receives what he asked for, he then gets an opportunity to use it and realize it's not what he needs. He doesn't get the outcome he imagined he would.

The real tragedy here is that the person in the client role understands his problem better than he's able to predict what will solve it. And the person who understands the technology is often the most qualified to solve the problem because she knows how the technology she's working with can help. What's more, most technologists honestly want to help. They want to know the things they're building are put to good use.

But, in the client-vendor anti-pattern, conversations about problems and solutions are replaced by discussions and agreements about requirements. No one wins.

One of the goals of stories is to break this anti-pattern.

One kind of relationship many of us have that does break this anti-pattern when it goes well is the one we have with our doctor. Try showing up at your doctor's office and giving her your "requirements." Tell her the prescriptions you'd like written and the operations you'd like scheduled. If she's nice, she'll smile and say, "That's interesting; tell me where it hurts."

In my head, I picture a continuum where on one side is the word *waiter*, and on the other is the word *doctor*. Try to make your working relationships much more like a good doctor-patient relationship, and much less like a waiter-diner's.

Product Owner as Producer

If you work in a more traditional IT setting, the notion of a product owner may seem confusing. For example, if you help build critical systems for a bank, the bank knows its real products are the banking services it sells to its customers. If there is a person with the official title of "product manager," it'll be his job to look after a specific type of bank account or credit product. The computer systems that support that service offering are just a piece of the puzzle. And often that same IT infrastructure supports lots of different banking products. Understandably, the bank doesn't see that infrastructure as a product, and there's often no one who owns it.

In these types of organizations, business analysts (BAs) are often placed in a "requirements gathering" role. They'll act as an intermediary between the developers and the business stakeholders like the product manager of a banking or insurance product. When those businesspeople need changes to the IT infrastructure that supports their product, they'll work with the BA to describe those changes. And here's where they might take on the client role as the BA acts in a vendor role, and that's where the anti-pattern kicks in.

In casual conversation, my friend David Hussman gave me a better metaphor for the relationship the BA should have with his business stakeholders—the same relationship that a music producer has with a band. This makes sense coming from David, who's both an Agile guru and ex-guitarist for the 1980s heavy metal band Slave Raider. He's worked with producers, and been a producer himself. In that relationship the band comes to the music business with passion, and hopefully some talent, but they don't know the music business or the mechanics of recording an album. The producer does, however. It's the producer's job to help that band make the most successful recording it can. Successful producers can turn raw talent into a polished, commercially viable recording artist.

As a business analyst in an IT context, that's your job. Take the vision of your business stakeholders and help them make it a success. You can't be just an order taker—you'll need to behave more like a doctor. And sometimes this means telling your stakeholders things they don't want to hear. But, if you're sincere about helping them succeed, they'll see it and value your help.

When acting as product owner for other stakeholders' ideas, take on the role of a producer who helps them succeed.

One potential anti-pattern is to make the business stakeholder take on the product ownership role. I say *potential* because it can work if the businessperson has lots of help and support from other team members, an aspiration to learn how to do the job of a product owner, and the time it'll take to do it. Product ownership isn't a trivial responsibility, and shouldn't be treated as something that could be done in your spare time. Instead of forcing another job on businesspeople, I'd recommend you find them a producer to help them succeed.

This Is Complicated

For an idea that at its core is simple, this whole story thing has gotten terribly messy. If anyone told you software development—or *any* product development, for that matter—was easy, they were lying.

Stories are many things at once. We'll use the word to refer to the card, to the chunk of software we build, and especially to the kind of conversations we have to make decisions about what we should build. Stories can describe very large opportunities, or the almost insignificant deliverable pieces that by themselves aren't necessarily meaningful to customers and users. Working with stories is a continuous process of conversation and discussion to break them down from big things to small things. And through all those conversations, we're keeping not only what we could build in focus, but for whom, and why. Story mapping is just one of the ways to help us break big things down while keeping the focus of the conversation on the people using your product and what makes them successful.

If this is all starting to make sense, then you've made that big, necessary mindshift. It's not a shift to use stories to document requirements, but a shift toward working with people more effectively, and together focusing on solving real problems with the products you create.

And that, I hope you'll agree, is a beautiful thing.

CHAPTER 13

Start with Opportunities

Let me point out again how stories are like rocks. And like a rock, when you break it into smaller parts, you can call those parts "rocks" too—just smaller rocks. But there's always that first rock. That's the one we'll need to look closely at to decide if it's worth breaking up or not. Let's call it "rock zero." And in our flow of stories, I'll call that an opportunity.

I'm using *opportunity* for ideas that we believe will solve a problem. I'm not just a glass-half-full guy. It's just that it's a bad idea to consider every idea as something we need to include in our product, because you know that there isn't enough time and people to build all that stuff. And, even if you did have the time and people, your customers would be overwhelmed.

Have Conversations About Opportunities

When we come up with ideas, these ideas are often pretty big—but not always. In story lingo, you could call them *epics*, but I prefer to call them *opportunities*. No matter what you call them, they're still stories, and the goal of the first conversations we have about them is to decide whether to move forward with them, or trash them. For each one of these opportunities, we can discuss:

Who they're for
> At this level, it's often different groups of users, customers, or a target market.

What problems we're solving

For each type of user, we can talk about what problems we're solving for them. We'll need to talk about how they solve their problems today by using manual tools, our competitors' products, or worse, our product that's causing them pain today.

What we're imagining

We may have some ideas about what the product or feature should be. We should discuss those ideas.

Why

It's a good time to discuss why it benefits our organization to build software for these users. Solving users' problems usually isn't enough. We also need to consider the ultimate return on this software investment and whether this investment is aligned with our current business strategy. I'm not saying we need to calculate return on investment (ROI), because anyone who can do that at this stage is likely full of something other than just stories. Just discuss in general terms how we imagine it'll benefit our organization if we build it.

Size

At this level, even when they're big, we can start to give some gut estimate of development time, although it won't be very accurate. It works best to look at the opportunity and compare it to something you've already done: "That sounds like it will be about like this other feature we put in the last release. That took a couple of weeks, so this may take about the same amount of time." To help decide if we should proceed with discussion on this idea, it's valuable to know if we're talking about something that'll take days, weeks, or months to build.

The whole stack of these stories is what I call an *opportunity backlog*. We aren't sure yet if we should build them, or at least we shouldn't be. Remember, there are always more ideas for things to build than we'll have time for. Find the opportunities aligned with your organization's business strategy and that solve problems for customers and users that are compelling. Have enough discussions to make a go/no-go decision.

Dig Deeper, Trash It, or Think About It

"Go" doesn't mean "We're gonna build this thing," it means we'll move the opportunity forward into deeper discovery discussion. During discovery, it'll take a lot more discussion—probably with others not in the room. If this is a new feature or an entirely new product, it'll take diving a lot deeper into customers and users and how they solve their problems today. Ideally, we'll talk to them directly. It'll take exploring and prototyping different solutions. It'll take lots of deeper discussions in light of what you and your team learn to make a decision about what specifically you'll need to build to be valuable to customers, users, and your organization. And, after all that work, you still might decide to kill the idea.

"No-go" is a great result of an opportunity discussion. Remember, there's always more to build than there is time. If the opportunity doesn't look promising based on your discussion, trash it now. It may be a good idea to involve the people who championed the idea in the discussion so hopefully they come to the same conclusion.

Your group may not have enough information to make either a go or a no-go decision. If that's the case, make a list of what you need to learn, and together get to work getting the information you need.

If you still can't make a go or no-go decision, you can always put it back into the opportunity backlog to discuss later. That's called procrastination, and I do it a lot.

The Opportunity Canvas

When looking at product opportunities, I've used Marty Cagan's Opportunity Assessment template as my starting point. Recently, I've really come to like using a *canvas*-driven approach. The canvas approach to looking at business models, as described in Alexander Osterwalder and Yves Pigneur's book *Business Model Generation* (Wiley), is an effective way for groups to work together to size up a startup business. But for me, and most of the people I work with, we're not looking at starting a new business or launching a new product. We're often looking at adding a next important feature to the product we have. That shouldn't stop you from using a similar canvas approach to sizing up product opportunities, however.

A canvas organizes information spatially. It's big and all in one place so a group can see and work with it, which is hard to do in a slide or printed document, and the organization allows you to see dependencies. Information is adjacent to other information it depends on.

A canvas looks like this:

And working together to gather information in a canvas format looks like this:

Using a canvas approach has real benefits like:

- You can see the important concerns of an opportunity in a single view.
- You can see the relationships between these concerns.
- Building shared understanding, ownership, and alignment by working together collaboratively to create a canvas leverages everyone's contribution.

As a product discovery team, initially fill out the canvas based on what you understand today. Involve stakeholders, subject matter experts, or anyone else you think can bring important information into the conversation.

Use sticky notes to make it easy to change your mind as discussion progresses. Iteratively improve the canvas as you learn more.

You could proceed through the canvas starting with the first box, and continue to the ninth. However, if you don't have good answers for a box, record what you *do* know, or your assumptions now, and proceed.

Fill Out the Canvas in One Flow, and Read It in Another

The boxes in the canvas are numbered in a logical order you can use for discussing an opportunity. But, if you're sharing the canvas with someone else, you may want to read it left to right, and top to bottom. You'll notice the left-to-right flow is from "now" to "later" in the output versus outcome model introduced earlier. You'll also notice that top to bottom moves from user needs to business needs.

This isn't a form to fill out. This is instead a set of topics to discuss and iteratively refine your understanding of. Remember: "design by community isn't design by committee." Involving lots of folks helps everyone learn faster, but ultimately, the go/no-go decision to proceed with an opportunity falls to the product owner. The best product owners leverage their teams to help make the decision, and usually find that they and their teams are in agreement.

Here's the flow of spaces in the Opportunity Canvas.

1. Problems or Solutions

Ideally, we should start with a clear problem we're trying to solve. However, the world is rarely ideal. We're often given a feature or enhancement idea and then need to work backward to understand the problem. Start with what you have.

Solution ideas
> List product, feature, or enhancement ideas that solve problems for your target audience.

Problems
> What problems do prospective users and customers have today that your solution addresses?

If you're building a product for entertainment like a game or tool to share fun stuff on a social network, they may not have a real "problem" to solve, just a desire to be entertained.

2. Users and Customers

What types of users and customers have the challenges your solution addresses? Look for differences in users' goals or uses that would affect their use of the product. Separate users and customers into types based on those differences. It's a bad idea to target "everyone" with your product.

3. Solutions Today

How do users address their problems today? List competitive products or workarounds your users have for meeting their needs.

4. User Value

If your target audience has your solution, how can they do things differently as a consequence? And how will that benefit them?

5. User Metrics

What user behaviors can you measure that will indicate that they adopt, use, and place value in your solution?

6. Adoption Strategy

How will customers and users discover and adopt your solution?

7. Business Problem

What problem for your business does building this product, feature, or enhancement solve for your business?

8. Business Metrics

What business performance metrics will be affected by the success of this solution? These metrics are often a consequence of users changing their behavior.

9. Budget

How much money and/or development would you budget to discover, build, and refine this solution?

Opportunity Shouldn't Be a Euphemism

I know your company probably doesn't use opportunities. In fact, if your company is anything like those I've worked with, you've got a roadmap filled with stuff you're supposed to build. You may even think of them as your "requirements." Making a no-go decision on any of that stuff may not be your call. The truth is, we really shouldn't turn all those clever ideas into software, no matter the job title of the person with the clever idea.

Use this first big story conversation to frame the work you and your team may be getting into. Even though the answer to the go/no-go question may be "Go," make sure you leave the conversation with shared understanding about the problems you're solving, for whom, and how your organization benefits from building software.

If it's not your decision, or anyone on your team's decision, to go ahead with this opportunity, then make sure you include those in the conversation who can make that decision. If they're not available, have the conversation anyway, and make assumptions about who, what, and why. Then share those assumptions with decision makers. I promise you that they'll correct you if you've got it wrong. Discussing those corrections will start the right conversation.

Story Mapping and Opportunities

As much as I like story maps, I wouldn't use a map to manage opportunities. Those opportunities are usually bigger chunks. And discussion about these big rocks usually drives toward the details we'll need in order to decide about moving them into deeper discovery.

But one thing that story maps are great at is giving you a really effective way to step back and look at the big picture for the product you have now. Use a map you create for your product today to find opportunities, or to consider the opportunities you already have in the context of your product today.

Try building a simple, very high-level map of your existing product. This is a "now" map similar to the one you built in Chapter 5 about starting your morning. (You did build it, didn't you?) These types of maps have been around in various forms for a while. They're often called *journey maps*. To make one for your current product's experience, just map the flow users take through the major activities they engage in. Use this map to give context to your opportunities. To do this, add each opportunity into the body of the map. Use a different color of sticky note or index card to clearly call them out. What you might see are opportunity "hot spots"—places in your users' flow where there's a higher density of ideas and likely pain from your users.

Look at the users engaged in each activity, and the frequency of that activity. Opportunities that affect high-frequency activities engaged in by critical users are likely opportunities you should be focusing on— sooner rather than later.

You can use this same map to add in cards for the things users complain about today. To balance things, look at the parts of the product that they love today, and add in those joys. If you find places where there's lots of pain for users, but you haven't yet identified any opportunities, you probably should.

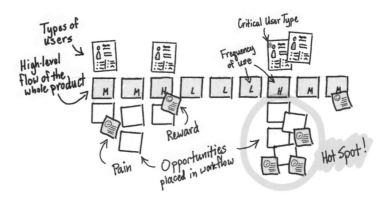

Journey Mapping and Concept Generation

Ben Crothers, Atlassian

Given that we offer over 10 different products, we have to make sure that we design, build, and improve upon those products in ways that match how our customers use them together, not one by one. As part of a project to discover how the products could work together in a better way, we formed a multidisciplinary team to map the entire end-to-end customer experience in finding, evaluating, purchasing, and using them, as well as getting help and adding more products and services.

This was huge. To help break it down, we mapped the experience at a high level first, and then broke into subgroups to expand on each section of that skeleton journey. We did this by initially filling a wall with the moments, actions, and questions that customers go through, color-coding as we went, and then going back over it, adding pain points, opportunities, and assumptions.

We gained a lot of insight by being able to trace an end-to-end story rather than just a feature-based experience. We quickly realized, for example, that some parts of the experience—such as setting up products or getting help—weren't isolated to one part of a linear journey, and needed to be catered for much more and in greater detail.

Various other stakeholders and teams were brought in to flesh out more detailed journeys that were all pegged to various points along the high-level skeleton journey, so that we captured and validated as much existing knowledge as we could.

Then we went absolutely nuts coming up with as many concepts as we could to improve upon and reinvent various parts of the detailed journeys. All of the concepts were distilled and written up on cards, and stuck on the wall in loose order along the journey.

Each team member explained each of his or her concepts, after which we all voted on the concepts' effectiveness with sticky dots, according to their feasibility, viability, and desirability.

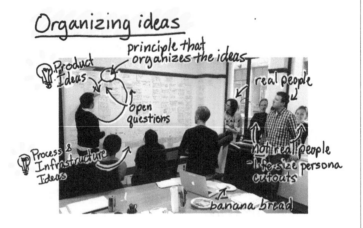

We were then able to craft an overall cross-product vision of an ideal customer experience, based on these journeys and validated concepts. The journey was also brought to life with a 20-page comic, which transformed the journey—and all the personas, scenarios, and concepts involved—into a single storyboard that made it easier to communicate to the whole organization. This informs many product enhancements that continue today.

What's really compelling for us is that many of those involved in developing and refining these enhancements now were also involved in generating the concepts to start with. Even though this exercise was done over eight months ago, that shared concepting and understanding makes things so much more efficient now.

Challenging Assumptions with Rehearsal Remapping

Erin Beierwaltes and Aaron White

1. One Map to Rule Them All

After customer visits, interviews, and explorations, the project owner had a journey map that he confidently believed covered the path to the best outcome for the customer. Business as usual for many teams. Now it was time to share with more people and get it going.

2. Question Everything

But after a few conversations, we started to question what we had missed. What simple assumptions had we made that could have bigger than expected impact? We needed a quick way to challenge our assumptions, find holes, *and* build shared understanding among everyone who would be a part of the project.

3. Set the Scene

We gathered the team, assigned personas (there were multiple), and described the desired outcomes that would naturally guide those personas to use the part of the product that would test our assumptions. We did *not* write step-by-step instructions. Our direction: "Simply, as this person, you would like to accomplish this goal." Rehearsal!

4. Rehearsal

While the actors played their parts and tried to reach their described goals, a few observers played the part of the silent audience.

The PO observed what paths were taken, answering a few questions, and avoiding leading anyone down a particular path. The IxD observed behaviors, comments, and reactions.

5. Rebuild the Map

We didn't show the original map, but instead walked all of the actors through building a new map that described how they accomplished their goals, sharing along the way how some took different paths.

6. Pains and Gains

After the rebuild, we asked each actor to share pains (things that challenged, frustrated, or confused them) and gains (things they thought were slick, cool, or intuitive). A real sense of new empathy, understanding, and excitement filled the conversation.

7. Observations

Finally, it was the audience's turn to ask questions about interesting behaviors they had seen. We were amazed at how many things the actors were unaware they had done, but that gave us a window into how someone might naturally try to accomplish something.

8. Profit!!!

After only 2.5 hours, we had built shared understanding about the real feel of the new solution in a way only a conversation could have. Actors spoke with real empathy for the customers they played, and the discovery team had gained huge insights into what was working and where more experiments might be required.

Be Picky

You're not helping anyone if you agree to take on everything. Aggressively trash opportunities that don't offer much hope of creating the outcomes you hope for. Work with business stakeholders to do this so they can help make those decisions.

If you've made a go-forward decision, it's time to roll up your sleeves and get to work. And that's what the next chapter is about.

CHAPTER 14

Using Discovery to Build Shared Understanding

When I see simple models that describe Agile development, they often start on the left side with a big list—the *product backlog*. Now, I'd consider that funny if I didn't know that some people consider it that easy. Getting a good actionable product backlog out of an opportunity is going to take a lot of hard work; it won't simply materialize for you. And it definitely isn't the result of capturing a list of things people want built. It's a deliberate process of discovery that initially focuses on learning a lot more about who, what, and why.

Discovery Isn't About Building Software

Discovery work isn't about building shippable software. It's about learning. It's about building a deeper understanding of what we could build. It's about asking and answering questions like:

- What *problems* are we really solving?
- What solutions could be *valuable* to our organization and to customers buying or adopting the product?
- What does a *usable* solution look like?
- What's *feasible* to build given the time and tools that we have?

It's asking and starting to answer all these questions about an opportunity that starts your first round of rock breaking. All the details about the product or feature you discuss become the titles of smaller stories.

And each of those smaller stories can result in even deeper discussions, and still smaller stories.

All these discovery discussions don't just result in more stories. Remember that story discussions involve creating lots of other simple models that represent what we understand. We'll need these other simple models to build shared understanding.

If the only thing you create while making sense of a big, ambiguous opportunity is smaller stories, then you're probably doing it wrong.

Four Essential Steps to Discovery

If I've got a big idea, or even a small one that needs some clarity, I follow this progression of discussions to move from the big idea to the details I'll need to best understand if we've got a solution worth building:

1. *Frame* the idea from a business perspective.
2. *Understand customers and users* and how you're helping them.
3. *Envision* your solution.
4. *Minimize and plan* to identify the smallest viable solution and how you'll build it.

1. Frame the Idea

If you really use an opportunity backlog, and really had an opportunity discussion to make your decision to begin discovery, then you're most of the way there. Use framing discussions to kick off focused discovery. Involve the people who'll work together to better understand this opportunity.

Use framing discussions to set bounds for the work you're doing. If you're clear on why you're building something and who it's for, you and your team will be better able to stop discussions about solutions that don't solve the problem you're focusing on, or aren't for the users you've targeted.

2. Understand Customers and Users

Use discussions about customers and users to gain more insight into the people your product or features are for, and how they benefit them. Involve those who have deep user understanding, and others who need to get it.

Sketch simple personas

I like creating simple *persona* sketches with a small discovery team to build shared understanding of my users. A persona is an example of your target user assembled from the facts and sometimes the assumptions you have about your users. Building personas helps us look at the software through the eyes of our users. Personas are handy tools.

Sketch simple personas

user type or role

name and a quick sketch

some context
- who is Chuck?
- why would he use our solution?

about
- charachteristics
- goals & pains
- activities

implications
- what's valuable to Chuck?
- how would what we believe about Chuck change the solution?

Chuck: Casual Web Surfer

← Sketching the persona on flipchart paper

I built this simple persona with a group at Mano a Mano, a nonprofit group that helps people in Bolivia by doing everything from building roads to supporting education and healthcare. Our discussion this day was about small, Internet-savvy donors—the sort of people who may not have a huge amount of money, but want what they *do* have to give to be used wisely. We'd expect people like Chuck to find Mano a Mano on the Web or hear about it via Twitter or Facebook.

We created this persona together as a group using flipchart paper. It's a fast, fun activity with lots of people shouting and contributing information.

Now, if you're an experienced UX designer who's created personas before, you may be feeling a little sick to your stomach right now. For the rest of you reading, good personas are built from good data gathered through solid research. UX people concerned about that might be nervous about team members just shouting stuff out and scribbling it on flipchart paper. It doesn't sound rigorous. So don't just shout your guesses. Discuss what you know and what you've observed. Tell stories. Involve people in the discussion who have firsthand experience with users. If you've done lots of research, bring it into the discussion with you. Identify the details most relevant to the opportunity you're building and put those into the persona. Filter out the noise. When you're done, have an honest discussion about how much of this is just a guess.

"We already have personas created. They're beautiful documents we've posted on the wall." I hear that a lot. But be honest with yourself. Most people haven't read them, have they? And half of the people who *did* read them did so just to poke fun at them. Maybe I'm being cynical, but I see that a lot.

Build personas together, collaboratively. Do this to build shared understanding with the team about who'll build the product. Do this to really consider the most relevant aspects of the persona.

Build lightweight personas together to build shared understanding and empathy within the team.

I create simple personas for each type of user who might use the feature we're discussing. If I'm moving fast, I may just list different types of users or roles using the software, and note a few details about them. Remember Gary in Chapter 1? One of the piles of cards right next to Gary was exactly that—a list of users and a few bullets of relevant information about them.

Create organizational profiles or orgzonas

If you're building a product that organizations might buy—for example, an accounting product—take the time to list different types of organizations and record some details about them. These are your customers—the people with cash in hand who need to get some value from your product. An organization type with some supporting details is often called an *organizational profile*. My friend Lane Halley first introduced me to creating example organizational profiles much like you'd create a persona. For fun, she called them *orgzonas*.

Map how users work today

You can go one step deeper and map the way your users work today without your product, or with your current product. If you were playing along in Chapter 5, you built a story map about the way you do things today. Doing this for the way your users work today will help your discovery team really understand the problems they're solving.

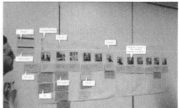

These photos from Duncan Brown of the Caplin Group show something they call a *narrative journey map*. It's a map that tells a story about the "now" side of the "now-and-later" model I started this book with. It doesn't describe our great solution; it describes the way people reach their goals today—faults and all.

The body of the map contains facts, observations, pains, and joys. When you map what you understand now, you'll see "hot spots"— areas in the flow where there are lots of problems. You'll also find rewards—the joys at the end of a set of steps that make your users' efforts worthwhile. You can build valuable products by taking away pains, or magnifying joys. Use this map as a springboard for brainstorming solutions, or for validating that the solution you have in mind really does solve problems.

3. Envision Your Solution

By now you've framed to be clear on why you're building this from a business perspective; you've dived deeper into users and customers so you know what their world looks like now. It's time to imagine the future—to envision the solution and how your target customers and users will make use of it.

Map your solution

This is where story maps shine, at least for me. I use the story map to imagine the life of my users with the solution we're building in place. Both Gary and the Globo.com team in the first two chapters built maps like this. As we discussed in the opening chapters, the steps people take in the story you tell form the left-to-right flow. Remember from Chapter 4 that those are user tasks—short verb phrases that, when read from left to right, tell the story. The finer-grained tasks and other details stack up vertically under each step. If it's a long story, distill groups of activities to create a three-level map.

Words and pictures

Have you ever been in a situation where you describe a product idea to a developer, and are pleasantly surprised when he says, "Oh, that's simple. It shouldn't take long to build." But, then when you really get going on it and start building it, you realize the developer was imagining something far simpler than you were. For example, you might have described a site to sell your stuff online. You might have been imagining something like eBay or Amazon Marketplace. But the developer was imagining something more like Craigslist, and that's why you were pleased with the estimate. I've learned over the last decade that words alone just aren't enough.

Visualize your user interface to build shared understanding of the solution.

If you've got UX designers on your team, now's a good time for them to start sketching. Sketch individual screens and post them above the map in the order they appear. You'll end up with something that looks like a storyboard.

Visualizing the Whole Experience

Josh Seiden, with artwork by Demian Repucci

One day I received a call from Robert, a recently hired design manager at a large, well-funded education startup. The company was in the early stages of a big project, it was hiring rapidly, and it was on a tight deadline to produce a huge system. Just one problem: it was having trouble figuring out how to approach the enormous design challenge it was facing. Could I help?

When I arrived in the office a few days later, Robert—both proud and overwhelmed—showed me around. The company had hired a large consulting firm to help it develop requirements for its project, and that firm had done an impressive amount of work. Every wall in the light-filled loft offices was covered with brown butcher paper, and each one of those sheets was in turn covered with index cards and Post-it notes: requirements, in the form of user stories. Thousands of them. As Robert walked me past the walls of stories, I noticed that all the stories were organized by functional module: a text editor wall, a grading application. And curriculum modules: a wall of science, a wall of English. I struggled to build a picture of the system in my mind.

Robert was in the process of building a design team, and also trying to segment the problem. As we talked through what his team needed, we realized we could use a story map to help organize the thousands of user stories in a way that would help the design and development teams operate from a shared vision.

Coincidentally, a few weeks earlier, I had sat in on a workshop facilitated by a team of storyboard artists. The goal of the workshop was to help entrepreneurs articulate a vision for their business ideas. Working quickly, these artists sat with the entrepreneurs, drawing their stories out of them and sketching out the ideas as storyboards —mini comic books that told each story with great clarity. I decided I wanted to combine this approach with story mapping, and called one of the artists who had impressed me in that workshop, Demian Repucci.

Over the next few weeks, Demian and I met with Robert and his team, as well as with the product managers of the various pieces of the system. Our focus was on high-level workflow—the major use cases in the system. As we met, Demian sketched in his notebook and I used index cards and Post-it notes to outline the use cases on the conference room walls. After the meetings, Demian would return to his studio to illustrate key moments, and I used Omnigraffle to produce clean versions of the story maps that we had drafted in our meetings.

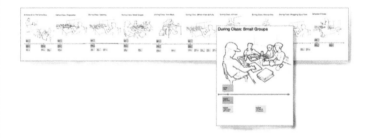

With Robert, we decided that the most valuable thing we could deliver was the organizing structure for the team, so we produced a series of posters that could be printed on 11×17 paper and taped to the walls to form the "spine" of the story map. The teams could then use that independently to organize their user stories in a new way. Instead of a module-centric view that doesn't lend itself to iterative development, we now had a usage-centric approach that could be sliced into cross-module releases.

One approach to envisioning the user experience that involves the whole team is a Design Studio approach. A Design Studio is a fast, simple, and collaborative way to involve a large group in deliberate ideation, which is a flashy word for coming up with lots of possible ideas. What you'll quickly learn is that no single person has the best ideas. Rather, the best ideas are often a combination of several people's ideas along with more discussion to build on them. A Design Studio (and simple ideation, for that matter) is the opposite of what most folks, including me, often do: go with the first idea that seems like it'll work. I first saw Design Studio described by Jeff White and Jim Unger (*http://portal.acm.org/citation.cfm?id=1358650*) and wondered why I hadn't always been doing it. I've done these involving development teams, stakeholders, and even customers and end users.

Whatever approach you use, combine ideas, refine them, and come to a shared understanding of what the software could look like.

An uncomfortable thing that happens here is that visualizing your solution will help you catch things you've missed in the map. You'll find you may need to add, change, or reorganize the map to support what you've visualized. Don't worry: that's a good thing.

Design Studio Recipe

A Design Studio is a quick, collaborative approach to ideation. There are lots of ways to do this right, but here's my simple recipe:

1. *Invite a group of people* whose opinions and ideas you'd like, and whose buy-in and understanding you'll need to build the product. Eight to twelve people is a good number.

2. *Describe the problem you're solving.* Review the work you did to frame the opportunity. Review personas and any "now" maps that describe how people work today. Review any solution maps you may have started, but be wary of saying too much. If they anchor their ideas on yours, you may be missing out on some of their great ideas.

3. *Optionally share examples and inspiration.* Discuss and show other similar products that are good examples. Discuss and show products that may not be the same, but that have good ideas in them that could be leveraged.

---

4. *Everyone sketch!* Give everyone paper, pens, maybe some sketching templates, and a fixed amount of time. I see as little as 5 minutes, and as much as 60. I like using 15 minutes.

5. *In small groups, share ideas.* I like doing this in groups of 4, so if you had 12 people, break that into three groups of 4. Person-by-person, share your best idea. Team members give feedback. Coach participants to give feedback on how well the solutions address the problem, not on how much they like them. Coach them to build on others' ideas. Continue person-by-person for a fixed time-box—30 minutes usually works for me.

6. *Ask each group to consolidate their best ideas* into a single sketched solution. This is the hardest part. Take 15–30 minutes for this.

7. *Ask each group to share their best, consolidated ideas* with the whole group. Discuss these.

8. *Thank everyone, and gather up the sketches and ideas.* You, your UX designer, or your core discovery team will need to leverage them to create a final, best, consolidated UI sketch. Remember, in the words of my friend Leisa Reichelt, "design by community is not design by committee." You'll have lots of good competing ideas here, and someone's got to make the tough call.

Photos courtesy of Edmunds.com   Photo courtesy of Lane Halley

Validate completeness

One of the things our heads are good at is filling in details. For example, when we see two frames of a comic strip, our brains fill in what happened in between. This is a cool trick for comic books, novels, and movies. But, when thinking through what software does, we'll often imagine the interesting features while neglecting the necessary stuff that happens in between. Overextending the movie metaphor, it's sort of like talking only about the car chases and gunfights, and leaving out the story that explains why all that action took place.

Telling the full breadth of your users' stories using a map helps you remember to talk about those critical details in between. You'll usually see that the really cool feature you were thinking of needed some setting up by the user early in the story, and resulted in some changes to reports and notifications later in the story. There may even be consequences for others of your new feature idea. For example, administrators may need to manage security concerns, or managers may like oversight on how the feature is being used by their staff.

Validate engineering concerns

Back to the filmmaking metaphor, if you are going to move on to make this movie, you'll need to start thinking about how and where you'll film it. You'll need to consider the kinds of special effects you'll need. At some point you'll need to go deeper than the story and consider the technical details of making your movie.

A story map of your software is helpful for the same kind of discussion you'd have making a movie. Discuss your solution map with engineers and architects before getting too far along. Seeing the big picture helps them think through bigger engineering constraints that could result in hopelessly flawed solutions. They can give you early warning that your solution may sound cool, but it's not feasible to build given your current architecture and time budget. They can often suggest alternative ways of doing things that'll give your users an equivalent experience, but be more cost effective to build.

These engineers for a large insurance company have been talking in front of this map for a long time. During the course of their conversation, they've found a snag in this big map about their product. The business rules engine in their product needs to change. Seeing the big picture helped them visualize and directly confront the complexity. They'll use that knowledge to talk about what they can plan to do early to help mitigate risks.

Play "What-About"

You've imagined the solution from a user's perspective, and visualized the user experience. Take some time to discuss what's going on underneath the user interface. Talk about tough business rules, complex data validation, and nasty backend systems or services you'll need to connect with. Add stories into the map that name these parts. Or make sure you make notes on the stories you have.

It's a good time to review what you've got with lots of other people as well. Share what you and your group have come up with. I promise you'll get people who ask lots of questions that start with "What about…" I love these people, although not always when they're right in front of me. But I love that they're helping me think of the tough stuff before I stumble on it later, when it'll be even more painful to learn.

The movie metaphor really works for me here. If I were going to make a movie, I'd want a screenplay and a storyboard—the sketches of key scenes that help me imagine the movie. If I were investing in a movie, I'd need to see at least that to get a clear picture of what the writers and directors were envisioning. If I liked the movie at this point, I'm going to need to learn a bit more about how much it costs, and how feasible it is to produce.

I'd hope they'd use those sketches to think more deeply about the movie. I'd want to know that they'd considered how many locations we'd need to film in and what they looked like. I'd want to know that they'd considered what kinds of sets, props, and special effects we'd need. As the important Hollywood investor, I'd need the screenplay, the storyboard, and lots of other details that supported a rough plan and an estimate. We'd need this so we could set a budget and a timeline for making the movie.

This is the sort of stuff you need before you start building your solution.

Ideas, Examples, and Journeys

David Hussman, DevJam

Many people overcomplicate the discovery process, but it can be quite simple and still remain powerful. Step past the mythical certainty of "requirements," and take a moment to explore the discovery of ideas using examples and journeys as your guide.

- *Use the following simple guide:* 1) suggest a product idea to explore, 2) select people you think will benefit from the idea, 3) create a collection of examples of them using the product idea, and 4) use those examples to create a map and the journeys you think they should take. Remember that as the product creator, you've taken on the onus of creating meaningful experiences and not just more features.

- *Ideas do not need to be brilliant.* Of course you want a great product, but often ideas deemed to be brilliant don't pan out, while others—which don't shine so brightly—grow in brilliance as you explore their use in the context of someone trying to accomplish something of meaning.

- *Selecting passengers is not rocket science.* Don't overcomplicate the selection. If you are unsure where to start, simply make a list of the people you think will benefit from your ideas. Frame them in a humane way so they come to life and stay alive in the mouths and minds of the product development community. After you have worked them a bit, select someone to work with and don't worry if it's the right person. Be ready to learn from exploring, and avoid worrying whether or not your selection is right—it probably is not.

- *Create a varied list of examples.* This is where many people lose control and accidentally stumble into complexity. Start with a simple or obvious example; the more concrete, the better. Then come up with a complex example, and don't fear setting the bar high. You are creating a range of constraints, you are not promising anyone the world. Again, make the complex example specific. If you're looking for how specific you should be, and you are courageous, replace the work example with a test, and you'll be one step closer to an automated validation vehicle.

- *Add a handful more examples that fit between the obvious and the complex,* and then start simple. Tell the story of the passenger using the simple example as your guide. Tell it to someone else, and have that person help you capture the stories on the journey. Where are your users when they start? What triggers them to engage? What do they do, specifically? How does it end? Use the various examples to explore the various journeys for your passengers.

- *Choose the journeys that will help you learn.* Worrying about where to start is yet another complexity well. Walk the map, selecting journeys that you think will teach you the most about your audience and their needs. Again, if you're worried that you are not making the right selection, you may be right. The best way to find out, and the best investment in learning, is to select a few journeys, build them, and watch people use them—in person or via real-time analytics.

- *Avoid the trap of product arrogance.* The difference between what you *think* people need and what they *really* need is the realm of product arrogance. Using the process laid out here, you can more quickly get to learning in context by building and validating one journey at a time.

Don't celebrate yet

By this step in the discovery flow, you should have begun to describe your solution's parts as individual stories. Each piece is a part of the big opportunity. If you're like me, you've used a story map to organize all the parts. If you're smarter than me, you'll have invented an even better way to organize all the parts—and if that's the case, you should get in touch right away. If you're a little dim, you'll just have a big pile. Or even worse, someone may have written a big long requirements document that obfuscates all you've learned. Please don't do that.

Whatever you end up with here, you're at the point where lots of people celebrate because they've "finished the requirements." Don't be those people. You've got a last and most important step to do.

4. Minimize and Plan

You've envisioned a solution with words and pictures, at this point, your team may be feeling pretty proud. But one of the big problems with discovery happens when we all work together to identify a fabulous solution with lots of bells and whistles that we all love.

I know what you're thinking. *Why would that be a problem?*

The problem usually comes in when we focus on making everyone happy, and at the same time fail to focus on small, specific target outcomes. The result is a solution that's much bigger than it needs to be.

Remember, our goal is to minimize the amount we build (our output) and maximize the benefit we get from doing it (the outcomes and impact). Your opportunity will break into lots of possible smaller stories. We certainly wouldn't build them all. That wouldn't be minimizing output, would it?

> *If you're not cutting away more ideas than you keep, you're probably not doing discovery work right.*

There's always too much

I'm sorry, but there is. If you've been involved with software development for any length of time, you likely already know this. I've tried for many years, over a decade really, to pretend it's not true. I've given up on that. You should, too. But don't worry: you've got some tools that'll help you identify something feasible to build given the time and people you have.

In Chapter 3, you read about Globo.com's approach to using a map to confront a tough deadline. The company focused on that deadline, embraced it, and identified an outcome that would let it be successful. Then it sliced up its backlog; that is, it cut away all the stories that weren't necessary for it to reach that outcome. This was its minimal viable solution hypothesis. And it wasn't just a crappy, half-baked version of the big idea—it was a really great version that was sharply focused on being successful for the Brazilian elections. The Globo folks believed it would be valuable to their business, their advertisers, TV networks, and their users. They'd thought about all their users, and were pretty confident they had a usable solution. And by slicing their map, they'd found a solution that was feasible to build given the time and teams they had. That intersection of valuable, usable, and feasible for a specific target set of customers, users, and uses is a viable solution.

Viable means successful for a specific business strategy, target customers, and users.

We can think past that first viable release to second and third viable releases, too. But we know that once that first release goes live, the world will have changed, and that's good. But it'll also mean we'll need to rethink the future releases in light of the new world we've created.

The secret to prioritization

Step in close, because I'm going to whisper this.

Not many people know this—or at least they behave like they don't. Maybe they're just playing dumb to throw people off.

If you've hung around in Agile development for a while you might have heard the phrase "prioritize stories by business value." The statement is true, sort of, but where you see the words "business value," you're supposed to fill that in with something specific. This is where you and your discovery team need to say specifically what is of value.

Let's look at Mad Mimi again. Gary needed to find a product that would be viable in a specific market soon, before he ran out of money. *Viable* for Gary meant he had an audience that liked the product and would pay for it. And he could begin to grow the product's audience and the revenue he earned as a consequence.

It's that business goal combined with financial constraints that required Gary to focus on specific users and user activities he'd support. Gary still had high hopes of creating the "music industry marketing interface" that gave Mimi her name. But he decided to focus first on the band manager promoting his band using direct email marketing to his fans. After he did that, the specific functionality he needed to focus on became clear.

If you were listening closely just now, you caught the secret to prioritization.

Specific business outcomes drive focus on specific users, their goals, and the activities they'll engage in with your product. Focus on those activities drives focus on the specific features and functionality users will need to be successful.

For Mad Mimi, Gary made a deliberate decision to focus on delighting band managers promoting their bands. *That's the specific value he chose to focus on.* He didn't use that ambiguous term "business value." He filled in that blank with what was of value to him.

The prioritization error that most people make is to try to prioritize features first.

Prioritize specific business goals, customers, and users, and then their goals, before prioritizing features.

The next time you catch someone asking which feature is higher priority without discussing business goals, target users, and their use, that's your cue to start asking questions. Try not to act too smug. Not everyone knows this secret.

Discovery Activities, Discussions, and Artifacts

There are a lot of activities and artifacts you and your team can create during discovery. Here's a quick table that'll give you some basic starting points for the kinds of things you could do. Don't do all these things, because it's likely too much. And don't do just these things, because there are likely equivalent or even better practices that suit your skills and context. But definitely don't just sit in a room and write lots of stories. That'd be crazy.

Frame the idea

Use these discussions to review why your business is building the software, who it's for, and how you'll measure success.

- Named business problems you're addressing
- Specific business metrics affected
- Short lists of specific customers and users
- Metrics that will allow us to measure whether people use and like this new feature
- Big risks and assumptions
- Discussions with business stakeholders and subject matter experts

Understand customers and users

Use discussions and research to understand customers and users, their needs, and how they work today.

- Lists of user roles and descriptions
- Simple user profiles or person sketches
- Simple organizational profiles or orgzonas
- Story maps about how people do things today—also known as journey maps
- User research and observation to fill in what we don't know

Envision solutions

Focus on specific customers and users, and then envision solutions that will help them. Visualize solutions with words and pictures. Validate those solutions with customers and users.

- Story maps
- Use cases and user scenarios
- UI sketches and storyboards
- UI prototypes
- Architectural and technical design sketches
- Architectural or technical prototypes
- Lots of collaboration with team members, users, customers, stakeholders, and subject matter experts

Minimize and plan

Identify what you believe is a small, viable solution. Estimate well enough to set a budget for delivering the solution. Create a plan for development that will minimize risk.

- Story maps used for slicing
- Estimation used for setting a development budget

Discovery Is for Building Shared Understanding

Do you recall working on a software project where no one quite understood the big picture? Do you recall a time when the team learned halfway through development about a big chunk of work they hadn't planned on? Often, when this stuff has happened to me in the past, we'll find that between all of us in the team, and the outside people we collaborate with, we had the answers. We could have easily foreseen problems we ran into if we'd have just gotten on the same page.

Gary's story in Chapter 1 is a bit about Gary and his delivery team not having shared understanding of the big picture. Even Gary—the guy who held the vision of the product in his head—didn't have a clear understanding of the size and complexity of his product. Visualizing his product as a bunch of simple models helped him and everyone he was relying on get the same big picture in their minds.

For some things you build, it may be enough to just get everyone on the same page about who your customers and users are, and the big picture of the solution you have in mind for them. But I need to warn you, your hypothesis about what you're building is probably wrong. Don't worry: there are a couple of strategies I want to tell you about that really make discovery practice work. And that's what the next chapter is about.

CHAPTER 15

Using Discovery for Validated Learning

I've misled you. Sort of.

Some of you may have been reading the last chapter, and other chapters before that, and you've been slowly reaching a boiling point because you know what I'm leaving out. Sorry about that.

The stories I told about MadMimi.com and Globo.com are both incomplete. The truth is that both of them used discovery conversations to identify what they believed was a minimum viable solution. But whether those solutions were actually viable or not was just a guess. In fact, all this stuff is a guess until we actually ship and observe what the market—our customer and users—actually does. Initial discovery conversations, along with story maps, helped them get to a good starting guess. But, for both of them, it marked the beginning of a much longer journey to really discover a viable product.

This leads me to one of the biggest mistakes people make, and that's actually believing their minimal viable solution will be successful.

We're Wrong Most of the Time

I'm as guilty as the next guy in believing my great ideas will be successful. The truth is that in the past I released lots of solutions I thought would be wildly successful, but they just weren't. They weren't dismal failures, either—they just didn't make much of a difference. When this happened I, and my company, learned to look the other way. It wasn't just me. We *all* thought the features we were adding would be valuable.

But in the end we'd added a feature a few people used, but most didn't, and we knew we'd end up supporting for the life of our product.

My belief, not rooted in any formal scientific research or studies, but just in my own failures and what I observe working with other companies, is that very little of what we build is successful or has the real impact we hope for. I figure around 20 percent max. Then there is another 20 percent of things we do that are genuine failures—solutions that result in a negative impact. I've seen a variety of organizations that release a new, better version of their website and see sales decrease, or release a new version of their product that customers try and then demand the old version back. That's the kind of failure I'm talking about.

But it's that 60 percent in the middle, give or take, that is neither success nor failure that's the big problem. This is the stuff that we spend valuable development money creating, and in the end wish we hadn't.

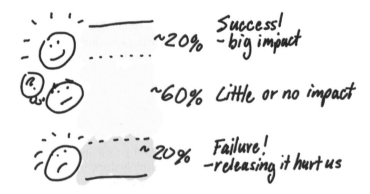

Research from the Standish Group published in historic "Chaos" reports explains that between 64 and 75 percent of features are rarely or never used.[1] And, depending on the source you look at, 75–90 percent of all software startups fail.[2]

1. Jim Johnson, Chairman of the Standish Group, "ROI, It's Your Job" (keynote), Third International Conference on Extreme Programming, Alghero, Italy, May 26–29, 2002.

2. Deborah Gage, "The Venture Capital Secret: 3 Out of 4 Start-Ups Fail," *Wall Street Journal*, September 20, 2012, *http://on.wsj.com/UtgMZl*.

All this is pretty disappointing when you think about it. No wonder just pretending it's working is the strategy of choice for most organizations.

The Bad Old Days

In the bad old days, I used to work a bit like this. I'd come up with a great idea, or in reality, someone else like my CEO or a key customer handed me *their* great idea. I'd get to work making sense of it and fleshing it out. Then my team and I would build it. It always took twice as long as we expected, but that's a problem to deal with in later chapters. We'd finish. We'd ship. We'd celebrate. Sometimes we celebrated, then shipped. But either way, we were done.

But then stuff actually started to happen. What usually happened was people complaining about what we'd delivered not working the way they wanted. Sometimes they didn't complain at all (which we'd find out later was a side effect of no one really using it). We'd then spend a lot of time pretending we were successful. For some of you, that might describe the way your company works today. And I'll be honest with you: it's still the way I often fall back into working. Don't tell anyone. I'm supposed to be an expert.

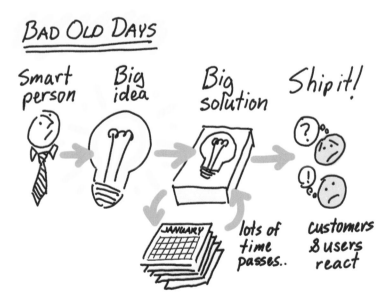

But there are better alternatives.

Empathize, Focus, Ideate, Prototype, Test

Years ago, a potential client contacted me and asked me if I could help it adopt a process called *design thinking*. This client had been using a typical Agile process, and was doing it really well—"well" in that it was delivering predictably and with high quality. But it had learned that "the faster you deliver crap, the more crap you get." That's a little harsh sounding. To put it another way, the client had learned that there was little correlation between the quantity of software it built, and the outcome and impact it got from it.

When this client called, I was known for my specialty in user experience design and Agile development. I thought to myself: "I'm a designer, and I'm thinking, so I must be design thinking." But I was wrong. That's not what the client meant. Luckily for me, I didn't say what I was thinking out loud.

Design thinking refers to a way of working originally described by a company called IDEO, and then later described and taught by Stanford University's d.school. These days, it's taught in a number of universities and used in lots of companies worldwide.

DESIGN THINKING

use face-to-face
time to find
problems worth
solving

identify lots
of possible &
impossible solutions

test solutions
with real users to
learn if they solve
the problem

Empathize Define
[Focus] Ideate Prototype Test

make sense of
what you've
learned & focus
on specific people
& problems

make solutions
real with protypes

one cross-functional
team moves through
the whole process

NOT a "waterfall"

Use phases as
thinking steps &
freely move back
& forth -> but timebox

A design thinking process has several steps that, as I explain them, seem like obviously good ideas. But, in practice, what I and most people tend to do is the exact opposite. No wonder things go bad so often.

The first step of a design thinking approach is *empathize*. It's not called research, which I'd normally expect from a design process. It's called *empathize* because a critical outcome of doing the work is to understand how it really feels to be a user of your product. To do this you need to go to where users are, meet them, watch them work, and ideally work alongside them. Now, of course, if you build software for surgeons, no one expects you to become an amateur surgeon. But do your best to understand what it's like to walk in their shoes. It's important to remember that out of traditional research, especially the quantitative hands-off stuff, we get data and not always empathy.

> *Talk directly to customers and users. Experience the challenges you're helping them with firsthand.*

The next step is called *define*. From the work we do during empathize, we learn a lot. But we need to make sense of it—to build shared understanding. And we'll do this using lots of collaboration to tell stories, share, and distill what we've learned. Then we'll choose specific people and problems on which to focus.

Use story maps here to map the way people do things today. Include in them details of what you saw and learned. Focus on the pain points users have, and the rewards they seek. Use simple personas to build a good example user that synthesizes what you've learned. Choose specific problems to focus on.

Really focus on one or a few problems. State them specifically.

The next step is *ideation*. If you were paying close attention in the last chapter, we talked about a simple practice called design studio. It's an example of a good ideation approach. In common business practice where the first person to come up with a viable idea is the winner, it seems a waste of time to come up with lots of possible ideas. If you remember that your first obvious solutions are, well, obvious, then if really coming up with an innovative solution is important, think past that.

I like using a story map as a backdrop for ideation. Use a map that shows pains, joys, and other information about users, and then brainstorm ideas directly into it. Write solution ideas directly on cards or stickies and inject them into the map where the solution is most relevant.

Deliberately come up with multiple possible solutions to customer and user problems.

The next step is to *prototype*. Now, we likely all know what prototypes are, but we often neglect creating them in the rush to get working products built. It's a pity, really. Small investments in simple paper prototypes help us think through our solution. They help us begin to experience it ourselves. Building simple prototypes out of paper, or the simplest of prototyping tools, helps us filter out a lot of ideas that just won't work. Beginning to simulate the actual act of using a product helps you continue to ideate—to come up with ideas to make the solution even better.

Build simple prototypes to explore your best solutions. Advance prototypes to a level of fidelity that allows users and customers to evaluate whether the solution really solves their problem.

The last step is to *test*. By that I don't mean check to see whether there are bugs. I mean learn whether your solution really does solve someone's problem. You might be surprised that it could do that even *with* bugs. When you've got a prototype that you believe solves the problems you've chosen to focus on, put that prototype in front of people who'll use your product. This isn't exactly "show and tell." And it's definitely not selling. Potential users need to recognize the prototype as something they could use to solve one of their problems. They need to use it to accomplish a real task. You can actually accomplish this by faking a lot of it.

Get your solutions in front of the people who will buy or use your product. Don't expect them to be a success at first. Iterate and improve them.

In addition to those five steps, part of design thinking is a way of working that emphasizes small, multidisciplinary collaborative teams working together quickly using simple models, sketching, and low-fidelity ways of documenting and communicating. You should recognize that as the discovery team and other collaborators I described in Chapter 12. You should recognize their way of working as one that emphasizes building shared understanding.

Using elements of design thinking helps us really understand the problems we're solving, so we don't solve problems we imagine people have. Prototyping and testing solutions before we invest big in building full-featured scalable solutions helps us validate that we're building solutions people really value and can use.

But design thinking alone can lead to some problems.

How to Mess Up a Good Thing

Design processes have been around a long time. Design thinking as a generalized approach to design has, too. And a design process done well can be a huge improvement over the bad old days. But don't confuse process with skill. There are some predictable ways that design processes fail. If you've seen a good design process take way too much time and result in a bad outcome, then you might believe these sorts of processes don't work. It's not the process.

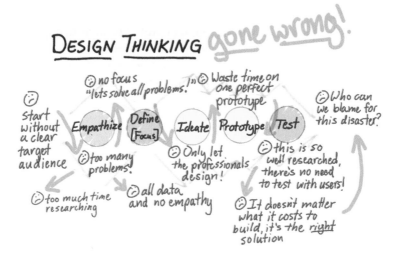

Here are a few great ways to mess up a design process:

- Start without framing the business needs and target customer well. This'll make it hard to prioritize who to focus on, and hard to tell if you're finding a good solution.

- Spend a lot of time doing thorough research and making sense of what you've learned. You'll never run out of things to learn—so why stop? Time-boxing might have been a good idea.

- Don't spend any time at all talking to people and learning from them. After all, we've got a lot of data, and really, our solution ideas are great. We just need to get going on designing them.

- Fail to focus on specific problem, and instead try to solve lots of problems for lots of people. The more problems you solve the better, right? Except that big problems often result in big solutions.

And trying to solve a problem for people with conflicting needs can result in a solution neither person likes.

- Consider multiple solutions, but only ask real designers to contribute solution ideas, because they're the only ones trained to have good ideas.

- Don't waste time considering multiple solutions, because the idea we have is so good.

- Beautifully craft a prototype that really looks real, but doesn't work well enough for customers and users to really use it. After all, when they see it, they tell us it "looks really lovely."

- Convince yourself and then others that this well-researched, professionally designed solution will work. After all, you've followed a rigorous design process. What could go wrong?

- Don't worry about how much it'll cost to build. It's the right solution, and any cost to build it is justified.

- When you deliver the solution to customers and users, and don't see the outcomes you expect, find the breakdown in the process that's at fault. Or better yet, find a person or group you can blame.

I'm being a bit snarky here, I know. But I'm a strong advocate for using design processes. And, oddly, I find I'm often the one complaining about them. I can also say that I've been guilty of almost all the failures listed. But, over the past few years, I've found a twist on typical design approaches that improves them.

Short Validated Learning Loops

Eric Ries is the author of a book called *The Lean Startup* (Crown Business). In his book Eric describes how he fell into the trap I described earlier as the "bad old days." As the CTO of a startup, he helped his company build what they believed to be a successful product. Only their target customers and users didn't see it that way. In fact, they mostly responded with a mixture of pleasant feedback, bad feedback, and outright apathy. Definitely not the outcome and impact they were looking for.

One of Eric's company advisors was Steve Blank. Steve had written a book called *The Four Steps to Epiphany* (K&S Ranch) in which he asserted that the first thing you need to develop isn't a product, it's customers. He described a process for progressively validating that you've found customers who are interested in a solution, and for then validating that the solutions you have in mind are the solutions they'll buy, use, and tell others about. Blank referred to this as a *validated learning process*.

Eric Ries's biggest contribution to product development is simplifying and "productizing" that thinking into this simple mantra: *build-measure-learn*. Eric emphasized reducing the time it takes to get through this simple learning cycle. One of the biggest flaws in traditional design processes is spending a very long time learning and designing—so long that you become very attached to the solutions, and then failing to validate that those solutions really do bring about the outcomes you intended. Where a typical design process may take weeks or months to validate a solution idea, a Lean Startup process usually takes just days.

What's in a Name

I need to tell you that I love most things about Lean Startup thinking. But one thing I don't love is the name. It's not all that Lean, and the concepts are way too important to just be used by startups.

Lean refers to the use of Lean thinking and principles as described by the Toyota Processing System decades ago, and Lean thinking as it's popularly used in lots of other contexts now, including software development. There are tons of good ideas to be found in Lean thinking, and Lean Startup only scratches the surface.

Eric tries to make the case that startups exist inside even the largest of businesses, that there are contexts of high risk and uncertainty that call for startup thinking. But it's my belief that if you catch yourself saying, "There's not much risk or uncertainty in this project," you need to remember that those are famous last words. There's always some amount of risk, and the learning strategies described in a Lean Startup process are pretty useful in most contexts. There's no need to try to justify to yourself or others that you need to behave like a startup.

How Lean Startup Thinking Changes Product Design

In the bad old days, we'd have come up with a big idea, built it, and hoped for the best.

If we were trying to break out of that trap using a rigorous design process, we'd have done our best to set aside our great ideas, and then dig deep into research to understand the problems we're solving.

Here's how I recommend we do things today, using Lean Startup thinking.

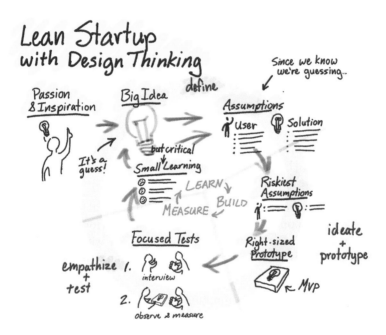

Start by Guessing

Yes, guessing.

In the bad old days, you'd have guessed and pretended you weren't. In a design process, you'd not have allowed yourself to guess. You would have anyway. But you'd have pretended you weren't. So just stop pretending.

It's actually not just guessing. It's a mixture of passion, experience, and insight—along with a fair dose of guessing—that gets the ball rolling. I take my assumptions and guesses about who my users are, usually by sketching simple prototypes. I'll describe how I think they work today by building simple "now" story maps. I'll do this collaboratively with other people who have firsthand experience with users and customers. And, in some situations I'll do this involving customers and users directly. So, in fact, many of our team's guesses aren't guesses at all. But it's not exactly research like we used to do, either. We'll spend hours to a couple of days doing stuff like this—never weeks or months.

After we've all got shared understanding about who will use the software and some focus in the problems we're solving, we then guess at the solution. We'll use principles of design thinking—deliberately coming up with and considering multiple solutions. But we'll try to converge quickly on what we think our best solution is. Sometimes we'll fail to decide on a single solution, and pick a couple. We don't wring our hands about this too much, because we know we're probably wrong anyway.

Name Your Risky Assumptions

Since we may have guessed a lot about our users and their challenges today, we'll name those guesses. Specifically, we'll work together to write a bulleted list of the things we believe are true, but if we find they aren't, then we'll need to rethink everything.

We'll do the same with our solution. We'll think about how we believe people will respond to it and how they'd use it. We'll form a hypothesis in our minds about how we think they'll behave with our solution. We'll also discuss technical risks—things that would threaten the feasibility of our solution.

Given a list of risks and assumptions about our customers, our users, and our solution, we'll identify what we think the few biggest risks are.

Design and Build a Small Test

Here's where things get *really* different.

In the bad old days, we'd have planned and built a whole product. In a design process, we'd have prototyped a whole product, or most of it anyway. But using a Lean Startup approach, where our goal is to learn something as quickly as possible, we'll do our best to make the smallest prototype possible. In lots of cases, it'll be hard to call it a prototype at all.

Here's an example from my friends at a nonprofit organization called ITHAKA. They make a product called JSTOR. If you've been enrolled in a US college in the last decade, you likely used JSTOR in your college library to find articles and books for a paper you had to write.

The students using the product wanted to easily use it from anywhere —at coffee shops, or at home, or when they traveled. But getting to JSTOR from outside the college could be a challenge for students. It required them to set up a username and password with their college so when they were sitting in a coffee shop, they could log in and get access to all the resources their university had licensed. The JSTOR team already had a solution, but it was a bit tricky to use. They wanted to test a new way of doing things.

They had these assumptions about those students:

- Worked from coffee shops and dorm rooms
- Didn't know they could access JSTOR from those locations
- Or, if they did know, they thought it was difficult

They had these assumptions about their solution:

- Would be easy to learn
- Would be obvious to students that they were getting full access to JSTOR without being at their library

To test their assumptions, the JSTOR team didn't need to build software—not yet. They needed to talk to students specifically about where they were when they were doing research, especially when they were using JSTOR. The team needed to confirm that students had the challenges that they imagined, and, given that, that students thought JSTOR's solution idea would address those challenges.

The team planned on talking to lots of students. And, to make it easier and more consistent to describe the problem and their solution to students, they created a simple design comic. If you haven't seen one, a design comic is exactly what it sounds like. It looks like a few pages from a comic book. But, instead of showing superheroes battling supervillains, it shows real people solving a real problem with your solution idea.

Here are a few pages from JSTOR's design comic (reproduced courtesy of ITHAKA, © 2014 ITHAKA, all rights reserved):

The test the team designed required that they spend a little time interviewing students to learn about their challenges today. And then, they'd review the scenario with the students to see if their solution looked like it would address the students' challenges. They didn't build a full prototype. They *did* have concerns that their solution would be really usable, and they couldn't learn that from a comic book. They also had a few technical concerns that would require writing some prototype code to test. But none of that mattered if students didn't have the problem, and didn't respond well to their idea.

That smallest possible solution to test is what Lean Startup refers to as a *minimum viable product*. Yes, Eric Ries knows it's not a whole product. But, when your goal is learning, it *is* the smallest product you could build to learn.

Measure by Running Your Test with Customers and Users

Put the test in front of customers and users. In early work this usually means schedule interviews and spend time with people. If you're creating a consumer solution, you can do *customer intercepts*, which is a technical way of saying go to where your customers and users are, stop them, and talk to them. I've tagged along with people I work with as they go to shopping malls, coffee shops, and tourist attractions.

JSTOR recruited students and grad students and spent 30–60 minutes talking with them first to interview and learn how they did things today so the team could confirm their assumptions about the problems they were solving. Then they stepped students through the design comic to get their response to the solution idea.

Rethink Your Solution and Your Assumptions

After running your test a few times, you'll begin to get predictable results. If you're dead wrong, you'll often learn that pretty quickly. Take back what you've learned. Roll those facts back into what you thought you knew about your users, and the way they work today. Use that to rethink your solution. Then, rethink your assumptions about users and solutions. Then design your next test.

After the JSTOR folks ran their tests, they learned that some students didn't have the problems they thought they did. Normally this would be disappointing news, because we all hate being wrong. But, in a Lean Startup approach, this is excellent news. It's excellent because they found they were wrong after a couple of days of thinking and working, as opposed to finding out after weeks of a team building software.

If you're using this sort of approach, your biggest challenge will be to learn to celebrate what you're learning as opposed to worrying about being wrong.

> *In a Lean Startup approach, failing to learn*
> *is frequently the biggest failure.*

In a Lean Startup approach, *build* means build the smallest possible experiment you can. *Measure* may be analytics gathered from working software, direct observations from interviews and face-to-face testing of prototypes, or both. *Learning* is what we do with the information. It's the rethinking of our assumptions and reforming what we believe to be a best solution going forward.

Stories and Story Maps?

You might be asking, "Where are the stories and story maps in all this?" And you'd be right to ask.

Throughout a validated learning approach, you'll be constantly telling stories about who your users are, what they're doing, and why. You'll use story maps to tell bigger stories about how people work today, and how you imagine they'll use your solution. When it comes time to build prototypes, you'll use stories and story conversations to agree specifically on what the prototype you're building should look like, and what you'll check to confirm the prototype is done. After you understand that stories are a way of working, you'll find it's difficult to tell when you are or aren't using them.

There is one big difference in the way we use stories during discovery, though. Usually when we're using them, we're talking with developers, testers, and lots of others about the software we intend to build and put into production. We'll work pretty hard to make sure we've got shared understanding. We'll get into a lot of details about how we'll build the software so we can learn enough to predictably estimate how long it'll take. Usually we'll talk about a number of stories so we can agree on how much we can get done in a two-week sprint or iteration. But the way we're working during discovery is faster. We hope to build simple prototypes in hours, not days. Even the prototypes we build using code and live data we hope will take days, not weeks. We're building to learn, and we expect most of our ideas to fail, or at minimum, need some adjustment to be successful. So we focus on working together quickly, agreeing quickly, and minimizing the formality.

During discovery and validated learning, you may be telling stories constantly, breaking ideas and work down into small buildable pieces, and agreeing on exactly what to build. You'll be doing it so fast that it won't be clear you're using stories. But you are.

CHAPTER 16

Refine, Define, and Build

So, now what? If stories are for planning and facilitating discussions in order to build software, all we seem to be doing is lots of talking.

Cards, Conversation, More Cards, More Conversations...

Your first bunch of conversations helped you make sense of an opportunity. You talked about who'd be using your product, and imagined how they'd use it to accomplish something valuable to them. Your conversations went deep enough to break the big opportunity into parts that were small enough that you could tell which parts were important to be in a next product release, and which didn't matter so much. You collected the stories that described that next viable release into a release backlog.

If you're clever, and I know you are, your next conversations went deeper into what the software might look like, how it would behave, and how it might knit into your existing product and software architecture. You had these conversations with a close eye on the risky stuff. You sliced up the stories into the parts that you could build early that would help you learn more, faster. And because you're clever, you segmented your release backlog into stories to take on early to learn, in the middle to build up, and later to refine.

But now it gets real. It's time to have our *best* last conversations.

Cutting and Polishing

We'd like to get to work building these things, and we know that building the software that our storytelling describes will go smoothly and predictably if we can concisely describe exactly what we'd like to build. But, after all these conversations, the stories we're left with feel a little rough around the edges. We likely haven't talked about any of them in enough detail to understand precisely what they are and what they aren't, and really predict how long they'll take to build. But we've got a magical machine that'll fix all this.

I want you to picture an elegantly designed little machine. We'll drop jagged, rough stories from our release backlog into a big funnel on the left side. Then, inside the machine, we'll hear a little grinding and clattering. But then out of a little spout on the right side comes small, polished little nuggets. These little nuggets are the things that team members can pick up and use to predictably build high-quality software.

This machine looks magic from the outside. But, on the inside, you and your team are having some serious rock-cutting and polishing discussions. The special, secret mechanism hidden inside this machine is a *story workshop*.

As you might recall from Chapter 11, story workshops are small, productive conversations where the right people work together to tell the stories one last time, and in the process make all the tough decisions about exactly what they'll choose to build. These are the deep story conversations that result in confirmation. Finally, we're getting to that third C in the *card-conversation-confirmation* flow. And it's this C that helps us really cut and add the polish to these rocks.

Workshopping Stories

You'll need a small group that includes a developer, a tester, and people who understand users and how the UI will look and behave—UI designers or business analysts in some organizations. This goes best when the group is small enough to work together effectively in front of a whiteboard. That's usually three to five people.

Details & Confirmation

Stories in

Right-Sized Stories Out

who? what? why? how?

Story discussions are more workshop than meeting

This is a workshop, not in a meeting. *Meeting* is the word that has become a euphemism for unproductive collaboration. A story workshop needs to be filled with lots of productive discussion, hand waving, whiteboard drawing, and sketching. We'll need to work together to decide exactly what we'll build. We've got to come out of this conversation with solid shared understanding, and we'll need space to have those productive words-and-pictures conversations.

In all those conversations prior to now, we talked through details, but hopefully we had the restraint to go just deep enough to make the decisions we needed to at the time. The decisions we're making now focus on answering the question: exactly what will we build?

It's during this conversation that you'll find out your story is too big. By that I mean it's bigger than the ideal size we like to see going into development—a couple of days or less to build. OK, it's not *always* too big. But, if you just assume it will be, then you'll be pleasantly surprised when it's not. Happily, you have exactly the right people in the room to help you break down this story into smaller stories that can be delivered, tested, and demonstrated in the growing product the team is working together to build.

Story Workshop Recipe

Use a story workshop to refine understanding and define specifically what the development team will build. The workshop is a product conversation—supported by lots of pictures and data—that helps the team make decisions and arrive at confirmation: the acceptance criteria for what we'll choose to build.

Ahead of the workshop, let the team know what stories you'll be workshopping. Post it on a wall, or otherwise broadcast it. Let team members opt in; that is, choose to participate or not.

Keep the workshop small to stay productive. Three to five people is a good size.

Include the right people. For this conversation to be effective, include:

- Someone who understands users and how the user interface could or should work—often a product owner, user experience professional, or business analyst
- One or two developers who understand the codebase you'll be adding the software into, because they'll best understand what's feasible to build
- A tester who'll help test the product—because he'll help ask the tough questions so that we consider the "what abouts" that others are often too optimistic to consider

Other people and roles may be relevant here, but remember that the right size for a good conversation is "dinner conversation–sized."

You may find that one person can wear two hats. For example, I often see a combination business analyst-tester in some IT organizations. But, if all the concerns aren't considered, pause the workshop and try to find someone from the team who can look after the missing concern.

Dive deep and consider options. Use the conversations to dive deep into:

- Exactly who the user is
- Exactly how we believe she would use it
- Exactly what it looks like—that is, the user interface
- Exactly how the software behaves underneath that user interface —those sticky business rules and data validation stuff

- Roughly how we might build the software—because we need to predict how long it will take to build—and happily, we're making things real enough at this point we can more accurately predict how long that will take

Remember that we need not consider anything absolutely required. If the discussion leads to solutions that are expensive or complex, step back and discuss the problems we're really solving, and other alternatives we could build to solve them.

Agree on what to build. After enough conversation to build shared understanding, move to answering the questions:

- What will we check to confirm this software is done?
- How will we demonstrate this software later when we review it together?

Talk and doc. Use whiteboards or flipchart paper to draw pictures, write examples, and consider options. Don't let your decisions vaporize. Record them on a whiteboard or flipchart where everyone can see. Photograph notes and drawings and then transcribe them later.

Speak in examples. Wherever possible, use specific examples of what users do, exactly what data might be entered, exactly what users would see in response, or whatever examples best support your story.

Split and thin. When discussing details and thinking about development time, you'll often find stories are larger than you like to put in a development cycle. Work together as a group to split up big stories, or "thin" out stories by removing unnecessary extras.

It's not working when…

- No one participates—when one person describes what's required and everyone else listens
- When we focus only on acceptance criteria and not telling the story about who does what and why
- When we fail to consider options both from a functional and technical perspective

Sprint or Iteration Planning?

Some Agile practitioners accomplish these critical story conversations during planning sessions like iteration planning or sprint planning. That works pretty well if you're working with teams that work effectively together and come into the discussion with a good understanding of their product. For teams I worked with for years, that's the way we did things.

But one of the biggest complaints I hear from Agile teams is that these planning meetings are often long, torturous affairs. At some point everyone agrees on what to build, even if they don't have shared understanding, just to make this torturous meeting stop.

Coming in from the Cold

Nicola Adams and Steve Barrett, RAC Insurance, Perth, Australia

> My first foray into the world of an Agile project team in my role as a business analyst was a cold, hard lesson in the power of collaboration over the written word.
>
> — Nicola Adams

The Context

Recounting a slice of the transformational journey from waterfall to Agile within RAC Insurance in Perth, Western Australia, Nicola—an experienced BA—was well versed in the traditional delivery approach to software development. Her role involved engaging the business, understanding the problem domain, and working with IT to document functional specifications to hand off for delivery. The communication lines were like this:

The focus had been on detailed specifications to try to leave no stone unturned. Recognizing that "developers don't read," mitigation strategies were employed (e.g., specification walkthroughs) with variable success. Lengthy time lags were typical from after specifications were completed to when the knowledge was needed to support development and testing.

What Happened Initially?

The natural affinity to written specifications was not easily broken. The concept of fitting requirements on the back of a card was hard to grasp. How could Nicola expect the developers and testers to deliver the required functionality, which she felt accountable for, if they didn't have sufficient information? The focus shifted to creating story narratives, little different from the functional specifications except in scale; the lines of communication did not change.

Nicola's elaboration session preparations included:

- Requirements gathering with business stakeholders
- In-depth analysis of requirements and data
- Creating story narratives (one to five pages each) documenting requirements, solution design, and acceptance criteria
- Reading the narratives to the team using a projector and asking for any questions

Unfortunately, the outcomes were not so great. The elaboration sessions were flat and uninspiring, with the majority of the team disengaged. In addition, Nicola felt she had insufficient time to prepare stories, and the team largely ignored the narratives during delivery.

After an elaboration session, Sam, a subject matter expert standing in for the product owner, remarked, "If this is an Agile project, I don't want to be involved!"

This needed fixing!

What Changed?

Steve, the project manager, facilitated a team retrospective to focus on the problem. This retrospective resulted in a number of key takeaways, including abandoning story narrative documents, including the business and delivery team in story elaboration, and ensuring a set cadence for backlog grooming and story elaboration.

Nicola went beyond simply applying the actions; she fully embraced the intent. The next story elaboration session was a seismic shift from what had preceded.

The team no longer sat bored and disengaged as they plowed through screen-projected story narratives. They were now huddled around visual models and artifacts, engrossed in real story conversations involving the product owner, business subject matter experts, and the delivery team.

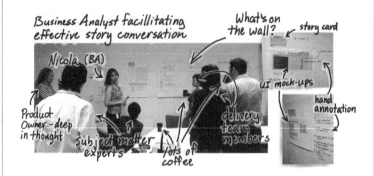

Business Analyst facilitating effective story conversation

What's on the wall?

story card

Nicola (BA)

UI mock-ups

hand annotation

Product Owner - deep in thought

subject matter experts

lots of coffee

delivery team members

The lines of communication had changed. Nicola was no longer the intermediary between business and IT; she was now a facilitator allowing conversations to flow between those who understood the business value, those who sat with the users to know what would be usable, and the delivery team who knew what was feasible:

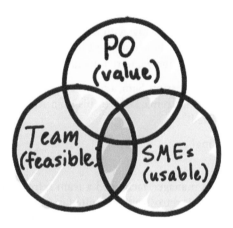

PO (value)

Team (feasible)

SMEs (usable)

The business and delivery team loved the new format and were now fully engaged, a shared understanding was created around the problems to be solved, group divergence and convergence enabled the team to arrive at optimum solutions within constraints, and Nicola felt under less pressure and had more time.

Nicola had come in from the cold!

Crowds Don't Collaborate

The torturous sprint planning meeting has become such a common dysfunction that many teams sensibly choose to have these story discussions in the days preceding the meeting. They often have these scheduled in their calendars as pre-planning meetings, backlog grooming, or backlog refinement meetings. But, too often, what happens is they've simply moved the same torture they hated during the planning meeting to a different day. To add insult to injury, team members are asked to take a break from their current productive work to sit through this torture. No wonder they're not excited about it.

The problem isn't that story conversations are hard. Well, actually they can be pretty hard at times. But all conversations are made tougher by trying to include too many people. If many of those people aren't interested or motivated to participate, you're doomed. You know the people I'm talking about—the ones pretending we can't see them playing with their smartphones under the table.

Allow team members to opt in to these conversations. If later they complain about the decisions made, make sure you invite them to be there next time.

If everyone wants to participate, try using a fishbowl collaboration pattern like the one described in the following sidebar. This way, interested people can drop by, participate if they want, and leave if they find they're not missing anything exciting.

Fishbowl Collaboration Pattern

If you've got people who sincerely want to be involved in the conversation, but adding them expands the conversation past a productive size, try using a fishbowl collaboration pattern. This'll give them a way to be involved with minimal impact to the outcome. What they and others often find is that being there wasn't as important as they thought. Over time you'll see that they're happy to let others discuss the details and then learn about the results in a later conversation.

The process works like this: three to five people work together in front of whiteboard or flipchart paper—they're the fish in the bowl.

Others in the room may observe but not speak. They're outside the bowl.

If someone from outside the bowl wants to participate, she can "jump in." But, when one outsider jumps in, one insider must simultaneously jump out.

In this way, the conversation stays small and productive, and others stay informed and involved. It's also a great way for learners to get up to speed without slowing down work.

Split and Thin

Remember the cake and cupcakes discussion from Chapter 8? Now's the time to break down those cakes to the smallest cupcakes you can. It's now—when we've got developers, testers, and others who can really build the software—that we can really imagine how we could break down the story.

Remember that software is "soft." Well, it's not soft like a sponge or a cupcake. Ideally, it's more like a rather large document or a book. If you were writing a book, like I'm doing my best to do right now, you wouldn't try to do it all at one time. You might sit down and write a chapter at a time. In fact I'll write a chapter at a time, and Peter, my competent, supportive editor, will review what I've written and make corrections and suggestions.

But then the chapter's not "done." Far from it.

I'll need to go back through and figure out where there should be illustrations. I'll need to figure out if I should add footnotes, references, glossary terms, or index items. Then other editors from the publisher will go back through each chapter, making final refinements. I've naturally split up the work to do it iteratively so that I can see the whole book take shape sooner.

You're reading the "Refine, Define, and Build" chapter. And if you're reading it now, it's hopefully fully baked. If I were to think about my final acceptance criteria, I'd say it should be:

- Edited and understandable by me
- Edited and understandable by my editors
- Supported by illustrations that help enable readers to visualize points
- Supported by an index readers could use to find terms in the chapter
- Supported by a glossary that readers could use to look up definitions of terms introduced in the chapter

Crap, that's a lot of work. Even as I type those things into the first draft now, I realize I've got lots of work to do. But I don't want to do all of it before moving on to the next chapter, because I'd like to see how the whole book is hanging together. So I'll break it into "cupcakes"—small, complete parts that aren't ready to ship, but that boost my confidence that I'm on the right track as I move through this book.

I'd break down my work into stories like this:

- Refine, Define, Build first rough draft
- Refine, Define, Build second refined draft
- Refine, Define, Build with illustrations
- Refine, Define, Build with reviewer feedback incorporated
- Refine, Define, Build index terms
- Refine, Define, Build glossary terms
- Refine, Define, Build final draft

Each one of those things I can tell a story about describes what it looks like, and thinks through the steps I (with Peter's editing assistance) must accomplish to finish each of these smaller versions and improvements to the chapter. And you can see that as each thing is completed, the chapter gets progressively more refined and closer to releasable. In theory, there's something you could see and consume after the first story in the list is done. But I wouldn't do that to you. It wouldn't be pretty, and your reactions wouldn't be good.

Finally, since I know you're on top of your game, you may have noticed that the list of smaller, cupcake-sized stories looks a lot like the acceptance criteria for the chapter. That's the magic here. It's the discussion of the acceptance criteria that reveals how we could break down the work into smaller parts we could create and inspect along the way.

It's important to inspect your work along the way so you can evaluate it and make course corrections. You should have seen the really stupid example I'd originally written here. But you'll never see it because I wrote it, inspected it, and then removed it.

In a traditional software process, that "inspecting and removing" stuff would be called bad requirements. But, when you've got your Agile hat on, it's just learning and iterative improvement.

Play Good-Better-Best

One of my favorite simple techniques for splitting stories more finally is the Good-Better-Best game. We played this game using a big story and sticky notes and ended up with this:

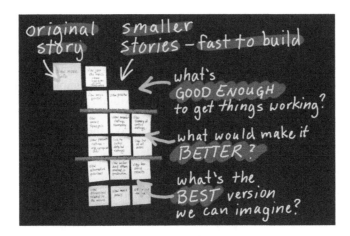

Good Enough for Now

Given a story, start by having a discussion about what's just good enough—barely sufficient, really, and probably not good enough that users or customers would love it. Write down characteristics that would make it good enough and treat them as separate, smaller stories.

In walking through an example that's something like IMDb.com (the Internet movie database), we discussed the "View movie info" story. We imagined a screen where I could look at movie details so that I could make a decision about seeing the movie. When we discussed Good, we came up with these simple things:

- View the basic info: title, rating, director, genre, and so on
- View the movie poster
- Watch a preview

Better

Then ask what would make it even better. For the movie database example, we ended up with things like:

- Read a movie synopsis

- Read member ratings

- Read reviewer ratings

- View a list of all the actors in the movie

Best

Finally, ask what would make it really fabulous. Don't be afraid to go crazy here. Remember, these aren't the requirements. This is just you and your team considering options. Some interesting things sometimes come from these discussions—things that might make the product really fabulous, but are surprisingly cheap to implement. For the movie database example, we ended up with things like:

- Watch alternative previews or videos about the movie

- Read trivia about the movie

- Read news about the movie

- See and participate in discussions about the movie

You can see how this progression of smaller stories helps build the "View movie info" story up from something that will let me just see it work, to stories that would improve it to make it really fabulous. If I were building this feature, I'd do the basics first across the whole application before I moved on to making things better and then best. I just feel safer meeting deadlines when I build that way.

When you're really having good story discussions, and I know you will, at the end of a *story workshop* you should have right-sized stories supported by lots of extra documentation and models, and by acceptance criteria that describe how you'll check this story to confirm it's done. Sometimes it'll take a couple of workshops supported by a little outside research, analysis, and design work to arrive at agreement, but that's OK. Cutting and polishing takes time, and a bit more patience.

Development Cycle Planning Recipe

Agile processes like Extreme Programming and Scrum use *time-boxed development*, where each development cycle starts with a planning session and ends with review. In many companies, they're some of the most loathed of meetings anywhere. They can be long and painful, and by the time team members leave the meeting, they're often ready to agree to anything just to get out of the room. It doesn't take a rocket scientist to guess that the quality of the plans they make isn't so good.

But it doesn't need to be that way.

Here's a simple recipe that should help you avoid the worst problems.

Prepare

Choose stories a cycle or two ahead. If you're a product owner, meet routinely with your core product team to discuss the progress of the solutions under way. Choose the stories that you'd like to take on next to move those solutions closer to release.

Workshop ahead of time. For those on the product team, make time to work together with team members ahead of the planning session. Dig into details, split larger stories, and consider multiple options. Look back to Mat Cropper's story in Chapter 7. When I spoke with Mat, one of the things he most looked forward to was the series of short, half-hour, ad hoc story workshops he had developers and testers get ready for planning.

Invite the whole team, and others whose help you might need during the upcoming development cycle.

Plan

Start by discussing the big goal for the upcoming cycle. You've chosen some stories to work in. How does that group of stories help advance the solution you're trying to deliver?

Review the stories you'll be discussing. Don't go into extreme detail here—just enough to give everyone the big picture. Look back to Nicola and Steve's story in this chapter. Look at the wall Nicola is standing in front of: lots of words and pictures to help team members imagine it, right? Isn't she smart?

Set a time-box for the delivery team to plan on their own. Remember, crowds don't collaborate. And the people building and testing this software need to do some real thinking to create their recipes for building these stories—just like Sydnie did in Chapter 10. Give the team an hour or so to break into small groups and work together on the stories. If you're a product owner, UI designer, or business analyst, stay close by. Observe if you like. But be ready to answer questions that'll help them move fast.

In small groups, create a plan for each story. Remember the three amigos discussed in Chapter 12? Make sure the small groups are like that. And, as a development team, decide how many of these stories can be successfully completed in the delivery cycle. Don't forget to take into account holidays and days off. I once had a team tell me their plan was off because of the upcoming Thanksgiving holiday, as if that holiday came out of nowhere and jumped up and surprised them.

All together, agree on the plan. At the end of the time-box, and after the team does their plan for each story, they'll need to come back and share their plan—not every detail, because that would be super-boring, even to them. What's important is for the team to be clear about what they believe they can get done in the cycle. They should take this plan and their agreement seriously, especially if they want others to consider them reliable and predictable.

Agreeing may take a little time, especially if all the work that needs to be done won't fit in the development time-box. It's lucky you know some tricks for slicing stories down thinner. Try dialing back a story from better to just good enough. That should make it fit.

Celebrate. You're done. In a past, we liked planning in the afternoon. We tried to finish a bit before quitting time. Then we'd celebrate by taking the rest of the day off. We showed up the next day refreshed and ready to start working on the plan we created together.

Use Your Story Map During Delivery

Use a map to build shared understanding with your delivery team. I often hear from team members working in an Agile process how much they like collaborating, and how productive they feel because every week or two they see and demonstrate working software. But then they follow that up with statements like, "I feel like I've lost the big picture. All I see are these little parts of the product we build." Use a map to give the team the visibility of the whole product or feature you're working on. They'll make better tactical design and development decisions if they understand the context those decisions fit into.

Use a Map to Visualize Progress

As you begin to build your product release, the map makes a good visual dashboard to show what you have and haven't built.

Some teams remove detailed stories from the body of the map as they bring them into development to complete. That way, when they look at the map, all they see is what's left to build.

Other teams like leaving the map in place and using pens or colored stickers to mark the stories they've completed. When they step back and look at the map, they see a visualization of what's done, and what's left to do.

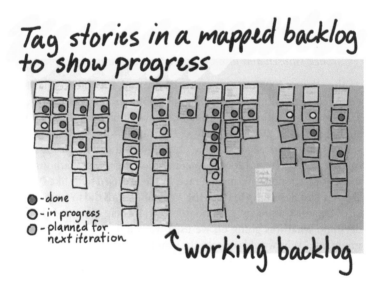

Use the map to identify the next stories to build. Every week, product owners will need-assess the progress of ongoing development work, and make decisions about what's important to focus on next. When the map visualizes progress, then it's a bit easier to scan it to look for areas that need more focus. It's sort of like being a painter. If you can step back and take in the entire painting, it's easer to figure out where to start working next.

Use Simple Maps During Story Workshops

Each development cycle, you'll identify stories in the map you should work on next. You'll carry those stories into those last best conversations you'll have during story workshops.

An easy visualization to build during that workshop is a simple map. You might be mapping only the three or four steps the user takes using a feature you're discussing. But being able to point to sticky notes on a wall that show the flow helps the discussion move faster. As you begin to discuss acceptance criteria, write them on sticky notes and add them into this mini-map. In the end, you'll have a simple visualization that supports the conversation you had in this workshop.

Visualize Your Working Backlog

Chris Gansen and Jason Kunesh, Obama Campaign Dashboard

As the Obama 2008 election campaign proved, the Internet has forever changed politics. Barack Obama's online strategy played a direct and significant role in his nomination and subsequent election. The strategy for the 2012 election was to provide tools that supported traditional grassroots organizing and fundraising, while using technology as a "force multiplier" to counteract the massive amounts of third-party money entering the race. While we used tools like Pivotal Tracker and Basecamp to track the work our teams did to support the 2012 Obama Campaign Dashboard, to really help everyone else understand what was going on we used walls full of sticky notes. You might ask, "Why would you take the time to mess around with a bunch of Post-its on the wall?" Here's why.

We had two different cultures working together in the same space on this effort. We were the folks in the corner who unscrewed the light bulbs so we could work in relative darkness; who brought in our own noisy keyboards; who wore gigantic headphones to drown out the buzz of cable television interviews, bells, and handclaps that permeated the open newsroom-style office; and who wore metal band t-shirts instead of seersucker suits. All the people who'd worked on previous campaigns, the guys in suits, came in with a traditional view of software development. "We describe the features we want, and you build them for us. Yesterday." They weren't used to receiving things incrementally and seeing them iteratively change and improve, and they definitely weren't used to making the tradeoffs required to get the stuff they really needed when it had the biggest impact. It's a

---

campaign. There's no extending the delivery date, except by act of Congress! The day after the election, it's over whether we're finished or not. And there was no way they'd get everything they imagined.

President Obama in suit and Jason in polo shirt, doing the most stressful product demo ever

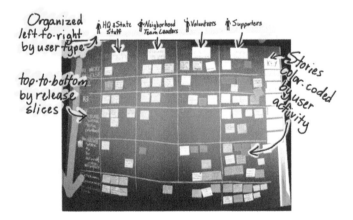

The first board

When we originally got started, we used some basic mapping approaches to describe the people using our system and the different kinds of things they'd need to do. We could then organize the work into releases over time. This worked OK, but it was hard for the people leading the campaign to really get engaged with thinking about the way people would work later, more than a year from the present day. Their heads were focused on what they needed to get done *now*. And they were making lots of guesses about what volunteers and group leaders would be doing. They had to, especially if we were reimagining the way they worked.

After seven months, we shipped a small, minimum viable product—just enough to release to our first users in Iowa. That's when everything changed. The immediate reaction was bad because what we released clearly wasn't everything people envisioned it would be. There were lots of important things missing. It had bugs. We heard a lot of "Why didn't you get it right the first time?" As much as we assured them we'd be fixing broken things and improving things every single week, they couldn't really buy it until they saw it. But as things quickly did improve, that really built trust.

That's where the big wall of stickies comes in. We used Pivotal Tracker and Basecamp, but all these other people weren't going to use those tools. We needed a fully transparent way that everyone could see what we were working on, and what was coming. Our wall of stories was organized left to right by calendar week, and top to bottom by priority. We were all focused on time. There was a big clock on the wall counting down the minutes until the election. They all knew that some things were less important now, and some even more critical as election day got closer. Every story on the wall was color-coded for the activity the idea affected—like Field Work, Team Building, Voter Registration, and Voter Turnout. There's a lot of purple in this picture because it's early, and Team Building, represented by the purple stickies, is more important than other things like Voter Turnout right now.

Absolutely fixed schedule

← not a Scrum reference

The countdown

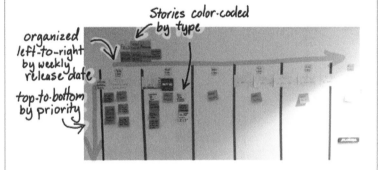

Stories color-coded by type

organized left-to-right by weekly release date

top-to-bottom by priority

Weekly releases left to right, priority top to bottom, color-coded by area of the product

When we added things to the board, we did it together with the people running the campaign. We talked about what was already planned for that week, and what the odds were of it making it into the week's work. We talked about the real problem being solved behind the feature idea. Together we decided how important it was relative to all the other things on the wall. When it came time to build the software, the developer responsible would work directly with the stakeholder who knew the most. They'd work together to figure out the details. Sometimes all it took was lots of scribbling on a whiteboard to agree. Sometimes we'd take a day and build some simple UI prototypes.

This big visual wall of sticky notes was critical for building a bridge between the people developing the software and the people who needed it. It's what they needed to help them visualize what was going on and when, and to actively participate in making decisions.

CHAPTER 17

Stories Are Actually Like Asteroids

If you're of a certain age, you may fondly recall playing an early video game called *Asteroids*. Stick with me here for a moment. I promise this is relevant.

In the game *Asteroids*, you're represented by a little ship floating deep in outer space. But you're stranded in a field of huge asteroids, and you need to shoot your way out to survive! If you shoot a big asteroid, it explodes into a few smaller asteroids. And, to make things more complicated, these smaller asteroids move faster, and in different directions—which makes it harder for you to keep from getting hit. If you shoot one of those smaller asteroids, it'll break into even smaller asteroids that move even faster in *different* directions. Pretty soon, the screen is full of asteroids of all different sizes flying in every possible direction. Happily, when you shoot the tiniest asteroids, they blow up completely and help clear away this mess.

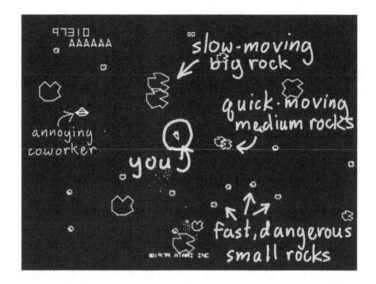

A really bad asteroid strategy is to shoot all the big rocks and break them down into small rocks. The screen fills with lots of small rocks flying every which way, and you'll die a quick and painful death.

A really bad product backlog management strategy is to break down all the big stories so they're small enough to fit into the next development cycle. Your backlog will fill with lots of small stories flying every which way, and you'll die. Well, you won't actually die, but you'll be buried alive in a lot of needless complexity. You and everyone else will complain about losing the big picture amid all these tiny details.

Break stories down progressively, and just in time.

At each story discussion and splitting stage, you'll do so with a purpose in mind:

1. *For opportunities* you'll discuss who they're for, what problems they solve, and if they're well aligned with your business strategy. It may make sense to split bloated opportunities at this point.

2. *During discovery*, you'll discuss the specifics of who uses the product, why, and how. Your team's goal is to envision a product that's valuable, usable, and feasible to build. You'll do lots of rock breaking here. Hopefully you'll move only the smallest number of stories you need forward into a release backlog that describes a minimum viable product release.

3. *When planning a development strategy*, you'll discuss where the risks are—risks that spring from concerns about what users will like and adopt, and risks that spring from real technical feasibility concerns. You'll break rocks with learning in mind, building what you need to first, to learn the most.

4. *When planning for the next development cycle*, you'll have your last best discussions to decide exactly what to build and make agreements on how you'll check the software to confirm it's complete. Each one of those agreements provides an opportunity to break down a story even further where each story satisfies as little as one agreement.

You can see that if you tried to have all four of these conversations in the same sitting, it'd be a long, grueling conversation. It'd take a wide variety of people to weigh in on different aspects. And you've probably gathered from my warnings and your own past experience that big groups of people don't work effectively together—at least not all in the same room at the same time. That's why we break stories down progressively over time with lots of conversations.

Reassembling Broken Rocks

In the *Asteroids* game, you have to be very careful about which asteroids you shoot because you can't put split asteroids back together once they're broken. But you *can* put split stories back together.

To avoid a backlog filled with lots of tiny stories, take a bundle of stories that go together, and write all their titles on a single card as a bulleted list. Summarize those titles with a single title on your new card. Voilà, you've got one big story.

This is pretty fantastic stuff when you think about it. The card, and the title written on it, is a tangible handle to lots of intangible ideas. Ideas are a lot more malleable than rocks or heavy documents. We sometimes forget that another name for software development is knowledge work. When we forget that and instead fixate on documents and process, it turns into something dry and secretarial. And when I work with people managing huge backlogs filled with tiny stories, it feels horribly secretarial.

Bundle Small Stories to Clean Up Your Backlog

I often run into product teams that have backlogs with hundreds of items in them. And, predictably, they tell me that they struggle to prioritize their backlogs. When I look into their backlogs, they're often filled with lots of little stories. Talking about each one of them to make a prioritization decision would take hours, or days in some cases. So don't.

If this were *Asteroids*, you'd have lost. But since it's not, try bundling up your small stories into bigger stories:

1. If your stories are in an electronic backlog, get them out onto cards or sticky notes. Whatever tool you're using should be able to print or export to a spreadsheet. I'll use a simple mail merge in a word processing program to create labels for all the stories and then stick them to a card, or print directly onto cards.

2. Ask for help from a group of team members who understand the system. Schedule a room with lots of wall or table space where you can work.

3. Give everyone a handful of story cards and ask them to start placing them on the tabletop or sticking them to the wall.

4. When you see a card that seems similar to one you're placing, cluster them together. Don't think too hard about what "similar" means—just go with your gut.

5. Do this organizing in silence, at least to start. You'll find that it's the conversation that slows things down. And it's good to learn to use the model and your body language to communicate.

6. Move and reorganize any card you want. It's everyone's model, so that means no one owns the position of a card. If something looks out of place, move it. If someone disagrees, he or she will move it back. That's your cue to discuss why.

7. After things settle into clusters, take a different color card or sticky and make a header for each cluster. On that card, write a better story name—one that distills why all these cards are similar. If you've written a distillation called "UI improvements," that may be too vague. "Improve entering and editing comments" would be better, assuming those UI changes were about comments.

8. The distillations become your new, bigger stories. The other cards become bullet points in its description. Add those

distillations back into your release backlog. Or, if they're deferrable, move them all the way back to your opportunity backlog.

Cluster ideas that seem similar

Small stories

New, bigger easier to manage stories

Distill: write a single sticky that pulls together the ideas in the cluster

This works fantastically well for deep backlogs composed of lots of little items. It's wonderful for deep bug lists, too. You know how there are always lots of lower-priority bugs that never get fixed? Bundle them with other higher-priority bugs in the same area of the system. When a developer goes in to fix the high-priority bugs, it's often trivial to hit the low-priority bugs, too. Your customers and users will thank you for it.

Don't Overdo the Mapping

I often hear from people trying to figure out this story mapping stuff that it's just "too much." When I ask them "What went wrong?" they'll tell me about creating a very large map of their whole system in order to discuss a simple feature. They're right: that's too much. So don't do that.

Map only what you need to tell a story about your feature.

For example, I was working with a company making some changes to the commenting feature in its collaborative document editing software. The team mapped document editing at a high level, and they only used a few cards for that. When they got to the area for commenting, they added more cards that summarized what their product did today using lots of bullets on a single card. Then they began to discuss changes they'd like to make, adding lots more cards for all the details and options they were considering.

When adding a feature into an existing product, map a little ahead of where the feature begins in your users' story, and a little beyond where it ends. Don't map your whole product.

Remember that story maps support conversations about your users and your product ideas. A good rule of thumb is this: if you don't need to discuss it, you don't need to map it.

Don't Sweat the Small Stuff

I've described this whole rock-breaking journey, and even cautioned you to treat those rocks like asteroids in the old Atari game so you're not tempted to break them down too fast. Hidden within all these strategies is the assumption that a lot of the stories we come up with are big. But, actually, a lot of them aren't. After you deliver a product or feature to users, you'll immediately find lots of little things that are dead obvious—things you wished you'd have thought of before shipping, but you didn't. At least that's what happens to me. For those things I don't have an opportunity discussion, or pull together a group to do product discovery, because it'd be obvious to everyone they should be done. For those things, I'll get them into a current release backlog and then as early as possible workshop them with team members so we can get them built. The same goes for bugs, and lots of little improvements.

Saving the World, One Little Fix at a Time

Here's my friend Sherif from Atlassian again. He was explaining to me that product team members pick up and work on lots of small fixes and improvements all the time. They worry about their users a lot there. And they know that lots of little bugs and imperfections drive their users crazy—and that drives them crazy. They say it's like dying a "death by a thousand paper cuts." So, on the wall near a team working on a product called Green Hopper is a bunch of tick marks. Every time a team member fixes one of these little things, he or she makes a mark on the wall. It looks like 47 of these little fixes will go out in the next release. If you use Confluence or JIRA, you can thank them later.

CHAPTER 18

Learn from Everything You Build

If you've got a traditional development hat tightly on, you might believe you're done when the software is built. But Agile development and stories are built for learning. We spend a lot of time before we build anything making sure we should build it, and agreeing together on what to build. And, after we build, we'll look again and ask if should have built it, and if it's good enough.

Let's talk about all the opportunities you have to learn after you build.

Review as a Team

Let's rewind to the celebrating part. At the end of a cycle of development and testing, celebration is in order. You've turned some ideas, lots of discussion, sketching, and hand waving into some honest-to-goodness working software. It would have taken a lot longer using a traditional requirements process. And you and your team would likely feel a lot less ownership of the result.

After a few high-fives, it's time to sit down as a team and take an honest look at what we've accomplished. If we're being honest with ourselves, we'll likely find some things we'd change to improve the software. For each of those things, we'll write another story and add it to our release backlog. We'll decide if these are changes we need to make right away, or changes we can defer 'til later during our endgame.

In processes like Scrum, this is called a *sprint review*. If you're a Scrum practitioner, you may have heard that everyone is welcome at this review, but I'm going to suggest you do something different.

The team that worked closely together, had those last, best story conversations, agreed on what to build, and worked together to build it needs time and a safe place to openly discuss their work. What others outside the team, including business leadership, think of the product is important and the team needs to hear their opinions. But those people weren't in the conversations that built shared understanding about the details of what to build. They weren't part of the discussions that created the detailed plans to build software. And they weren't working alongside the team as it turned all these discussions and agreements into working software. We need to first evaluate if we've built what we envisioned at the quality level we hoped for and in the timeframe we planned. Do this in a *team product review and reflection*.

Team Product Review and Reflection Recipe

The team that worked together to understand the stories—and to make a short-term plan for building them—must stop and reflect on the quality of their work. Use a short workshop to accomplish this.

Constrain this workshop to include only the people who worked together to understand and plan the work. Include the product owner and any others on the product team, as well as developers, QA, and anyone who did active delivery work. Yes, I'm saying that it's OK to exclude business stakeholders. We'll share with them soon enough. But right now we need a safe place to talk.

Bring food. Years ago in my team, this workshop simply couldn't start if we didn't have bagels.

Use this workshop to *review three things: the product, the plan, and the process.*

Product

Start by discussing the software built as a result of the stories. Make sure you bring it up on a screen, and get a chance to try it out. *All* of it. In big teams, it may be the only chance everyone has to see one another's work.

Grade your quality subjectively as a team. Grading will drive out lots of good discussion.

- *Discuss the quality of user experience.* Not just how the UI looks, but how it feels to use. Is it as good as you expected? Grade yourselves on a scale of 1–5, with 5 being best.

- *Discuss the functional quality.* Did testing go smoothly, or were there lots of bugs? Do testers expect to find more bugs as more software is added, or as they get more time to test? Grade yourselves on a scale of 1–5, with 5 being best.

- *Discuss the code quality.* Did you just write code that will be easy to maintain and grow? Or did you just write your next batch of legacy code? Grade yourselves on a scale of 1–5, with 5 being best.

Write stories to correct quality issues you see in the product.

If you're engaged in both discovery and delivery work, and you should be, discuss your discovery work of the last cycle. What did you do? What did you learn?

Plan

If you were working in a time-boxed iteration or a sprint, you started by making a plan and a prediction for how much you could get done. Was it a good one?

- *Decide which stories are and aren't done.* This may be harder than you think. Having this discussion helps your team build a common definition of what they consider to be done. Does "done" mean there are automated tests? Does it mean that all manual testing is done? Does it mean that product owners or UI designers have reviewed it?

- Total the number of stories you agree are done. This is your *velocity*.

- Total the stories started and not completed. If it's a lot, it'll signal you need to work on your planning. I call this amount the *over-hang*. Someone I used to work with called it *hangover*, because it makes your head ache.

- Discuss the amount of time budgeted on *discovery work*. Did you use the time? Did you use more time than you budgeted? Using too little will hurt you later when you don't have things ready to build that you feel confident in. Using too much may hurt your chances for delivering what you've committed to on time.

Process

Discuss the way you worked over the last development cycle. Could you make changes to the way you're doing things to improve quality? To improve your ability to predictably plan? To just make it more fun to be at work every day? Because if you're having fun, I promise you'll be able to go faster.[1]

- Start by discussing changes you tried last cycle. Did they work? Do you want to keep them, or kill them?

- Discuss changes you'd like to try during the next cycle. Don't take on too much. Small changes are best. Trying to change too much at once is similar to trying to take on too much work at once. You'll disappoint yourself.

That's it. You've successfully learned from the stories you've built, and *all* the work you've done for that matter.

---

1. This process improvement discussion is commonly called a *retrospective*, and there are lots of great approaches to performing one. If you'd like to look at a more comprehensive recipe of retrospective approaches, try the book *Agile Retrospectives* by Esther Derby and Diana Larsen (Pragmatic).

Review with Others in Your Organization

When the team has given their product a fair evaluation, widen the audience to include anyone else in the organization that's interested. This group will need some insight on the discussions you had as a team and any tradeoffs you made. Remember, the stories you've translated to working software are likely little rocks chipped off of a larger vision of the finished product. People outside the team may be expecting to see that finished product. They're likely to point out what's missing because they weren't part of the planning sessions where you decided what to defer until later. Expect that. And help them understand how the pieces you've just built fit into the bigger plan. Do this in a *stakeholder product review*.

Stakeholder Product Review Recipe

There are lots of others in the organization who are likely interested in what you're working on, and what you've accomplished. You'll need to make this work visible to them. Unlike your team, these others probably don't know the details of what you chose to build, nor where they fit into the big picture. So, you'll need to plan on connecting what you accomplished and learned back to the product. This is also an excellent opportunity to learn from them, and to get their support.

Invite everyone who's interested. This is a big public review. Anyone interested is welcome. Make sure your whole team is there. Seeing others' reactions to what they've done, either positive or negative, helps remind them that what they're doing matters.

Bring food. I promise everyone will like what you have to say when they're loaded up with carbohydrates. Even bad news goes down easier with cookies.

You'll review two categories of information: the discovery work you've been engaged in, and the stories you've delivered.

Review Discovery Work

Reviewing discovery is critical. The best time to get feedback from stakeholders is before you've invested lots of time building something. If you're showing real lessons learned from putting software in front of customers and users, they'll value learning what their customers actually think. The only thing that trumps an executive opinion is a cold, hard fact.

- Discuss each opportunity you've taken up briefly: who it's for, why we're building it, and the outcomes you expect if it's successful.

- Discuss and show the work you've done to understand the problem and the solution.

- Discuss and show prototypes and experiments you've run. Discuss what your customers and users are saying about your solution.

Review Delivery Work

It's been my experience that stakeholders are focused on what and when you'll release to customers and users. They should be because it's not until after you release a viable solution that you'll be able to observe real outcomes. They'll be interested in progress made toward that goal.

Review the delivery work you've completed at a solution-by-solution level. Think of the minimum viable solution as the big rock that's more relevant to stakeholders.

For each solution:

- Review the solution's target customers, users, and outcomes. It's good to remember why we're building this and what success means.

- Discuss and show the results of stories built for each solution. Stakeholders will offer feedback. Hopefully if they had a chance to give feedback when you were doing discovery work, the feedback at this point will be, "Yup, that still looks good."

- Discuss the stories holistically. If you're using a strategy like the *Mona Lisa* strategy, you'll need to explain to them why the software looks incomplete at this point. Remember that they may want to see a square inch of a complete portrait, and not the software equivalent of a sketch of the whole canvas.

- Share with them your progress toward getting this solution releasable. How much work is left? What have you learned while building the solution that will affect its successful delivery?

Be prepared to write stories for new opportunities, or for changes you'll need to make.

It's possible that others in the room unfamiliar with what you're building and why will suggest things that aren't a good idea.

Respectfully. and gently remind them of the target audience and outcome for the solution, and why what they're suggesting might be a great idea, but doesn't support the outcome you're currently focused on.

Keep your work visible to everyone in your company. Help them be excited about what you're doing and learning.

Enough

I'm confident when I use a product I like that I'm not appreciating all the little details and decisions that went into it. In fact, if it's working really well, I hardly notice the product at all. I don't notice how my mobile device loses and reestablishes an Internet connection. I don't notice how when I change the position of something in the mobile app of my task management software that the web version seems to be immediately in sync. But these are important qualities. And I'd notice if they weren't there. You as a team have been stewing in lots of details. But, oddly, you may not want users and others to notice them. In fact, you may want to notice that they don't notice them.

You'll learn the most from the stakeholders in your organization, customers who buy your product, and individual users who'll use it when you put enough software in front of them that they can clearly see how it'll help them reach one of their goals.

For stakeholders
Enough software may be the addition of a feature critical to acquiring new customers. Or enough may be information on what you've learned about the details that must be in that feature to be competitive.

For customers
Enough software may be the addition of a feature that will represent real value for them when they or their organization begin to use the new software.

For users
Enough software may be the addition of software that allows them to reach one of their goals using your product.

If you did your rock-breaking process well, you ended up with lots of small, buildable parts. Each of those parts allowed you and your team to learn something. But, if you were doing it right, those small parts are likely not enough to be relevant to other groups.

In my mind, I picture this as small bits of software we build piling up like LEGO bricks. I load all those bricks onto an old-fashioned scale, the kind with two platforms and a counterweight on one side. What I weigh this growing pile of software against is a bigger LEGO brick that represents *enough*—enough to allow a user to complete a task or reach a goal; enough for customers to see it as part of their value proposition; enough for business stakeholders to see how it helps our organization reach a business goal. When enough software piles up and tips the scales, it's time to test that software with users, review it with customers, or review it with business stakeholders.

You as a team of close collaborators need to review the results of every single story to learn and improve not only your product, but also the way you plan and the way you work together. When getting feedback and learning from other groups, be sensitive to what is enough for those groups.

Learn from Users

We may have been pretty confident that we were building the right things when we started, but to stay confident it's important to test the working software with users.

Notice that I said *test* here. We don't learn much from users by playing "show and tell"—that is, by demonstrating it to them and asking them to imagine using it and decide if they'd like it. It's a little like looking at a new car on a showroom floor and trying to decide if you'd enjoy driving it. Test-driving your software will help users really evaluate if it's solving a problem they have. As a team, we'll learn more by watching them use it. If you and your team were having good story conversations, you likely talked about users, why they'd value what you were building, and how they'd use it. It's watching them use it that really validates those hypotheses.

When you've got enough software to allow users to accomplish something meaningful to them, it's time to test. You may not be testing something completely new. You may have made changes or enhancements to something your product already does. Spend time with users to observe them using your software doing realistic work.

Learn from Release to Users

You've built small amounts of software and reviewed every bit of it as a team. You've periodically reviewed it with stakeholders insider your organization, and with customers who'll buy or adopt your product, and with users who'll use it. But, if you remember where this book started, it's not the software we really wanted—it's the outcomes we get after the software is delivered and put into use.

When you feel like you've built enough that you're confident you'll get those outcomes, then it's time to release the software into the world.

I picture one more scale that's piling up with bricks of software that I've tested with users, iteratively improved, and I'm now confident could be released. I'll balance that growing pile against yet another, larger brick that also represents enough—enough to release and be successful with its target audience. When I've got enough, it's time to release.

You'll need to plan to learn from each release. Please don't release software and sit around waiting for your customers and users to complain. Those complaints are outcomes. But they're often lagging indicators of how they really feel and how well your product will really do. For each release, discuss as a team how you'll measure or observe the users of your product to see if you really got the outcomes you expected. Discuss and decide how you'll:

- Build metrics into your product that allow you to track usage of new features
- Schedule time to observe users as they use the new release

As a team, routinely discuss what you've learned, and then take your ideas for improvement and write more stories. Some you'll see as important enough to implement right away. And others you'll see as opportunities to add to your opportunity backlog.

Outcomes on a Schedule

There are some companies and some software that allow us to release whenever we have enough. But for a great number of companies and products, if not most of them, we need to release on a schedule. If we've been using our development strategy effectively, we've laid down a foundation in our early opening-game stories, built up the product using midgame stories, and when it comes time to release, we're playing our endgame stories.

Now I need to remind you of a few more truths about software development.

Software is never really done.

You'll finish implementing the software for each story your team takes on during a short development cycle. But you likely won't finish every story you imagine at the outset of development, or identify as you learn each cycle. If you've used an effective development strategy, however, the software will be as good as it possibly can be at the time it's released.

Outcomes are never insured.

In spite of all the work you've done to validate that you're building the right things, people using your product often don't behave as predicted. Plan to learn with each release. Plan to make changes based on what you've learned.

Improvements made after release are the most valuable.

It's those unpredictable things that you'll observe when users begin to adopt and use your software frequently that yield the most insight. If you plan for time to really measure and observe outcomes, you'll be rewarded with people who really love your product and a product that's really valuable for your organization.

Use a Map to Evaluate Release Readiness

You'll complete your product release story by story. As you draw near the date you promised to deliver—and there's *always* a promised delivery date—for each major user activity ask, "If we had to ship right now, what grade would we give ourselves?" If you use letter grades like my kids get in school, you'll end up with a report card for your product.

For example, if you looked at a product or feature with five major activities a few weeks before its promised release date, and saw a report card of *A*, *A-*, *B+*, *D*, *B+*, you might want to take the remaining weeks and focus on the part in the user's workflow that's currently graded a *D*. If in the end you release with *A* s and *B* s, that's pretty good. Of course, straight *A* s would be better, but getting it out on time may be more important.

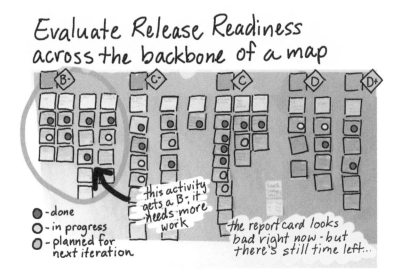

As you draw near the release date of your product, work together to assess release readiness. I promise you, everyone wants to know.

This book is almost done. If you've read this far, you may have some opinions about its release readiness. You could go back to the table of contents and write your letter grade on each chapter. Take a smartphone photo and send it to me. I'd love to see it.

The End, or Is It?

Just like a good software product, this book isn't really done. Throughout the book are lots of great examples contributed by people I've met who tell me about the cool things they're doing with stories and story mapping. I've got a lot more stories on my hard drive, too, and it's killing me that I don't have time to get them refined and included in the book.

There are also a lot more details I could discuss about stories and story maps. And I'm sure you've got unanswered questions about using stories in your own context. As I reach the close of this book, I worry about that, too.

As someone who's been a developer, a UI designer, and a product manager, I can tell you I've rarely been happy at product release. And that's because it's then that I know about all the things I couldn't include, and about all the little things that could be better with just a bit more time to polish. If you really care about what you're building, I expect you'll feel that way as well.

I'll repeat the da Vinci quote I used earlier in Chapter 4:

Great art is never finished, only abandoned.

I'll stop short of saying this book is great art. But I will say I've abandoned it when there's more that could be done. I'll leave that *more* to you, and expect to hear from you when you've discovered your own better ways for working together to create great products.

Acknowledgments

This was one of the hardest parts of this book to write. I've been blessed enough to enjoy the support of a huge number of people throughout my career. I have and continue to receive so much encouragement from everyone I meet and work with. So, what scares me is that as soon as I start thanking people, I'm going to leave someone out. If I've left you out, I am very sorry, and I suspect you're in good company.

And, another thing is that I'm pretty sure I don't have any original ideas. I've heard it argued that there are no original ideas left. But for me specifically, everything I know I've learned from the wise people I've worked with over the past two decades. From these insightful friends and peers I've learned and applied new ideas and practices. Through long discussions with them, I've learned to interpret and deeply understand the experiences I've had when practicing my craft. It seems hard to take credit for any of the ideas in this book since I know most were borrowed or simply stolen from others.

Whenever I do have what I believe to be an original idea, I'm reminded of *cryptomnesia*. It's a fun word that applies to the accidental plagiarism that reputable people like George Harrison and Umberto Eco are guilty of. Cryptomnesia occurs when a forgotten memory returns without it being recognized as a memory. The crytomnesiac believes the great idea they've just come up with is new and original, and not the forgotten memory of something they've read, heard, or otherwise experienced. The people I'm thanking below are quite likely many of the people I've unintentionally stolen from.

So with that preamble, I'll get started:

I'd practically given up on writing a book. I've had a real problem when I was trying to write over the past ten years. I seemed to be able to write short articles, or give a talk, but as soon as I tried to write anything longer than a couple thousand words, things went sideways. I can best describe my book writing as taxidermy. That is I'd take something living and beautiful and then kill it and stuff it. The best I could hope for is that it would be lifelike. Peter Economy broke me out of that cycle. It was his years of experience writing and his always positive and supportive attitude that helped me find a written voice that worked. I'm grateful to Peter. If you're struggling to get a book written, you should call Peter.

Martin Fowler, Alan Cooper, and Marty Cagan are all heroes of mine. I've had the pleasure of meeting with, working with, and enjoying long conversations with all of them. Their thinking has influenced mine throughout my career. Two of the three thought it was a bad idea to have three forewords in the book, but I'm glad I insisted, and they agreed. They represent the voices of engineering, user experience, and product thinking that I see as critical to creating successful products. I think it was critical that you, the reader, heard from each of them.

Alistair Cockburn has been a friend and mentor of mine for over a decade. I'm quite certain that much of what I believe are my great ideas were stolen directly from Alistair and my long conversations with him. Calling the model of story cards I put on walls and tabletops a "story map" came from one of these conversations. As I was trying to explain to Alistair what it was I recall saying "it's just a map of stories." "Then, why don't you call it that" Alistair said. That instead of the other silly names I'd been tossing around.

What I started doing with cards years ago to tell stories and build product backlogs came from bastardizing practices I learned from my friend Larry Constantine. The practice of story mapping and how I think of user experience would never have come about without the opportunity to learn directly from Larry.

David Hussman has been my wise friend, supporter, and a kindred spirit to me for years now. It's watching David tell stories and receiving his encouragement that's helped me find the voice I have today. David was creating story maps before they were called that.

And, I'd never have gotten a book completed without the support of Tom and Mary Poppendieck. Tom in particular has read some of my worst taxidermy over the past decade, and still offered words of encouragement. A few months ago, he refused to leave my house until I sent my final draft to O'Reilly. If he hadn't, I'd have kept twiddling with the book, never considering it good enough.

Other friends that stand out as supporters and sources of good advice along the way include Zhon and Kay Johansen, Aaron Sanders and Erica Young, Jonathan House, Nate Jones, and Christine DelPrete.

Special thanks to Gary Levitt, all the people at Globo.com, Eric Wright from Liquidnet, and all my friends at Workiva for letting me tell their stories in the first chapters of this book.

Countless times over the years I've been stopped by people who wanted to tell me their stories about how they'd used story mapping or applied a piece of advice I'd given them. My guilty secret is that I learn more from them than I think they get from me. I was happy to get contributions from just a fraction of them for this book. Special thanks to those that could get me a contribution given very short notice: Josh Seiden, Chris Shinkle, Sherif Mansour, Ben Crothers, Michael Vath, Martina Luenzman, Andrea Schmieden, Ceedee Doyle, Erin Beierwaltes, Aaron White, Mat Cropper, Chris Gansen and Jason Kunesh, Rick Cusick, Nicola Adams, and Steve Barrett.

There's a big group of people that I spoke with and learned from that I simply didn't give enough time to meet my unreasonable deadline. These people include: Ahmad Fahmy, Tobias Hildenbrand, Courtney Hemphill, Samuel Bowles, Rowan Bunning, Scout Addis, Holly Bielawa, and Jabe Bloom. To these people and all of you reading this, I still want your stories. Perhaps I'll release a special directors cut of the book that includes all these deleted scenes.

In the final stretch of getting this book done, I received valuable detailed reviews from Barry O'Reilly, Todd Webb, and at the last minute from Petra Wille. All of their detailed comments helped me smooth out the rough edges in the book.

Finally, thanks to Mary Treseler and the production team at O'Reilly for putting up with my delays and funky schedule, and sticking with me to the bitter end.

References

Adlin, Tamara, and John Pruitt. *The Essential Persona Lifecycle: Your Guide to Building and Using Personas.* Burlington: Morgan Kaufmann, 2010.

Adzic, Gojko. *Impact Mapping: Making a Big Impact with Software Products and Projects.* Surrey, UK: Provoking Thoughts, 2012.

--. *Specification by Example: How Successful Teams Deliver the Right Software.* Shelter Island: Manning Publications, 2011.

Armitage, John. "Are Agile Methods Good for Design," Interactions, Volume 11, Issue 1, January-February, 2004. *http://dl.acm.org/citation.cfm?id=962352.*

Beck, Kent. *Extreme Programming Explained: Embrace Change.* New York: Addison-Wesley Professional, 1999.

Beck, Kent, and Michael Fowler. *Planning Extreme Programming.* New York: Addison-Wesley Professional, 2000.

Cagan, Marty. *Inspired: How to Create Products Customers Love.* Sunnyvale: SVPG Press, 2008.

Cheng, Kevin. *See What I Mean: How to Use Comics to Communicate Ideas.* Brooklyn: Rosenfeld Media, LLC, 2012.

Cockburn, Alistair. *Agile Software Development.* New York: Addison-Wesley Professional, 2001.

--. *Writing Effective Use Cases.* New York: Addison-Wesley Professional, 2000.

Cohn, Mike. *User Stories Applied: For Agile Software Development.* New York: Addison-Wesley Professional, 2004.

Constantine, Larry L., and Lucy A.D. Lockwood. *Software for Use: A Practical Guide to the Models and Methods of Usage-Centered Design.* New York: Addison-Wesley Professional, 1999.

Cooper, Alan. *The Inmates Are Running the Asylum: Why High-Tech Products Drive Us Crazy and How to Restore the Sanity.* Indianapolis: Sams – Pearson Education, 2004.

Gothelf, Jeff. *Lean UX: Applying Lean Principles to Improve User Experience.* Sebastopol: O'Reilly Media, 2013.

Jeffries, Ron, Ann Anderson, and Chet Hendrickson. *Extreme Programming Installed.* New York: Addison-Wesley Professional, 2007.

Klein, Laura. *UX for Lean Startups: Faster, Smarter User Experience Research and Design.* Sebastopol: O'Reilly Media, 2013.

Ries, Eric. *The Lean Startup: How Today's Entepreneurs Use Continuous Innovation to Create Radically Successful Businesses.* New York: Crown Business, 2011.

Sy, Desiree. "Adapting Usability Investigations for Agile User-Centered Design," Journal of Usability Studies, Vol. 2, Issue 3, May 2007. *http://www.upassoc.org/upa_publications/jus/2007may/agile-ucd.html.*

Tom Demarco et al. *Adrenaline Junkies and Template Zombies: Understanding Patterns of Project Behavior.* New York: Dorset House, 2008.

Yates, Jen. *Cake Wrecks: When Professional Cakes Go Hilariously Wrong.* Kansas City: Andrews McMeel Publishing, 2009.

Index

A

acceptance criteria, 94
  agreeing on, 147
  for Refine, Define, and Build chapter, 227
activities, 75
  prioritizing in the backlog, 86
Adams, Nicola, 222
Agile development, 1
  learning from everything you build, 127
  product owner, 155
  RAC Insurance in Perth, Australia, 222
  Scrum process, 148
  story mapping and, 2
assumptions, 35
  challenging with rehearsal mapping, 176
  conversations about, 105
  naming your risky assumptions, 212
  rethinking after running your test, 215
Asteroids video game, 239
Atlassian, 113

B

BA (see business analysts)
backbone (story map), 23
  distilling your map to make, 75
backlog, 6, 93
  flat backlog trap, 22
backlog grooming, 148
backlog refinement, 148
bad requirements, 90, 127
Beck, Kent, 2, 89, 128
beta customers, 44
Blank, Steve, 209
breaking software down into smaller parts, 133
budget, time budget for development, 57
build-measure-learn cycle, 47, 210, 215
building software
  building less, xli
  building to learn, 41, 127
  continuing conversation as you build, 148
  iterative builds until MVP is produced, 44

We'd like to hear your suggestions for improving our indexes. Send email to index@oreilly.com.

learning from everything you
build, 247–257
planning to build less, 134, 196
planning to build piece by piece,
54
the wrong way, 44
business analysts, 110
in requirements gathering role,
163
in three amigos, 160
Nicola Adams at RAC Insurance,
222
business models, canvas approach to,
170
business value, prioritizing stories by,
197

C

Cagan, Marty, 47, 156, 170
canvas approach to sizing up opportunities, 170
card-conversation-confirmation flow,
218
Cardboard, 117
cards
contents of, 109–120
building shared understanding,
116
different team roles, different
conversations, 109
radiators and ice boxes, 114
remembering, 118
tracking huge amounts of information, 110
using tools, 116
what's really on story cards, 114
writing desired product features
on, 93
changing the world, xxxvii
choosers, xli
client-vendor anti-pattern, 162
business analyst in requirements
gathering role, 163
coach for team use of user story mapping, 85
Cockburn, Alistair, 70, 114, 127
code quality, 125

confirmation, 94, 147, 218
Confluence, 113
Connextra, 98
conversation, 93
about opportunities, 167
checklist of what to really talk
about, 104
continuing while building, 148
different roles, different conversations for, 109
diving into story details during delivery, 146
documenting using tools, 118
having best last conversations, 217
including too many people, 225
keeping valuable, usable, and feasible in discussions, 161
product owner responsible for all
story conversations, 155
tool for breaking down stories, 140
using after release to evaluate
product use, 153
using using story template to start,
99
words and pictures in, 95
Cs, 92, 218
cards, 93
confirmation, 94
conversation, 93
customer intercepts, 214
customers
conversations about, 104
describing your customers, 9
enough software for, 253
evaluating built software with, 150
understanding, 183, 199

D

da Vinci, Leonardo, 59
dates on story cards, 115
decomposition, 12
defining, 205
delivery
diving into details of each story,
146
reviewing in stakeholder product
review, 252

DeMarco, Tom, 102
dependencies on story cards, 115
descriptions of stories, 99
descriptions on story cards, 115
design by committee, 156
design by community, 156
design processes
    changes to, from Lean Startup
        thinking, 210
    messing up, 208
    traditional, big flaw in, 210
Design Studio, 189
    recipe for, 189
design thinking, 204
    defining, 205
    empathizing, 205
    ideation, 206
    prototyping, 206
    testing, 207
    way of working, 207
details
    exploring, 14
    filling in for story map, 72
    leaving until big picture is comple-
        ted, 12
development cycles
    discussing in team review, 250
    planning for, 241
    planning recipe, 230
development partners, 42
development strategy
    planning, 241
    slicing out, 83
discovery, 47, 181–200
    activities, discussions, and arti-
        facts, 199
    collaboration of discovery team
        with others, 158
    cross-functional teams finding
        right solution, 157
    discovering a minimum viable sol-
        ution, 144
    discovery team member in three
        amigos, 160
    discussing opportunities, 168
    envisioning your solution, 186
    essential steps in, 182
exploring ideas using examples
    and journeys, 194
framing the idea, 183
minimizing and planning, 196
questions to ask and answer, 181
reviewing in stakeholder product
    review, 251
story discussion and splitting, 240
time budgeted for, discussing in
    team review, 250
understanding customers and
    users, 183
using for validated learning, 201–
    216
using to build shared understand-
    ing, 200
documenting conversations, 6, 107
documents
    perfect, trying to write, xxxiv
    similarity of good documents to
        vacation photos, xxxv
    using to aid memory, xxxvi

E

empathizing, 205
endgame strategy, 63
enough, 253
envisioning the solution, 186, 199
epics, 140
estimation
    conversations about how long, 107
    estimate, size, or budget on story
        cards, 115
    estimating development time, 168
    in client-vendor anti-pattern, 162
    measurement as key to good esti-
        mates, 56
    time estimates for development, 53
evaluating built software, 149
    continuing after product release,
        153
    with business stakeholders, 152
    with users and customers, 150
experiments, minimizing, 48
Extreme Programming, 97
    spikes, 146

F

Fabricant, Robert, xxxix
finishing on time, 51–65
    envisioning the whole product, 59
    iterative and incremental thinking,
        62
    managing your time budget, 57
    not releasing each slice, 56
    opening-, mid-, and endgame
        strategy, 63
    other secret to good estimates, 56
    planning to build piece by piece,
        54
    risk, importance of, 64
    secret to good estimation, 53
    slicing out development strategy in
        a map, 64
    telling feature's story step by step,
        52
fishbowl collaboration pattern, 225
flat backlog trap, 22
focusing on outcomes
    slicing out a minimum viable
        product release, 27
    slicing out a release roadmap, 28
FORUM Credit Union, 31
framing the idea, 8, 183, 199
framing the problem, 83
functional quality, 125
functional walking skeleton, 55
functional-level tasks, 70

G

Globo.com, 21
go/no-go decision, 144, 168
    on opportunities, 173
goal level, 70
goals
    minimizing amount to be built, 9
    ordering by importance, 8
Good-Better-Best game, 229
guessing, starting product design
    with, 211

H

how, conversations about, 106

I

ideation, 206
impact, xli
    maximizing, xli
incremental strategy, 60
incremental thinking, 62
information icebox, 114
information radiator, 113
iteration planning, 222
iterations, 62
iterative, defined, 62
ITHAKA, 212

J

Jeffries, Ron, 92
JIRA, 113
    cumulative flow diagram gener-
        ated by, 120
journey maps, 80, 173
JSTOR, 212

L

large-scale development context, us-
    ing story mapping, 85
Lean Startup, 210
    build-measure-learn, 215
    designing and building a small
        test, 212
    how it changes product design,
        210
    measuring by running test with
        customers and users, 214
    naming your risky assumptions,
        212
    rethinking solutions and assump-
        tions, 215
    starting by guessing, 211
    validated learning over working
        software, 128
The Lean Startup (Ries), 35
learning
    after you build, 247
        enough, 253
            learning from release to users,
                255
            learning from users, 254

outcomes on a schedule, 255
review as a team, 247
review with others in the organization, 251
best learning practices, 103
development or research for (spikes), 146
in Lean Startup approach, 215
validated (see validated learning)
learning faster
building to learn, 41
customer/user reactions to prototype, 41
discussing the opportunity, 38
doing it the wrong way, 44
iterating until product is viable, 44
minimizing your experiments, 48
prototyping to learn, 40
validated learning strategy, 46
validating the problem, 39
learning strategies
building to learn, 127
slicing out, 83
Levitt, Gary, 5
Liquidnet, 37
literals, xxx

M

mapping the big picture, 83
maps, 72
(see also story mapping; story maps)
narrative journey map, 186
using simple maps in story workshops, 234
using to evaluate release readiness, 256
visualizing progress with, 233
measurement
importance to good estimates, 56
in Lean Startup, 215
metrics on story cards, 115
running product test with customers and users, 214
using metrics to learn if/how people use the product, 153
meetings, 219

midgame strategy, 63
minimizing and planning, 196, 200
prioritization, 197
minimum viable product (see MVP)
minimum viable product experiment (MVPe), 47
minimum viable solution (see MVS)
minimum, defining, 33
Mona Lisa strategy, 128, 134
morning map exercise, 78
MVP (minimum viable product)
differing definitions of, 32
iterating until viable, 44
minimizng your experiments, 48
MVPe (minimum viable product experiment), 47
MVS (minimum viable solution), 34, 138, 201
discovering, 144

N

narrative flow, 25, 72
finding the flow, 74
narrative journey map, 186
NASA Mars Climate Orbiter, crash of, xxxii
no-go decision, 144, 169
nonfunctional requirements, xxxi

O

Obama Campaign Dashboard, 234
Obama, Barack, 234
opening strategy, 63
opportunities, 167–179
being picky about, 179
canvas approach to sizing up, 169
flow of spaces in, 171
digging deeper, trashing, or thinking about, 168
go/no-go decisions on, 173
having conversations about, 167
in story discussion and splitting stage, 240
starting with, 143
story mapping and, 173
Opportunity Assessment template, 170

opportunity backlog, 143, 168
organizational profiles, creating, 185
Osterwalder, Alexander, 170
outcomes, xxxix
    evaluating if target outcomes were
        met, 153
    maximizing, xli
    on scheduled releases, 255
    prioritizing instead of features, 29
    slicing out tasks relevant to, 76
outcomes, focusing on, 27
output, xxxix
    minimizing, xli
overhand, 250

P

patterns, 4
personas, sketching, 183
Pigneur, Yves, 170
planning
    development cycle planning
        recipe, 230
    development strategy, 241
    evaluating in team review, 249
    for next development cycle, 241
    sprint or iteration planning, 222
planning to build less, 21
    creating smaller experiments and
        prototypes, 34
    definition of MVP (minimum via-
        ble product), 32
    finding a smaller viable release, 30
    prioritizing outcomes rather than
        features, 29
    slicing out a minimum viable
        product release, 27
    slicing out a release roadmap, 28
predictably unpredictables, 55
prioritization
    prioritizing outcomes, 29
    prioritizing user stories in the
        backlog, 86
    secret of, 197
problem, validating, 39
product backlog, 93, 181
product development
    goal of, xxix

product discovery, 47
    identifying a valuable, usable, and
        feasible product, 156
    Workiva example, 52
product managers, 109
product owners
    as producers, 163
    leading small, cross-functional dis-
        covery team, 157
    responsibilities of, 155
progress
    tracking using tools, 119
    visualizing using a map, 233
project managers
    conversations for, 110
    identifying valuable, usable, and
        feasible product, 156
Project Phoenix, 17
prototyping, 40, 206

Q

quality
    discussions about, 125
    examining for each soltuion built,
        150
questions
    identifying and discussing in con-
        versations, 105
    to ask and answer in discovery,
        181

R

RAC Insurance, Perth, Australia, 222
refining, defining, and building, 217–
    237
    cards and conversations, 217
    cutting and polishing, 218
    including too many people in in
        story conversations, 225
    splitting and thinning, 227
    sprint or iteration planning, 222
    using a map to visualize progress,
        233
    using simple maps in story work-
        shops, 234
    using your story map during deliv-
        ery, 232

workshopping stories, 218
rehearsal mapping, challenging assumptions with, 176
Reichelt, Leisa, 156
release backlog, 146
release roadmap, 29
release strategy, slicing out, 83
releases
    learning from release to users, 255
    on a schedule, 255
    using a map to evaluate readiness, 256
remote collaboration, tools for, 117
requirements, xxxviii, 89, 162
    bad requirements, 90, 127
    business analyst in requirements gathering role, 163
    misinterpreted, xxx
    stopping conversations, xlii
reviews
    team review of software builds, 247
    with others in your organization, 251
Ries, Eric, 35, 47, 209
risk
    exposing in story maps, 57
    importance of dealing with, 64
rock breaking, 137–154
    epics as big rocks, 140
    lifecycle, 142
    similarity of stories to rocks, 139

S

scaling user story mapping, 87
scope creep, 26, 127
Scrum process
    backlog grooming or backlog refinement, 148
    sprint review and retrospective, 150
    sprint reviews, 247
sea-level tasks, 70
sequence, identifying, 10
shared understanding, 11
    building, xxxiii

building in large groups, mapping as aid to, 22
building using cards' contents, 116
building with customers and users, 82
building with the team, 52
defined, xxxii
essential for good estimates, 54
mapping helping big groups with, 22
using discovery to build, 181–200
size, importance of, 137
solutions, 34
    being wrong about, 201
    conversations about better solutions, 106
    envisioning, 186, 199
        playing What-About, 192
        using story maps, 186
        using words and pictures, 187
        visualizing the whole experience, 187
    rethinking after tests in Lean Startup, 215
    reviewing delivery work completed for, 252
specifications, 222
spikes, 146
sprint planning, 222
sprint review, 247
sprint review and retrospective, 150
stakeholder product review, 251
stakeholders
    business stakeholder in product ownership role, 164
    conversations about, 104
    enough software for, 253
    evaluating built software with, 152
status on story cards, 115
stories, xliii
    baking like a cake, 131–136
        breaking down a big cake, 133
        creating a recipe, 132
    breaking client-vendor anti-pattern, 163
    defined, 3
    defining user stories, 85

diving into details of during delivery, 146
epics, 140
exploring alternative stories, 72
focusing on breadth before diving into its depth, 12
focusing on storytelling, 142
goal of using, xxix
in validated learning, 215
many components of, 165
product owner responsible for writing all stories, 155
right size for, 137
similarity to asteroids, 239
    not sweating small stuff, 244
    reassembling split stories, 241
    splitting stories, 240
similarity to rocks, 139
splitting and thinning, 227
    Good-Better-Best game, 229
starting with opportunities, 143
taling through and finding holes in your thinking, 11
telling better stories, 97–108
    creating vacation photos, 107
    template zombies and the snowplow, 102
    using Connextra template, 97
telling the whole story, 3
telling, not writing, 91
themes organizaing groups of stories, 142
using to drive the making of anything, 128
story mapping, xxi, 165
and opportunities, 173
as aid to discovery, 145
creating a story map, 67–83
    distilling your map to make a backbone, 75
    exploring alternative stories, 72
    now and later maps, 79
    organizing your story, 71
    slicing out tasks relevant to a specific outcome, 76
    summary of important concepts, 77

trying the morning map exercise, 78
understanding how customers work now, 81
using story maps, 84
writing story a step at a time, 67
describing your customers and users, 9
exploring details and options, 14
exposing risk, 57
focus on telling, not writing, stories, 91
focusing on outcomes, 27
for a feature, 52
framing your idea, 8
helping you spot holes in your story, 25
increasing frequency and fidelity of, 58
Kent's simple idea, 89
not overdoing, 243
scaling user story mapping, 87
six simple steps to, 83
talk and doc, 6
telling your users' stories, 10
think, write, explain, and place, 7
story maps
backbone, 23
in validated learning, 215
map across multiple teams to visualize dependencies, 23
map in narrative flow across many users and systems, 24
map in whole deliverable releases, 24
mapping your solution, 186
using during delivery, 232
story number, 115
story tests, 94
story workshops, 148, 218
agreeing on what to build, 221
conducting, 218
diving deep and considering options, 220
including the right people, 220
outcomes of, 230
recipe for, 220

splitting and thinning stories, 221
three amigos, 160
using simple maps, 234
storytelling, building an oral tradition
of, 123
subtasks, 71
summary-level tasks, 71

T

talk and doc, 6
in story workshops, 221
tasks, 68
aggregation into activities, 75
levels of detail, 70
telephone game, xxx
template zombies, 102
testers, 110
in three amigos, 160
testing
designing and building a small test
(Lean Startup), 212
learning if your solution solves a
problem, 207
meaningful chunks of working
software with users/customers,
151
user testing of software builds, 126
user testing of working software,
254
The Learning Connection (TLC), 17
themes, 142
three amigos, 159
three Cs, 92, 218
cards, 93
confirmation, 94
conversation, 93
time-boxed development, 231
title (on story cards), 114
tools
documenting models or examples
created in conversations, 118
for documenting conversations,
112
organizing stories into themes, 142
tracking planned work and its progress, 119

using the wrong tool or the tool
wrong, 116
using to externalize product visu-
alizations, 116
tracking, using tools for, 119
triad (core discovery team), 158
True, Doug, 32

U

UI designers, 110
Unger, Jim, 189
user experience quality, 125
user stories, 97
(see also stories)
user tasks, 68
users, xli
conversations about, 104
describing your users, 9
enough software for, 253
evaluating built software with, 150
researching typical users for a
product, 85
testing software builds, 126
testing working software with, 254
understanding, 183, 199
creating organizational profiles, 185
mapping how users work today, 185
sketching simple personas, 183
UX designers
in three amigos, 160
visualizing the whole experience,
187

V

vacation photos, 107
similarity of good documents to,
xxxv
validated learning, 128
using discovery for, 201–216
being wrong most of the time,
201
design process, messing up,
208
empathize, focus, ideate, prototype, and test, 204

Lean Startup, changes to product design, 210
  short validated learning loops, 209
  stories and story maps, 215
  the bad old days, 203
validated learning strategy, 46
validating the problems, 39
valuable, usable, and feasible products, 156
velocity, xxxix, 250
vendors, client-vendor anti-pattern, 162
viable, defined, 33
visualizing ideas, 107

W

what, conversations about, 104

What-About game, 25
  playing, 192
White, Jeff, 189
who, 104
  conversations about, 104
  in conversations about opportunities, 167
why, 104
  conversations about, 105
  in conversations about opportunities, 168
Workiva, 51

Y

Yates, Jen, xxx

About the Author

Over his past two decades of experience, **Jeff Patton** has learned there's no "one right way" to design and build software, but there's lots of wrong ways.

Jeff makes use of over 15 years experience with a wide variety of products from online aircraft parts ordering to electronic medical records to helping organizations improve the way they work. Where many development processes focus on delivery speed and efficiency, Jeff balances those concerns with the need for building products that deliver exceptional value and marketplace success.

Jeff has focused on Agile approaches since working on an early Extreme Programming team in 2000. In particular, he specializes in integrating effective user experience design and product management practice with strong engineering practice.

Jeff currently works as an independent consultant, agile process coach, product design process coach, and instructor. Current articles, essays, and presentations on variety of topics in Agile product development can be found at *agileproductdesign.com* and in Alistair Cockburn's *Crystal Clear*. Jeff is founder and list moderator of the agile-usability Yahoo discussion group, a columnist with StickyMinds.com and IEEE Software, a Certified Scrum Trainer, and winner of the Agile Alliance's 2007 Gordon Pask Award for contributions to Agile Development.

Colophon

The animal on the cover of *User Story Mapping* is a lilac-breasted roller, often considered one of the most beautiful birds in the world with its pastel plumage, striking field marks, and long tail streamers. It's the national bird of both Kenya and Botswana, and is relatively common and widespread throughout much of southern Africa.

These birds are typically solitary or are found in pairs, but may stay in small family groups during the winter months. They perch on high vantage points at the very tops of trees and poles, and stay still while watching for prey to approach. After dropping onto a victim, they may beat their prey against a rock or on the ground to kill it before swallowing it whole.

The birds are monogamous (believed to mate for life) and the name "roller" actually comes from the aerial displays the birds use during mating season. Lilac-breasted rollers will dive from a considerable elevation, and then roll in the air while simultaneously letting out a loud call to attract a partner.

Many of the animals on O'Reilly covers are endangered; all of them are important to the world. To learn more about how you can help, go to *animals.oreilly.com*.

The cover image is from Braukhaus Lexicon. The cover fonts are URW Typewriter and Guardian Sans. The text font is Adobe Minion Pro; the heading font is Adobe Myriad Condensed; and the code font is Dalton Maag's Ubuntu Mono.

Get even more for your money.

Join the O'Reilly Community, and register the O'Reilly books you own. It's free, and you'll get:

- $4.99 ebook upgrade offer
- 40% upgrade offer on O'Reilly print books
- Membership discounts on books and events
- Free lifetime updates to ebooks and videos
- Multiple ebook formats, DRM FREE
- Participation in the O'Reilly community
- Newsletters
- Account management
- 100% Satisfaction Guarantee

Signing up is easy:

1. Go to: oreilly.com/go/register
2. Create an O'Reilly login.
3. Provide your address.
4. Register your books.

Note: English-language books only

To order books online:
oreilly.com/store

For questions about products or an order:
orders@oreilly.com

To sign up to get topic-specific email announcements and/or news about upcoming books, conferences, special offers, and new technologies:
elists@oreilly.com

For technical questions about book content:
booktech@oreilly.com

To submit new book proposals to our editors:
proposals@oreilly.com

O'Reilly books are available in multiple DRM-free ebook formats. For more information:
oreilly.com/ebooks

Lightning Source UK Ltd.
Milton Keynes UK
UKOW06f2017180216

268669UK00001B/1/P

9 781491 904909